Remaking China's Public Philosophy for the Twenty-first Century

Remaking China's Public Philosophy for the Twenty-first Century

JINGHAO ZHOU

Foreword by Derek H. Davis

PRAEGER

Westport, Connecticut
London

Library of Congress Cataloging-in-Publication Data

Zhou, Jinghao, 1955–
Remaking China's public philosophy for the twenty-first century / Jinghao Zhou ; foreword by Derek H. Davis.
p. cm.
Includes bibliographical references and index.
ISBN 0–275–97882–6 (alk. paper)
1. Political culture—China. 2. China—Politics and government—1976–. 3. China—Social policy. 4. China—Economic conditions—2000– I. Title.
JQ1516 .Z45 2003
320'.6'0951—dc21 2002193049

British Library Cataloguing in Publication Data is available.

Library of Congress Catalog Card Number: 2002193049
ISBN: 0–275–97882–6

First published in 2003

Praeger Publishers, 88 Post Road West, Westport, CT 06881
An imprint of Greenwood Publishing Group, Inc.
www.praeger.com

Printed in the United States of America

The paper used in this book complies with the Permanent Paper Standard issued by the National Information Standards Organization (Z39.48–1984).

10 9 8 7 6 5 4 3 2 1

This book is dedicated to the bright future of China, as well as to my mother, sister, and brother, who live there.
This book is also dedicated to my wife, Sai Gong, whose love, devotion, and caring enabled me to complete this work.

Contents

Foreword

China's future is uncertain. China now stands at a crossroads: It can enter modernity and join the community of nations that embrace freedom and democracy, or it can continue down a path of totalitarian repression justified in the name of preserving Chinese community. Most Chinese see these options clearly, but only the people appear ready to make the turn toward freedom and democracy. The ruling Chinese Communist Party seems bent on retaining its power, control, and privilege.

It is true, of course, that China is showing some signs of entering the community of free nations, as it has revamped its economy along capitalistic lines. But is this enough? Hardly. It is a good start, and it may be that China will be unique in transitioning slowly from totalitarianism to democracy—although the people may not have the patience for such a transition, even assuming it becomes an intentional strategy. What remains to be done is a very comprehensive revamping of China's entire political order, its educational system, and its policy toward religion; indeed, of its larger public philosophy. This will take time, and as long as the Communist Party remains entrenched in power, it is not likely to initiate a comprehensive shift in its fundamentals.

Change will come only as a result of pressure, exerted from within or without, that demands it. The pressure from within is there, in seed form. The Chinese have a tradition of revolution, but it is a quiet form, given traditional Chinese manners and respect for authority. The Tiananmen Square protests of 1989 illustrate this. The student uprising was dramatic and serious, but those brave young people were not prepared to do anything more than speak forcefully yet retire quietly if the ruling authorities were in no mood to listen. Pressure from the outside is possible, but China is a formidable foe of any nation wishing to force change, and nations are more inclined to be friendly to China due to its increasing economic strength and respected military ability.

But change is very possible, and convincing the ruling authorities of the wisdom of change is likely the best course. Thus enter the efforts of people like Jinghao Zhou. He is part of an emerging generation of loyal, patriotic Chinese who work with grace and intelligence to bring about needed reforms. It is possible that this movement, now only inchoate, will grow like a tidal wave and lead eventually to the changes that must happen in China.

This wonderful book, *Remaking China's Public Philosophy for the Twenty-first Century,* is part of this emerging reform movement. It is an excellent piece of scholarship, the first I know of to offer a comprehensive program for revamping China's entire public philosophy along democratic lines. Zhou explains how to reorder China's ideology, economy, politics, religion, and educational system. He does not call for a slow, gradual transition, but for a massive overhaul in which all of these dimensions are reordered simultaneously. He also presents all this in a global context, suggesting that a new China will improve the entire international social and political order. I am hopeful that this book will gain a wide readership. It is important and timely, and it should be read by anyone interested in China's future.

Derek H. Davis
Director, J.M. Dawson
Institute of Church-State Studies,
Baylor University

Preface

This book uses the prism of "public philosophy" for the first time, in either the United States or China, to examine Chinese society, modernization, globalization, and democratization as a whole. Central to this book is the role of China's new public philosophy in the process of China's democratization. Why did I write this book? First of all, this book reflects my personal experience in China. When I was young, like other innocent Chinese people, I believed that the Communist Party of China (CPC) was the sole savior of the Chinese people, and that I was lucky to live in the communist era. Unfortunately, our beautiful fairy tale was smashed by reality. When the Cultural Revolution broke out in 1966, formal education in China was stopped. Instead of going to school, I witnessed chaos, cheatings, killings, and persecutions. Surrounded by the so-called red terrors, we could not secure our own property, privacy, and life. All of this originally generated my thinking about individual dignity and worth. At the age of sixteen, I was assigned to work at the largest factory in Jiangsu Province. In the eyes of most Chinese, I was a lucky man, because my being a worker in the Cultural Revolution, in addition to providing a stable income and benefits from the government, implied that I became a revolutionist. However, deep in my heart, I really wanted to receive a higher education. Due to my family background, I did not qualify to be recommended for university study in the revolutionary era. Self-study was my only choice, even though the so-called white expert road was not encouraged at that time. (Those who pursued professional careers or intellectual studies in the Mao era were regarded as capitalists, white was the symbol for capitalism, and red was the symbol for socialism. Chinese professionals were viewed as taking the "white expert road.") In 1971, I began writing literary works, including novels and poems, and expressing my concerns on social issues, but I found that it affected society little. I then wrote essays for newspapers and radio broadcasting, but writing political essays under the party's censorship system was extremely frustrating. I gradually realized that changing the social system is the prerequisite to restoring individual dignity in China.

After China restored the university entrance examination system in 1977, I passed the exams and began my formal education in the Department of Philosophy at Nanjing University. It was a great reward for my self-study! This time I felt that I really was fortunate to study at the top university in the first class after the Cultural Revolution. Philosophy programs in Chinese universities emphasize not only traditional philosophy but politics, ethics, and ideology. My motivation to study philosophy was to seek a workable way to improve the Chinese political system. After I graduated with a bachelor of philosophy degree, the government assigned me a teaching job. A teacher in China is required to teach what the party wants, especially in the humanities and social sciences. Obviously, this was not my original intention when I studied philosophy. Then I planned to take the exams to pursue the Master of Philosophy, but the head of the party and the president of my college harshly criticized me for my "bourgeois motivation" and warned me that I would lose my job if I failed to pass the exams. I was determined to take the chance, and once again I made it. The Department of Philosophy of Wuhan University was one of the top four in China, partly because the first president of Wuhan University, Li-Da, was a delegate of the first conference of the CPC. His book *Mass Philosophy* was used to enlighten readers regarding Chairman Mao Zedong's revolutionary ideas.

To promote educational reform, in 1984, the Association of Graduate Students of Wuhan University with Fu Dan University organized a national conference for graduate students entitled "The New Technological Revolution and the Direction of Graduate Students' Education." As an organizer and host, I was asked to give a speech at the opening conference. In my speech, entitled "The Challenges of the New Technological Revolution to Marxism," I raised more than a hundred questions on Marxism and concluded that it no longer fit the needs of the Chinese people, and that Marxism as an official ideology must be replaced by a new ideology in order to serve China's modernization. At that time, I believed that China's political system would change within the communist political system if more and more people challenged Marxism and the CPC. Based on this belief, in the 1980s I published over fifty articles on Chinese society and ideology from different perspectives; eight of them were reprinted by leading academic journals and newspapers, including *Xinhua Wenzai, Chinese Philosophy Year Book, Youth Digest*, and *Guangming Daily*. My naïve attempts inevitably failed within the communist system. The Tiananmen Square Incident of 1989 clearly showed that the party is the fundamental obstacle to Chinese political reform. After the incident, a great number of Chinese intellectuals walked away from politics and shifted their interests from politics to business. However, for me the Tiananmen Square Incident of 1989 was a turning point, leading me to rethink the true meaning of democracy.

The second reason for this book is an outcome of my scholarly research on Chinese society and politics from a philosophical perspective. In the United States, I practiced ministry in a church and law in a law firm after I earned my master of science in divinity degree. These experiences helped me to better understand Western democracy. Although my beliefs may have wavered, and I wandered spiritually, I never forgot my original intention in coming to the United States. I was fortunate when, in 1997, Baylor University offered me the opportunity to pursue a Ph.D. in Church-State Studies. This opportunity enabled me to revisit China's past, present, and future through a new lens. Thus it actually guided me to restart my scholarly work in the United States. Having done research on China's democracy, and drawing on my personal experiences in China, I have reached the conclusion that the CPC is the last fortress of antidemocratization in China. The CPC was responsible for the failures of socialist practice at any levels under the Mao regime. In order to maintain the party's power, the CPC launched the reform movement, but its achievements are basically limited to the economic arena. The CPC has resisted political change for more than twenty years. At this point, the party is also responsible for delaying the process of democracy in the post-Mao era.

China's economic growth rate has been the fastest in the world for two decades, but at the same time, China is also the world's largest communist country. It seems that this fascinating phenomenon challenges my central argument that the CPC is the fundamental obstacle to democratization. Therefore, it raises some serious questions: Has the CPC changed its identity and brought the party into the postcommunist stage? Can the CPC be the dynamic driving force of Chinese society in the twenty-first century? How long will the CPC be able sustain the current economic growth rate? Can both economic prosperity and political democratization be fulfilled under the leadership of the CPC? Needless to say, the party will not voluntarily surrender its power anytime soon. What can we do in the process of democratization under party rule? Neither nihilism nor radical revolution is the answer. An "inside revolution" (non-violent revolution) is the only way to accelerate China's democratization in the transitional period. The inside revolution is an initiative to develop a new public philosophy through educational programs and religious missions. It is why I call for remaking China's public philosophy for the twenty-first century.

It is strongly emphasized in this book that the ultimate purpose of remaking China's public philosophy is to dissolve the one-party system.

However, Marxism and the CPC are two sides of the same coin. It is impossible to remove Marxism from its position as the state ideology without terminating the one-party system. One cannot understand the CPC without understanding Marxism. According to the latest version of the Constitution of the People's Republic of China (1982), Marxism is the official Chinese ideology and the guiding principle of the CPC, and the CPC is the sole leadership of the Chinese people of all nationalities. Nowadays, the CPC has no intention to give up Marxism and its sole leadership. On July 1, 2001, at the meeting to celebrate the eightieth anniversary of the founding of the CPC, Jiang Zemin firmly pointed out that Marxism is the fundamental guiding principle of the consolidation of the CPC and the development of the country. According to Jiang, the CPC is the representative of the requirements of the development of China's advanced productive forces, the orientation of the development of China's advanced culture, and the fundamental interests of the overwhelming majority of the Chinese people (three representative theory).

At present, Marxism is still the state ideology, the party is still in power, and state ownership still dominates the Chinese economy. The concept that China became a capitalist society or that China has entered into a postsocialist society is false. It is impossible to make China a capitalist society and a democratic system in the framework of the one-party system. Although sooner or later the CPC will fundamentally change its nature as the reform movement deepens and the Chinese people awaken, the Chinese government would better serve the Chinese people and international society if the one-party system were dissolved earlier. China cannot sustain its current economic growth rate if the party does not fundamentally change its political system.

The manuscript of this book was completed in March 2002, before the Sixteenth National Conference of the CPC in November 2002. Western scholars and societies used to place hopes on the post-Mao era and the post-Deng era. Although China has been experiencing much change, the political identity of China remains the same. In writing this book, I pointed out that the Sixteenth National Conference of the CPC would not affect the nature of the CPC, even though the conference for the first time adopted a new slogan, "Chinese Political Civilization." I also asked several questions: What would happen in the post-Jiang era? Would the CPC step into the post-communist era and make China a real member of the global village after the conference? We now have the answer: The party is the PARTY. When the party is the PARTY, it will not change its nature. The failure to control the spread of severe acute respiratory syndrome (SARS) in China and to more than twenty-six countries in the world was essentially the unavoidable consequence of the censorship and Communist political system that reflects the nature of the PARTY. China's democratization will not be realized until the one-party system has been changed. When and whether the one-party system is dissolved depends on the process of remaking China's public philosophy. Although it takes time to realize the goal of China's democratization, in essence, the Chinese people are leaving the track of communism. I have visibly and rationally seen that China is departing from the traditional communist society model. Before the sixteenth National Conference of the CPC, I visited China for two weeks, personally experiencing the changes.

First, the signs of the party are disappearing. Before the reform movement, the CPC was a supreme power, controlling the entire Chinese society. The authority of the party was not only reflected in its organizations; it was also visible. There were picture billboards and posters at roadsides and in public places. The signboards of party branches hung at the front of every work unit. Television and movies were also filled with party images. The party was everywhere. Its images were as common in China as McDonald's restaurants and gasoline stations are in the United States.

My first stop in China was Shanghai. It was about twenty miles from Pudong International Airport to my hotel. On the way, I kept a close watch on the roadside, finding nothing except innumerable commercial advertisements visible throughout the cab ride. In the hotel, at least forty TV channels could be accessed, including CNN (although my friends told me that CNN is only available at hotels). Most Chinese TV programs follow Western styles, including soap operas, talk shows, and commercials. Even news reports are much less political than before. In order to get macroimpressions, I took a bus traveling from Shanghai to Nanjing through Zheng Jiang, Changzhou, and Suzhou, the most developed regions in China, then took a train returning from Nanjing to Shanghai. On this trip, I found that the visible signs of the party had been completely replaced by commercial buildings, housing, shopping malls, and commercial signs and advertisements. In these cities, I spent at least two days walking the streets, trying to find visible signs of the party, but I failed to find any. All party signboards at the front of work units, including businesses, factories, hospitals, schools, universities, department stores, grocery stores, and residential committees, had disappeared. The only exception was that the signboards of the party committees at the district level or above remained. If I were not a native Chinese, I could not find the CPC, and I might not even realize that China is a communist country. Wherever I went, every city was filled with commercial smells. Needless to say, the market economy in China is greatly expanding, no matter what it is—a socialist market economy or a capitalist market economy. When the market is expanding, the party is losing its territory. If China continues its rapid pace of marketization, the time will soon come when the party's power monopoly will be over.

Second, people can raise a different voice in public. Before I came back to the United States, my friends treated me to a dinner. We had five people at the table who are officials in different positions. The restaurant, which was very crowded, is located in a very beautiful place in the southern part of China. In such a public place, the Chinese people never before raised different voices, voices conflicting with official opinions. At the beginning we only chatted, recalling old events, which reminded us of old memories. In this same place, we used to sit together and write poems to express our political ambitions. Twenty years later, the lake remains as it was before, while we work in different countries. We were filled with a thousand mixed feelings, but we kept them silent for a while. Finally, I broke the silence, talking about my life in the United States and mixing in political ideas. I knew I should not make any political statements in such a public place. I looked around to see the other tables' reactions. Fortunately, nothing happened. I looked at my friends, asking with guilty feelings, "Did I get you guys in trouble?" "Not at all, friend," they replied, smiling, "Who cares now?" When they said "Who cares?" I understood that it had a double meaning: Who cares about politics; and, Who cares about the party, because the party is no longer sacred in Chinese eyes.

Third, party cadres are jittery and seeking other jobs. As an independent institution, the party committee at the district level or above had its own building, in which the party committee ran its authorities over governments and subordinate units through different departments. The main cadres of every party branch in work units took full-time positions, engaging in so-called political and ideological work. In previous years, many people were eager to get this kind of job because the job was easy and great privileges came with it. Mr. Tang was a faithful party member who joined the party at age eighteen. (According to the Constitution of the CPC, eighteen is the minimum age for party membership.) Now, he heads a party committee at a factory. I knew his office was the most luxurious one, indicating that his power is at the top in the factory. Following the old path, I arrived there, but I found that his office apparently had been taken over by the general manager of the factory (or so I guessed, because the factory has carried out a system of overall responsibility). Mr. Tang's new office was the last door on the third floor. After I knocked on the door and waited for a while, he opened the door and led me in. "What are you doing?" I asked directly, because I knew the party's door remained open to welcome visitors. "You can figure out what I am doing, even if you haven't lived in China for a long time." "You must be doing something for yourself, I guess." "Yes, I am doing my second job, *chao gu* (playing stock)." He continued, "I have no choice. I try my best, but prepare for the worst before my position is eliminated. You know that *gai zhi* (owner-system change) has been going forward on a large scale. The government requires all small and medium-sized enterprises to go private. Nobody knows what roles the party will have in work units. So my job is unstable and my future is unpredictable." Through my investigation, I have learned that some party cadres have already been persuaded to retire; some are unemployed; some shifted their positions from political work to professional work; and some are secretly doing a second job, like Mr. Tang. It is evident that party cadres at work units no longer concentrate on party work. In work units, there is no regular party meeting; party members are not required to write confessional reports; party offices are absent visitors; and party jobs no longer attract the people. The party in work units actually exists in name only. Most of the time, party cadres at the grassroots and district levels just stay in their offices, doing nothing. The public opinion in China is that full-time party cadres are not necessary at work units. However, some party cadres who work at provincial levels are still very confident and work very hard, focusing on ideological work. They believe that the party is the sole leadership of China and will survive well into the twenty-first century. I puzzle over how the party can manage to implement its policy on the grassroots level under such conditions. As they say in Chinese, *pi zhi bu cun mao jiang yan fu?* (With the skin gone, to what can the hair attach itself?).

Fourth, a large number of party members no longer believe in communism. In China, I asked party members some questions: "Who is the author of the Manifesto?" "What is communism?" "What is the final goal of communism?" "What are the general tasks of the party at present?" It seemed that they found all these questions funny and naïve and, therefore, beneath their consideration. Before the reform movement, the Chinese people thought that the party was doing a sacred mission, and most party members had serious commitments to the party. Now, however, members no longer have serious faith in the party and in communism. They told me that their original intention in joining the party was not to attain the goal of communism, but for their personal interests. In their words, "Communism has nothing to do with me!"

So why has party membership increased, up to 64 million? First, the ratio of party members to the overall Chinese population actually is in decline. China had 900 million people and 50 million party members in 1976. At that time, 5.5 percent were party members. Today, China has 1.3 billion people and 64 million party members. So at present only 4.9 percent of the Chinese population are party members. Second, a large number of party branches are actually paralyzed. In urban areas, party branches at small work units do not function at all. About 65 percent of Chinese people still live in the countryside. After China carried out the household responsibility system in 1978, every rural household made the economy its the top priority. In addition, there is a floating population of about 20 million and 47 million unemployed individuals in China. It is certain that some of them are party members who are no longer active, although it is difficult to get an accurate percentage. Third, the stratum of party members has been changed. Based on the *Research Report on Social Rank in China,* published by the Academy of Social Sciences of China in 2002, the Chinese people can be divided into ten basic social ranks: (1) government officials at different levels who are decision makers, making up 1.1 percent; (2) middle- and high-level managers in the middle and large enterprises, making up 1.5 percent; (3) big private owners, making up 0.6 percent; (4) professionals, making up 5.1 percent; (5) general office workers, making up 4.8 percent; (6) small business owners, making up 3.2 percent; (7) commercial services people, making up 14 percent; (8) industrial workers, making up 22.6 percent; (9) peasants, making up 44 percent; and (10) the unemployed, making up 3.1 percent. In the postindustrial era, the most advanced social ranks are professionals, managers, big private owners, and general office workers. The four social ranks altogether make up only 11 percent of the total Chinese population. However, those people, in contrast with other social ranks, are less interested in becoming party members.

Fifth, Chinese elites have lost interest in joining the party. The party established a very high standard for accepting members before the reform movement. Whoever wanted to join had to go through the following stages: submitting an application, handing in confessional reports, being evaluated and interviewed, having an extensive background investigation, filling out the formal application, being voted into the party branch, and, finally, becoming a reserved party member. One qualified to become a formal party member after the oath ceremony if she or he made no mistakes over the course of one year. Although it was a very complicated and long process, the majority of the Chinese people tried very hard to seek the possibility to join the party, because *dang piao* (the title of "party member") was critical for professional advancement.

When I talked to non–party members, including Chinese officials, intellectuals, college students, businessmen, workers, and peasants, I asked them whether they were interested in joining the party. Most of their answers were negative. The reason is very simple: The reform movement has opened up many ways for the Chinese people to reach their goals. Becoming a party member is only one of the ways, yet this way is uncertain in the future. In order to have a stable and good life, most Chinese people believe that three things—intelligence, education, and money—are the most important. The slogan "time is money" already has become popular. The Chinese people look upon party activities as "extra tax"; that is, the don't find them necessary. They like to spend their time not on party activities, but on receiving education, making money, and having fun. When I asked them the question, "Why don't you join the party?" they always answered with another question: "Why do I need to join the party?" Because they are capable of making their life comfortable without *dang piao*, they do not like to be restricted by the political and spiritual shackles. Obviously, *dang piao* is no longer attractive to the Chinese people, especially to talented people and the younger generation. Under these circumstances, the party must persuade people to become party members through different means, including through reducing the requirements to become party member. Nonetheless, it is still not easy for the party to increase its membership. I found that people who have less education, fewer professional skills, and less money are more interested in becoming party members.

According to a Chinese official report, on the eve of the anniversary of the CPC in 2002, Mr. Xue-feng Wen, a graduate student of the class of 1999 at the University of National Defense and Technology, had become a news figure and was invited by the official Chinese media to talk about the topic, "Why rejoin the party?" According to the reports, Mr. Wen is an excellent student at the university and was accepted as a reserved party member in 1997. A year later, the party branch urged him to submit his application to convert to a formal party member, but he refused to do so because he was displeased by the party's corruption. His refusal resulted in the cancellation of his qualification of party member. However, in March 2001, he changed his mind and submitted applications to become a reserved party member three times. Finally, his application was granted in December 2001. He thereby became a model the CPC can use to propagandize that Chinese intellectuals love the party. This example simply illustrates just how difficult it is for the party to convince Chinese intellectuals to join. Thus the party can no longer represent the most advanced culture and advanced productive forces in China. In order to increase the numbers of party members, Jiang has encouraged private owners to join the party. It does not necessarily mean that China has already entered into the postcommunist era. On the contrary, this will lead to serious new political and economic corruption, if the one-party system continues to operate, because the new policy will open a way for Chinese officials and businesspeople to work together to make dirty money.

At present, the party is still in power, but its power is diminishing, its reputation is declining, the party branch at work units is becoming paralyzed, the Chinese elite are leaving the party, and the communist faith is disappearing. Even though the party has managed to survive into the twenty-first century, few Chinese people even within the party truly believe in communism. Moreover, the party's reputation has seriously been hurt by widespread corruption among the party cadres. It has become a popular phenomenon that corrupt and evil officials carry huge amounts of government money with them as they escape from China to foreign countries. The Chinese government lost at least 52 billion U.S. dollars between 1997 and 1999. Therefore, it is a real question whether the party can represent the will and the interests of the majority of the Chinese people. That is why I persistently oppose the one-party system. There will be no democratization in China without terminating the one-party system by remaking China's public philosophy. Although the new leader Hu Jingtao will continue to implement Jiang's three representative theory, he will push the reform movement one step forward. I very optimistically predict that the one-party system will be dissolved in the first half of the twenty-first century, and, as a result, China will rise as a giant in the world. By that time, the Chinese people will enjoy both economic prosperity and the most advanced social and political system—the modern democratic system.

Acknowledgments

The idea of this book was initially inspired by Dr. Derek H. Davis, director of the J.M. Dawson Institute of Church-State Studies, Baylor University. It would have been impossible for me to complete this multidisciplinary study without his guidance, encouragement, and serious editing. I owe him more than I can ever acknowledge. In writing the first draft of the manuscript, Dr. H. Stephen Gardner, professor of world economics, offered scholarly insight and valuable comments. Dr. John N. Jonsson, professor of world religions, provided a great vision on the global significance of Chinese culture and unique approaches to the incorporation of Eastern culture and Western culture. Dr. Christopher Marsh, director of Asian Studies, gave his kind support and detailed comments.

I want to thank Dr. Nikolas Gvosdev for his assistance in polishing my first draft of the prospectus. Frank McAnear was the first reader for the first half of this book, and I benefited immensely from his critique and corrections. I want to thank Wanda Gilbert and the team at Impressions Book and Journal Services for their administrative assistance. I want especially to thank Kara Mitzel, grants coordinator of Corporate and Foundation Relations at Hobart and William Smith Colleges. Before I submitted my manuscript, she carefully read it, made corrections, and offered thoughtful suggestions.

I want to thank Greenwood Publishing Group for offering me this great opportunity to publish this book. I very much appreciate Halley Gatenby's help in the final stage of the book. Her professional editing was a crucial step leading to the completion of the book. My thanks also goes to Hobart and William Smith Colleges. I am very grateful to the colleges for offering me an assistant professor position that enabled me to complete this book.

Finally, I also want to thank my wife, Sai Gong, who took on the extra burden of taking care of my health and the housework during my writing. This scholarly work embodies her contributions.

CHAPTER 1

Introduction

The year 2001, the first year of the twenty-first century, was not only a historical turning point for every country in the world but also was meaningful to the democratic wave in the new century. That year marked the tenth anniversary of the collapse of the former Soviet Union. The collapse of the Soviet Union proclaimed that the cold war era had ended and a new democratic wave had been launched. That historical event also indicated that peaceful revolution is the best way to unseat a communist regime. The collapse of the Soviet Union, of course, had a profound impact on the People's Republic of China. Before China broke off its official relationship with the Soviet Union, China viewed the Soviet Union as the second home of Marxism, as an older brother, and as the socialist model. When Beijing broke off relations with Moscow, China tried to establish a China-centered socialist camp. The Communist Party of China (CPC) learned from the fall of the Soviet Union and became more cautious in promoting the reform movement in order to further strengthen its communist power, but, in fact, this incident once again—following the Tiananmen Square Incident of 1989—undermined the Chinese people's belief in communism and resulted in a spiritual crisis.

Although today only a few communist countries are still functioning in the world, the Chinese government still firmly upholds the communist model. According to the Constitution of the People's Republic of China, the CPC is the sole leadership of the Chinese people of all nationalities. The party at present tightly controls all of China through the one-party system. In 1921, when the first conference of the Communist Party of China was held in Shanghai, the party had only fifty members. On the conference's eightieth anniversary, the general secretary of the party, Jiang Zemin, declared that the party is the representative of advanced productive forces, culture, and the Chinese people. His conclusion is the well-known slogan, Long live the great Communist Party of China! Unarguably, China has made magnificent achievements since the reform movement. In 2001, China continued to expand its role and position in international society: It joined the World Trade Organization, won the right to host the Olympic Games of 2008, and received permanent most-favored-nation status from the United States. The Chinese economy has kept growing and has attracted even more investment from Taiwan. According to a recent survey conducted by the Taiwan journal *Tianxia*, about 1 million Taiwanese are planning to reside in the mainland in 2002. Many analysts have predicted that China will become a very competitive market in the near future. It is no wonder that quite a few analysts warn that China is a great threat to Western countries. Is communism rising up again as economic reform is expanding? Can the party guide China to both economic and political prosperity? How can democratic societies direct China's development in playing positive roles in the global village? Can the communist government be a partner of democratic societies?

A half-century ago, the world alignment was very clear: Nazi and anti-Nazi. Then, following World War II, the world was again divided into two camps: capitalist and socialist. Both sides believed that they represented an ultimate truth and the hope of human society that would finally redeem all humankind. Nevertheless, fifty years later, Nazism had been eliminated as a power, and communism had failed both in theory and in practice. The Communist Party in socialist countries actually no longer interests people. After the former Soviet Union joined the Western democratic alliance, Eastern European socialist countries, as satellite states, followed Moscow's step and established democratic systems. In China, the massive student protest of 1989 in Tiananmen Square was a good try to unseat party rule, but this attempt failed with bloody consequences.

Nowadays, democracy has become the main trend of human society. The twenty-first century is the century of democracy. Beyond China, North Korea, Vietnam, and Cuba still survive as communist countries. However, the 2001 terrorist attack on the United States on September 11 blurred the boundary between democratic countries and communist countries. The United States put some political and ideological differences aside to seek an extensive united front against terrorists. On the other side, the CPC suppresses political dissidents at home in the name of antiterrorism. When U.S. president George W. Bush attended the Shanghai Conference of Asia-Pacific Economic Cooperation in October 2001, he highly praised Jiang's achievements in the reform movement. In return, Jiang surprisingly gave tacit consent to U.S. military bases in Asian countries. Some commentators described that Sino-American relationship as a honeymoon. Interestingly enough, even after the U.S. government withdrew from the 1972 Anti–Ballistic Missile (ABM) Treaty, Russian officials said that U.S. secession from the ABM treaty would not exacerbate bilateral relations, and Beijing officials responded that it might work out in some ways. It seems that the ideological differences between the two camps have been dramatically narrowed. Is it true that the world already has entered a new era, as some analysts have claimed, an era of antiterrorism? Could it be said that the conflict between democracy and communism no longer exists? Could it be said that the fight against terrorism is a new standard for forming coalitions? Could it be said that communist China has become a permanent strategic partner of democratic societies? The Bush administration has regarded China as a "strategic competitor" and a "strategic adversary," but it has treated Russia as a partner. Russian president Vladimir Putin made a special trip to the United States in November 2001 and developed a personal relationship with George W. Bush. This visit reaffirmed that the cold war is over and once again shows the differences between communism and democracy at the critical moment of world history following the terrorist attacks of September 11. At this moment, China is still not in the inner circle of international society.

It is clear that any type of terrorism is not a demonstration of religious faith, but evil and a crime. The conflict between civilization and terrorism represents neither the conflict between Western and Eastern cultures nor the main conflict of contemporary time over the long term. The elimination of terrorism is only part of the solution to make peace. There will be no permanent peaceful world without global democratization. Communist China is becoming an economic power and supporting antiterrorism, but potential and realistic conflicts between communist China and democratic societies are visible and foreseeable. What is the best solution to establish a permanent peaceful relationship between democratic societies and China? In other words, what is the best way to make China a democratic society? Which way should China go—and which way will it? These issues have caught the world's attention because they are so important to the process of global democratization. Remaking China's public philosophy is the best way to make China a democratic society, peacefully, in the twenty-first century.

RAISING THE ISSUE OF REMAKING CHINA'S PUBLIC PHILOSOPHY

Modern democracy was born only 200 years ago. When the Industrial Revolution awakened human beings and ushered in a new era, the bourgeoisie, as a new leadership in the new era, guided people to build up the democratic system. In the middle of the nineteenth century, Karl Marx and Friedrich Engels, as representatives of communism and the working class, challenged the democratic system, proclaiming in the *Communist Manifesto* that the socialist system is the true democratic system and predicting that capitalist society would inevitably die. Because Marx and Engels's theory met the needs of the working class in the primary stage of capitalist society, it gradually became a movement and spread all over the world. The by-products of World War II, socialist governments gained power in many developing countries, especially in Asian societies. Although the communist Soviet Union joined the Allies to fight Nazism, communism and democracy essentially contradict each other. After World War II, the dominant forces realigned, and world affairs have thus become more complex. Since the 1980s, the democratic system has dramatically shown its advantages and has deepened its roots in the former socialist countries. History incontrovertibly proved that the democratic system is superior to the socialist system and is essential to economic prosperity and political stability. Modern democracy is the most advanced political system in history and the main driving force of contemporary society, though the Chinese government consistently denies it.

The People's Republic of China, one of the world's largest countries with a population of 1.3 billion, is one of last few communist countries in the world. China was once the world's most advanced civilization, but it gradually became a backward country after the fourteenth century. The full explanation for China's fall must consider the Chinese political system. Chairman Mao Zedong, the founder of the People's Republic of China, believed that socialist people could do everything that they wanted and proclaimed that only socialism could save China. He shut China's doors to the rest of the world, practicing a self-reliant socialist system and campaigning for the class struggle for twenty-six years. As a matter of fact, a radical form of socialism brought China to the edge of economic collapse. Twenty-six years of painful reality gradually was waking the Chinese people from Mao's utopian dream and made them rethink the Chinese way of life. After Mao died in 1976, the Chinese people had a chance to see the rest of the world. The sharp contrast between China and democratic societies shocked the Chinese people. Under high pressures from domestic and international societies two years after Mao died, the Chinese government began launching the economic reform movement. Since the 1980s, China's economic growth rate has been the fastest in the world. The living standard of the majority of the Chinese people has significantly improved. China has emerged with a new visage in the East in many areas, including housing facilities, architecture, urbanization, higher technologies, and lifestyle. However, within China, Marxism and Maoism remain the official ideology, and the CPC is still the sole party to hold power. It continues to dominate every aspect of Chinese society. So far there is no sign to show that the party has any intention of fundamentally reforming its political system.

Several questions emerge. How long can China maintain its current high economic growth rate without fundamental political reform? Can economic prosperity automatically bring a high culture to the Chinese people? How can China strengthen its civil society and be compatible with international civil society? How can China effect its all-around modernization and enable the Chinese people to fully enjoy modern civilization? What is the fundamental obstacle to Chinese democratization? What is the dynamic driving force for China to transform from an authoritarian regime to a democratic system? How can China integrate with global civil society and the international democratic village? What direction must China take in the twenty-first century? Above all, how can China transform its one-party system into a democratic system? Answering these questions is possible only if China seeks to reexamine, redefine, and remake its public philosophy. Some analysts claim that world politics stepped into a new era after September 11. Moreover, some scholars claim that the old line between democracy and socialism disappeared, and a new line between democracy and terrorism emerged. By this argument, China's democratization is no longer important to international society and the Chinese people. In reality, although the Bush administration has continued to push the Chinese government to improve human rights, it also changed its tone and has referred to the U.S. relationship with the Chinese government as a "strategic partnership." There is no doubt that terrorism is a great enemy to world civilization. China shares common interests with democratic countries in fighting terrorism, but the fundamental differences between communist China and democratic systems did not simply disappear after September 11. Fundamental differences, including but not limited to political systems, ideology, human rights, and the model of the reform movement, still exist between the two camps—democratic societies and China. In the long term, the war against terrorism will not be completed without international democratization. Likewise, China cannot realize its modernization without democratization. A more serious problem is that the Chinese government has put more restrictions on the Chinese people and the reform movement in the name of antiterrorism. Therefore, it is necessary to call world attention to the fact that the Chinese people now face a more difficult task in promoting the process of democratization while fighting terrorism.

It is a very interesting phenomenon that the oldest countries in the world, such as China, India, Egypt, and Greece, are not the most developed countries. China changed very little over more than 2,000 years, especially its political system. Many China scholars interpreted this phenomenon from quite different viewpoints, including geographic, economic, scientific, cultural, and political perspectives, but they failed to make a case based on public philosophy. In other words, they have not made efforts to explore the role of public philosophy in the development of society because they overlooked the very important fact that China had changed its public philosophy little after Confucianism was established as orthodoxy in the Han dynasty (206 B.C.–A.D. 220). Even after Western cultures flowed into China in the nineteenth century, indigenous Chinese public philosophy remained in the dominant position. Sun Yat-sen's Three People's Principles were a significant move away from traditional Chinese public philosophy from a historical perspective, but they were a mixture of Western democracy, Confucianism, and communism. Due to Sun's death shortly after the revolution of 1911, the Three People's Principles never touched the grass roots in China before the Nationalist government withdrew from mainland China in 1949. Marxism, the foundation of the CPC, was imported from the West, directly from the Soviet Union, although Mao Zedong mixed it with ideas of the peasant's revolution and Confucianism. Influenced by these kinds of public philosophy, all Chinese governments from ancient times to the communist regime have kept a highly centralized political system. The distinguishing characteristics of Chinese political systems can be characterized as one leader, one party, one ideology, and one voice. There is enough evidence to argue that the old Chinese public philosophy restrained China from becoming a developed country.

The Chinese people did not realize the significant role of public philosophy until modern times, marked by the first Opium War of 1840. Western gunboats for the first time in Chinese history forced China to open its door and to sign unequal treaties after China lost the first Opium War. This greatly humiliated the Chinese people, but it also generated enormous nationalism in China. The Chinese people then began to seek a resolution to strengthen China. They went through three stages and finally realized that the public philosophy was the foundation of Chinese modernization. The first stage, the Self-Strengthening Movement from 1861 to 1895, promoted military and technological modernization without political change; the second stage, from 1898 to 1915, witnessed the acceptance of Western political institutions without a change of public philosophy; and, finally, the intellectual revolution of 1917–23 touched "the inner core of intellectual life,"[1] that is, changed the public philosophy. In that third stage, while realizing the importance of public philosophy, the Chinese people's cultural fervor arose and fiercely attacked traditional culture. The May Fourth Movement of 1919 was the product of cultural fervor and the symbol of changes in China's public philosophy in the cultural framework. By holding high the slogan of democracy and science, the May Fourth Movement fiercely attacked old Chinese culture and introduced Western culture into China. Meanwhile, Chinese intellectuals conducted a great amount of discourse on the relationship between Chinese culture and Western culture and China's modernization through public forums. The changes in public philosophy promoted Chinese society to go through the transition from a monarchical system to a modern nation-state. Unfortunately, the evolution of China's public philosophy was interrupted by three civil wars from 1927 to 1949. During this period, Marxism and communism were widely accepted by Chinese peasants and the working class, because the blueprint of communism was the better choice as compared to the nationalist government.

After the CPC came to power, Marxism became the official orthodoxy. Mao was regarded as the sole representative of Marxism in the Chinese context. Marxism-Maoism was described as an absolute truth in Mao era. Anyone who challenged Marxism was subject to severe punishment. Therefore, the Mao era could also be called an ideological glacial epoch. After Mao died, the Chinese people once again began to seek modernization and repeated the same pattern of the three cycles in the nineteenth century. During the first stage of the reform movement, the Chinese government emphasized only the development of the Chinese economy. The party stated that the goal of China in the twentieth century was to realize four modernizations: of industry, of agriculture, of national defense, and of science and technology. Therefore, Four Modernizations became the main slogan used by the party to inspire the Chinese people for China's socialist construction. Some Chinese elites realized that the Four Modernizations were meaningless without a fifth modernization—democratization. Upon this realization, the Chinese reform movement entered into a second stage, in which China started to reform its political institutions. The Tiananmen Square Incident in 1989 clearly indicated that China could not fulfill its political reform without remaking its public philosophy. What is the next stage—the third stage? Obviously, an intellectual revolution and public philosophy reform must inevitably take place. It is a necessary stage for China's democratization to remake public philosophy.

However, some Western scholars regard culture as the basic force to promote social progress, because a nation is a cultural system. Michael J. Mazarr classifies four distinct models of cultural influence in social progress: "cultural values as broadly determining individual and national success; culture as an influence on decision making; culture as the principal determinant of economic and social structure; and culture as the dominant variable in conflict and international relations today."[2] Francis Fukuyama argues that cultural differences will become the chief determinant of national success: "Liberal political and economic institutions depend on a healthy and dynamic civil society for their vitality." Moreover, "a thriving civil society depends on a people's habits, customs, and ethics," which are shaped by culture.[3] Due to the fact that the term *culture* includes aspects of both material and ideological civilization, it is a circular argument to say that culture determines social progress. Therefore, some scholars disagree with the idea of cultural determinism and assert that socioeconomic policy is the key issue. Culture for them is not a primary driving force for a society, but a secondary force. Democracy is not primarily brought about by culture but by modernization and globalism. Moreover, Samuel P. Huntington set forth the completely opposite viewpoint: that the world is moving into a period of civilizational clashes in which cultural differences will necessarily be the main source of conflict, leading to ongoing skirmishes and wars.[4] Looking back into history, cultural conflicts and human society are twins. Cultural conflicts will not bring human society down. Instead, it is one of democratic societies' characteristics—pluralism—that will help every nation to establish their identities.

Some scholars seek a third way as a new social theory to guide social development. The third way "differs from both the market fundamentalism of the right and the statism of the socialist tradition."[5] According to Anthony Giddens, the strengthening of civil society is a foundation of the politics of the third way.[6] From Jurgen Habermas's viewpoint, economic system, market, civil society, and culture are not the keys to building up a democratic system. He emphasizes the relationship between philosophy of law and political theory, pointing out that democracy and the rule of law are internally related because social stability and integration require that people believe their society is legitimate; the legitimacy of a regime is grounded in the consent of the people, and law derives its validity from consent, that is, the consent of the governed in modern society.[7] Of course, law is very important to regulate societies, but laws are made by human beings and implemented by human beings. Therefore, public philosophy is the base for a society to make good laws. It is a dangerous society that is regulated only by law without following good public philosophy.

What is the best theory to guide the development of society? What term should be employed as a key concept to combine other aspects of social structure to form an integrated theory that fits the Chinese context and guides the process of Chinese democratization? Public philosophy is the key concept to form a new theory, and remaking China's public philosophy is the key to Chinese democratization in the twenty-first century, because remaking China's public philosophy is the way to change the interior lives of the Chinese people. The Tiananmen Square Incident of 1989 showed that dramatic revolution is not always the best way to unseat a communist regime and establish a democratic system. Remaking China's public philosophy will promote China's democratization peacefully in the twenty-first century.

THE SIGNIFICANCE OF REMAKING CHINA'S PUBLIC PHILOSOPHY

Up to this point, there has been no scholarly work completed, either in China or in the United States, that has used the prism of public philosophy to examine Chinese history, the process of Chinese modernization, and the relationship of China's reform movement and the process of democratization. Public philosophy comprises the inner connections that exist among a nation's civil society, its economy, its political system, its ideology, its civil religion, its culture, and its educational program.

Theoretically, China specialists have been paying considerable attention to the issue of the impact of economic reform on the political process, culture, and communist ideology. Their studies provide the theoretical foundation for the Chinese government to shift the focus from class struggle to economy and to promote the economic reform program. China needs an integrated theory to explore the mutual relationship between economic development and political change. If research on China remains tied to this approach, practically, it will favor the party's resistance to political and ideological change; and theoretically, it will result in economic determinism, with no ability to arrive at a workable solution for China's problems in the twenty-first century. It is time for China specialists to address the issue of how remaking China's public philosophy will impact social evolution, the reform movement, and the process of democratization.

The term *culture* is a very broad concept that includes all material goods and the system of ideas. Culture is like a basket that can hold everything. Therefore, it is difficult to expound upon a clear relationship between culture and other aspects in the development of society if we determine culture to be the basic concept to exploring a political theory. Also, cultural change is a slow process, and culture only influences economic and other areas indirectly. The economy is the productive base of a society, but the economy functions only within a specific system and is guided by specific theories. A new public philosophy is the theoretical precursor for a new society. In history, the Renaissance led the Industrial Revolution; the Age of Reason in Europe paved the way for the French Revolution. Both the Declaration of the Rights of Man (1789) and the American Declaration of Independence inspired generations to build up democratic societies. In contemporary times, the reform movements in Taiwan and South Korea are clearly directed by new public philosophy. Liberation movements in Africa and South America are also guided by new public philosophy, such as liberation theology and black theology. A new public philosophy stimulates people to draw on their historical experience and explore a new way to reconstruct social structures, economic systems, and political power, and to reformulate the relationships among individuals, society, and government, on the one hand, and between the state and society, on the other.

Practically speaking, remaking China's public philosophy is the best way to promote China's modernization and democratization peacefully. Among many needed reforms, the Chinese political system needs to be changed first. For more than 2,000 years of Chinese history, since the first emperor of the Qin dynasty (221–201 B.C.), China has been governed under an autocratic system. Although different dynasties carried different titles and followed different ideologies, the system was essentially autocratic whether it was ruled by an emperor, the Republic of China, or the People's Republic of China and whether it was guided by Confucianism, Marxism, Maoism, or the Four Basic Principles. In Chinese history, no one autocratic government has found a way to solve China's real problems, nor has one government had the sincere intention to fundamentally alter the traditional Chinese political system. Of course, in world history, no country has established a modern democratic system within an autocratic system, because the democratic system fundamentally contradicts the dictatorial system. The autocratic system must be abolished first in order to establish the democratic system. Any advanced political change in autocratic societies is to enlarge the people's power and reduce the government's power. Certainly, the Chinese communist regime is absolutely unwilling to give up its power voluntarily or to share that power with the Chinese people. Therefore, it is necessary to call for remaking China's public philosophy and changing the one-party system.

Drawing on the lessons of the history of reform movements in China, a new public philosophy for China is the precondition for the needed reform movement to be successful. There are two types of reform movements in Chinese history: reform from "bottom up," and reform from "top down." Reform movements from the bottom up, including Chinese peasant uprisings and student movements such as the May Fourth Movement of 1919, the April Fifth Movement in 1976, and the Tiananmen Square Incident of 1989, usually were supported by broad masses of the people. Most of these reforms failed because the needs of the masses contradicted the will of the ruling class. Reform movements from top to bottom include movements for economic policy, such as Wang Anshi's reform in the Song dynasty; movements for new technology, such as the "Self-Strengthening Movement" of the 1860s and 1890s that were characterized by Westernization; and movements for new political systems, such as the Hundred-Days-Reform of 1898 and the Three People's Principles of the nationalist movement. This type of reform was usually organized by officials, but the common people received only very limited benefits even when the reform was successful because this type of reform movement largely represents the will of the ruling class.

No one reform movement in Chinese history was successful and brought China democracy. The emperors and the top government leaders did not support the reform movements in order to prevent any challenges from society; the ruling class resisted the reform movements in order to keep its own privileges; and the political systems did not allow the reform to go too far. Most important, both the common Chinese people and the ruling class lacked the consciousness of reform. A new public philosophy can remake the mind-set of both common people and the ruling class to provide the theoretical foundation for reform movements both "bottom up" and "top down." In recent years, various cultural forms have coexisted in Chinese society, though Marxism is still the official ideology under the Constitution. It is urgent to systematically outline the new China's public philosophy in order to nurture the new consciousness of the Chinese people in this turning point of history, and to guide the ongoing Chinese reform movement toward democratization.

Why is a new public philosophy important for China's democratization? This book is based on and tests the following major hypotheses: First, the political system that will evolve in China in the twenty-first century is a critical issue for the global village because China has the world's largest population, occupies a strategic area, is the world's third-biggest nuclear power, and has the world's third-largest economy in terms of gross national product (GNP). While China increasingly is asserting a more proactive global role, it remains the world's largest communist country, with 64 million party members. Only a democratic system can guarantee that China will play a positive role in the global village. Otherwise, the party will threaten domestic and international democracy.

Second, economic power is not a full expression of power; a powerful country is an integral combination of economy, science, politics, culture, education, morality, and spirituality. Any country, especially a large country, that develops only its economic and military force without a high level of spiritual life and democratic commitment will threaten global civil society. The terrorist threat can relax the tension between communism and democracy temporarily, but it cannot eliminate the fundamental conflict between the two.

Third, democratization with a new public philosophy is a logical goal for human history. There is no legitimate authority without democracy and a new public philosophy. There is no new public philosophy without support from a democratic system. In China, the communist regime has been in a transition period from totalitarianism to authoritarianism, but it is still uncertain whether China will evolve from an authoritarian regime into a democratic one. The signatures of members of the Chinese government on international documents do not guarantee that the Chinese government will put the principles laid out in those documents into practice; China's WTO accession does not automatically make China a capitalist-based democracy.

Fourth, no socialist country in the world, including the Eastern European nations and the former Soviet Union, automatically turns into a democratic system without a profound reform movement, either gradual or radical. China's reform movement is ongoing, but the Chinese government tries to restrict the reform to the economic arena. From Deng Xiaoping to China's current top leaders, no one has wanted to reform the Chinese political system because no one has been willing to give up his power and the CPC's privileges. However, the Four Modernizations, even if successful, cannot guarantee a democratic life for the people. Political reform also does not automatically change any deep-rooted system of ideas, because democracy cannot of itself bring about high culture. A new public philosophy should include democratic theory and a corresponding belief system. There is no true democratization without a new public philosophy in China.

Fifth, viewing reform movements toward democratization worldwide, the main cause for the failure of reform movements generally is the lack of a consciousness for reform in both common people and officials in different ranks of the bureaucracy. A new public philosophy is promoted by elites, and voluntarily accepted and practiced by both the common people and officials. The function of a new public philosophy is to nurture a new consciousness for both the common people and public officials. The new public philosophy will provide a clear vision of a reform movement; transform the Chinese individual into a new form of human capital as a precondition for modern democracy; guide the process from an authoritarian regime to a democratic system; minimize the differences between Chinese and international society in political, cultural, moral, and spiritual life; and, finally, join the global democratic alliance, so that China can coordinate with international society in the areas of market economy, human rights, religious freedom, and international law.

THE THEORY OF PUBLIC PHILOSOPHY

The term and theory of public philosophy have been developed by Western scholars, but they have not been used in the social science fields in China. The term *popular philosophy* stands for a completely different concept that was used for the first time in the 1920s, after the Russian Revolution of 1917. In order to spread Marxist philosophy, Chinese revolutionary intellectuals, such as Li Da, interpreted Marxism in popular literature and enabled Chinese peasants and workers to understand Marxism easily. The popular philosophy became popular once again during the Cultural Revolution in China to meet the needs for workers, peasants, and soldiers to study Maoism; that is, Marxism with Chinese characteristics in the Chinese context. Therefore, the term *popular philosophy* in the Chinese context actually refers to Marxism and Maoism. The term *public philosophy* is also different from the term *public policy*. Public policy is the basic policy forming the foundation of public law. China is a party/state or party/society country in which public policy is made by a small ruling group or one top leader. The inner circle of the party—the Standing Committee of the Political Bureau—is made up of only about twelve to twenty persons. Within this pyramidal political structure, public policy in China is promoted from top to bottom. The Chinese people have no rights to participate in the process of making public policy but are required to implement public policy. Therefore, there is a wide gap between public policy and the will of the Chinese people. The development of public philosophy is, however, from the bottom to the top and represents the trend of history toward the future of society. The common people voluntarily accept and practice public philosophy.

Many China scholars have been aware of spiritual and cultural vacuums in recent years in China. Confucianism was swept away by the communist revolution; Marxism lost its appeal to the Chinese people; and the Chinese people no longer put their faith in the Communist Party and government. Nationalism is not as useful as it once was because imperialist countries such as the United States and Great Britain have become friends. Moreover, after the Tiananmen Square Incident in 1989, many Chinese people lost their strong appetite for participating in politics and began taking a more realistic attitude toward their daily life. In order for people to make money, prostitution has become a part of the consumer market, corruption has become a popular phenomenon in Chinese government circles, and gambling occurs in thousands of families. Many high-level Chinese officials have made money by using their powers and have accepted bribes. The Chinese political system does not promise to bring them to justice; in fact, it sometimes protects them. Obviously, Deng's pragmatic theories—"Cats Theory" and "Cross River Theory"—are only a short-term vision for the beginning of reform. China needs to remake its public philosophy for the twenty-first century to establish democratic mechanisms.

What should be the new public philosophy in China? Some scholars assert that China should follow a universal pattern toward democratization. Some scholars insist that Western democracy should be applied to Chinese culture. Meanwhile, the Chinese government stresses the theory of the Four Modernizations, the so-called socialism with Chinese characteristics. Some Western scholars deny these concepts and prefer to talk about "post-socialism," which refers to the special condition of socialism on the new historical stage. Arif Dirlik suggests that post-socialism actually is the end of socialism. Post-socialism is a new way that derives its inspiration not from traditional utopian ideas but "from the impulses to liberation that represent present responses to problems of oppression and inequality."[8] From another perspective, some Chinese scholars try to explore the relationship between the Chinese reform movement and the development of a society by examining the key role of human capital in the society. In *Gradual Revolution,* Hui Wang expounds on the relations of human capital and the reform movement in China. According to Wang, although the reform is gradual, it is a revolution because it is changing the principal characteristics of the Chinese economic system, especially those of the planned economic system, as it moves toward a market system. He maintains that the most important reason for China to take the gradual approach of reform is that human capital is the most important component in the reform movement. To reform human capital, there must be a gradual approach, because such reform is a slow process. According to Wang, there are three types of capital in a society: material capital, such as circulating funds, fixed funds, property, and land; system capital, such as industrial organization, enterprise systems, market systems, and administrative systems; and human capital—individuals, including decision makers, officials, businesspeople, workers, peasants, and so forth. Wang reveals the inner relations of the three forms of capital and points out that human capital is the most important capital for the processes of the reform movement and society, because the quality of the individual determines the environment of the reform and the process of the reform.[9] Because his emphasis is only on human capital itself and the relations of human capital and the reform movement, the issue he raises touches the basic aspect of public philosophy but not its full meaning.

In order to develop a theory of public philosophy to remake public philosophy, it is necessary to draw from the model of public philosophy in the United States. In the beginning, the theory of public philosophy in the United States was intended to be a new political theory to improve traditional political theory by an accommodation of civil religion. From the second half of 1950s, the United States endured a dramatic change in every aspect of society. Robert F. Cuervo has called this period "an era of self-reflection and reassessment."[10] In this transitional period, the theories of civil religion and public philosophy were developed by modern political thinkers from different perspectives to articulate political order and comprehend social dimensions. The contest between civil religion and public philosophy was the most important topic to interpret the American democratic tradition, including the "constitutional-legal tradition" and the "prophetic-utopian tradition."[11] As early as 1954, John Courtney Murray, S.J., touched on the theory of public philosophy, but he called "public philosophy" the public consensus that deals with the constitutional consensus. The public consensus is "an ensemble of substantive truths, a structure of basic public knowledge, an order of elementary affirmations that reflect realities inherent in the order of existence."[12]

Walter Lippmann was the first U.S. scholar, in *Essays in the Public Philosophy* (1955), to set forth the term *public philosophy*. He argued that the political regime needs a consensus of common truths that should be reflected in the state's public orthodoxy and institutions. He closely connected public philosophy with natural law and democracy and essentially tried to restore the idea of natural law and reason: "The Public philosophy is known as natural law";[13] and, "This philosophy is the premise of the institutions of the Western society."[14] He added, "The public philosophy was in part expounded in the Bill of Rights of 1789. It was re-enacted in the first ten amendments of the Constitution of the United States."[15] He examined the relations of liberty and democracy and the causes that precipitate the decline of democracy, pointing out that the loss of the public philosophy had caused a profound political problem. He hoped that both liberty and democracy could be preserved before one destroyed the other. According to Lippmann, it is impossible to operate a modern democratic institution without a public philosophy of natural law. He believed that public philosophy could be revived. One important cause of the decline of public philosophy, for Lippmann, is the French political theorist Jean-Jacques Rousseau's view of man. Because man is born naturally good, according to Rousseau, man needs only develop his faculties and vocational skills, not necessarily receive an education, to inculcate a public philosophy. Therefore, the revival of the public philosophy depends on whether its principles and the old philosophy can be reworked for the modern age.

Gerhart Niemeyer in 1971 suggested the use of the concept of a "political realm" to articulate the aspect of political order, in order to incorporate the theory of civil religion. Niemeyer examined public myths in *Between Nothingness and Paradise* and found the essential theological dimension existing in U.S. society; the problem was that the traditional political term *society* was inadequate to express the theological dimension. He suggested using the term *political realm* to articulate political order and understand theological truths and the public myths.[16]

Richard J. Bishirjian made it clear in 1978 that "a public philosophy, not civil religion, should be the primary vehicle by which the American nation's self-understanding of its ultimate meaning is articulated,"[17] because national life is indeed informed by public myths "that articulate the commonly shared beliefs of society's members."[18] According to him, the public philosophy should search for "the origins of social order," public truth, common good and beliefs, and international order.[19] An inquiry into the common good is required of public philosophy. The function of public philosophy is to turn humankind's untrue life into a true life.[20] Bishirjian set forth four principles of public philosophy. First, public philosophy is based upon the common truth. Political community cannot endure without public philosophy. Second, "the public good is not necessarily in agreement with public opinion."[21] The mere common sharing of a preference is not "the basis of a public philosophy."[22] Third, "public philosophy is the act of the souls" and "committed to the common good."[23] Fourth, public philosophy is not economic and material but touches upon and is compatible with the theological truths reflected in our public myths.[24] Commonly shared beliefs "must reflect an experience of a higher order of goods than the material."[25] Bishirjian found that the modern U.S. social structure is ordered by both a public philosophy and civil religion.[26]

Forty years after Lippmann claimed that the United States had lost its public philosophy, in 1996, Michael J. Sandel pointed out a similar problem. Tracing the history of U.S. politics, Sandel argues that Americans remain frustrated with politics, that U.S. public life is rife with discontent, and that U.S. politics has lost its civic voice. He states that neither Democrats nor Republicans have spoken to the concerns of the American people during the past half-century. The concerns at the heart of our discontent are the relations of individual and community as well as the decline of morality. In order to solve these two social problems, public philosophy should be restored in a new social context. However, Sandel further narrows the definition of public philosophy, putting it at the same level as political theory: "By public philosophy, I mean the political theory implicit in our practice, the assumptions about citizenship and freedom that inform our public life."[27] Furthermore, the public philosophy of U.S. politics is the liberal tradition of thought and theory.[28] The central idea of public philosophy is that "government should be neutral toward the moral and religious views its citizens espouse."[29]

In sum, all of these public philosophers agree that public philosophy is an undeniable social dimension of contemporary U.S. society and plays a very important role in the development of democracy. They also agree that public philosophy is closely tied to a political order, and that the lack or the loss of public philosophy causes profound social problems. Therefore, public philosophy needs to be redefined and restored in order to preserve our modern democracy. However, they have not reached an agreement on the issues of the basis and content of public philosophy and the relation of public philosophy to civil religion. Although these differences do not constitute an obstacle for us to develop the theory of public philosophy, it is important to understand the relationship between public philosophy and civil religion.

There are three viewpoints that address the relations of public philosophy and civil religion: (1) public philosophy is only a political theory, and civil religion is a different type of theory, but both are important to articulate and support political order; (2) civil religion provides an ultimate meaning for public myths and ultimately articulates a political order; and (3) public philosophy is a primary vehicle to articulate a political order, but it accommodates both political theory and civil religion. As a matter of fact, it is impossible to draw a clear line between public philosophy and civil religion. Nevertheless, understanding what civil religion is about and the general relationship between public philosophy and civil religion is helpful to developing the theory of public philosophy in the Chinese context.

It is widely acknowledged that Robert N. Bellah is the founder of the theory of U.S. civil religion in the contemporary United States, though some political thinkers, such as Machiavelli (1649–1527) and Hobbes (1588–1679), discussed civil religion before the term was first used by

Rousseau. In *The Broken Covenant: American Civil Religion in Time of Trial*, Bellah presents his ideas about U.S. civil religion and tries to interpret the relations of the individual and society through a transcendent vision from above, not from below. He examines the original myth of America from the birth of its independence and concludes that the covenant was broken: "Today the broken covenant is visible to all."[30] He argues that the United States would lose its social and political balance without a divine covenant. Therefore, it is very important to introduce civil religion to American life, because any society rests on a common moral understanding that must rest upon a common religious understanding. Both "moral and religious understandings produce both a basic cultural legitimation and a standard of judgment for a society."[31]

What is civil religion for Bellah? On the one hand, civil religion is not "about political theory or about ideology," "but about religion and myth."[32] On the other hand, civil religion is closely connected with "the liberal side of our heritage and its most important expression, the Constitution."[33] Although he makes it clear that "American civil religion is not the worship of the American nation but an understanding of the American experience in the light of ultimate and universal reality,"[34] it is not difficult to hear that his voice is similar to some public philosophers' voices. While public philosophers stated that the United States had lost its public philosophy, Bellah claimed that the United States had broken its covenant. Thus the revival of public philosophy and the recovery of the covenant become the connection between public philosophy and civil religion. At this point, Bellah's book is "a contribution to both public philosophy and public theology."[35] Probably for this reason, Bellah actually blurs the distinctions between public philosophy and civil religion. Some scholars point out that Bellah's civil religion becomes a political religion, "the new god in Bellah's civil religion is man, whose will be done by collective action." In Bellah's work, the United States was the new Eden, a paradise, and chosen by God.[36] Based on this, therefore, Bishirjian concludes that "the civil religion is an attitude of mind carried by a special section or class within Western democratic society, the intellectual class."[37]

Michael Novak, in *Choosing Our King: Powerful Symbols in Presidential Politics* (1974), offers a definition of civil religion that links public philosophy and civil religion: "a public perception of our national experience, in the light of universal and transcendent claims upon human beings, but especially upon Americans; a set of values, symbols, and rituals institutionalized as the cohesive force and center of meaning uniting our many peoples."[38]

Richard John Neuhaus went further and advocated that public philosophy is a part of civil religion. Civil religion is a religion because civil religion has the full characteristics of religion: cultic aspects, recognized leadership, participation, a statement of beliefs, and a moral code.[39] According to Neuhaus, civil religion includes three aspects: operative values, public piety, and public philosophy. The United States does not lack the operative values and public piety: "What is missing is a public philosophy." Moreover, American life has been missing public philosophy for a very long time.[40]

No matter how many differences exist among these scholars, both public philosophy and civil religion are important supporters of the modern democratic system and play an important role in the development of the American way of life. The United States would lose its social and political balance without either one of them. That is why U.S. political thinkers call for either the restoration of public philosophy or the recovery of the covenant.

A NEW PUBLIC PHILOSOPHY IN THE CHINESE CONTEXT

To develop a new public philosophy in the Chinese context, it is very important to bear in mind that the U.S. status quo is quite different from the Chinese context in terms of history, ideology, economics, politics, religion, and education. In its short history, the United States has consistently maintained a democratic system within a capitalist society. Liberalism and conservatism constitute the mainstream of contemporary U.S. political theory. In the U.S. context, the notion of public philosophy is close to a political theory. China, to the contrary, has passed through several different systems in its history, including the patriarchal system, the feudal system, the nationalist system, and the socialist system, in which many schools of thought have interacted with one another to promote the development of society. At this point, it is very difficult to narrow public philosophy to the same level of political theory in the Chinese context.

U.S. culture is grounded in Judeo-Christian traditions and belief. U.S. society is ruled not only by people and common law but also by a higher law. Although church is separated from state according to the Constitution of the United States, religion has infiltrated every aspect of social life. Civil religion has played a political role in the United States and actually becomes a political religion in some respects. However, China was not governed by people, common law, and a higher law, but by a ruler or rulers, the top leader's speech, and party policy. In premodern China, emperors acted as both secular rulers and the mandate of heaven. At present, on the one hand, the party essentially regards religion as an alien force in society and the potential enemy of the socialist system; on the other hand, the top leader—the general secretary of the party, from Mao to Jiang—has performed as the incarnation of the sacred. The Chinese people are forced to accept the communist civil religion. Therefore, the communist government is not checked by independent religious forces but is supported by the communist civil religion. It becomes a brutal government when the communist political system and communist civil religion work closely together, because the communist government can do whatever it wants as the government represents an absolute truth in the name of God. It is impossible for China to establish a truly democratic system without religious liberty and freedom.

Different countries under different systems share something in common. The social structure of a society can generally be divided into four levels or aspects: economy, politics, ideology, and religion. The four social aspects produce four corresponding institutions: corporations, the state, schools, and the church. What is the most important aspect for the evolution of a society and democratization? The economy is the system of economic activity in a country or region. Economic activities must proceed within a political system. According to H. Stephen Gardner, "The economic performance of a country is determined by its economic system and environment, and by the policies of its leaders."[41] Public policy plays a more important role in contemporary economic activity than do other elements of economy, yet public policy is the product of politics. Politics is a set of activities engaged in by a government, a politician, or a political party. The state is the body or the process of governing that controls the administration of public policy. Politicians and governments are deeply influenced by ideology in the process of decision making. Ideology is a set of doctrines or beliefs that form the basis of a political, economic, or other system. Ideology in a democratic system is always mixed with religion. It is a common phenomenon that political theory and religion constitute an integrated public philosophy to preserve a given democratic system. Religion is a belief in and reverence for a supernatural power regarded as the creator and governor of the universe. Religion provides a general identity to individuals by helping them cope with questions of ultimate meaning in their lives and the social and political order. When religion plays a political role, it becomes a civil religion.

Obviously, in a social structure, politics occupies a higher level than economics. Religion occupies a higher level than ideology. Therefore, politics and religion are the main melody to a social evolution. Understanding the relationship of state and religion is key to articulating and understanding the meaning of human beings and social order. The theory reflecting a society's political and religious activities as well as the relations of state and church is called the public philosophy. Through the lens of the need to alter China's public philosophy, it can be seen why democratization is important to China and how to achieve democratization in China from both Eastern and Western perspectives. It should be noted that education is also an important element, which permeates every aspect of the social structure, in promoting the development of a society. Education is not only based on the four social aspects but also serves and directs the development of the four aspects. Every aspect of social structure has its own historic ground. Therefore, public philosophy is both theoretical and historical. To develop public philosophy in a Chinese context, we should find the inner links between Chinese history and public philosophy. A better comprehension of Chinese history is helpful for understanding the complexities in remaking China's public philosophy.

Based on this logic, in chapter 2 we will study the basis of Chinese public philosophy from a historical perspective, examining the characteristics of historic China and old Chinese public philosophy as well as the links among economics, politics, ideology, religion, and education. My central argument in chapter 2 is that 2,000 years of Chinese patriarchal tradition still deeply influence Chinese ideology, economics, politics, religion, and education; the Chinese communist system is a neopatriarchal system; and the party is the last fortress of antidemocratization. It is necessary to remake China's public philosophy in all five dimensions simultaneously; that, of course, will result in the reconstruction of Chinese traditional culture. This does not mean that Chinese traditional culture is no longer meaningful to the Chinese people, or that it must be completely eliminated. To the contrary, China will lose its cultural roots if it denies all of its past, although Chinese traditional culture as a whole is not compatible with democratic principles at the political level.

The five aspects—Chinese ideology, economy, politics, religion, and education—are carefully examined in chapters 3–7. In chapter 3, we will study three types of Chinese public philosophy in chronological order; review the development of three epochs of Confucianism in Chinese history; analyze the place and role of Confucianism in contemporary China; interpret Sun's Three People's Principles—the people's livelihood, democracy, and nationalism; and investigate the advantages and disadvantages of Marxism through an examination of the development of Marxism in China from 1919 to 1979. Correspondingly, Confucianism, Sunism, and Marxism have played different ideological roles in the three periods of premodern China, the Republic of China, and the People's Republic of China. Confucianism became the orthodox Chinese ideology during the Han dynasty and dominated China for more than 2,000 years. Confucianism as a whole does not fit Chinese democratization, but it contains many good elements that can serve Chinese modernization. Sun set forth the Three People's Principles and laid the foundation of democratic principles, but the principles were never put into practice on the mainland. After the nationalist government settled in Taiwan, it learned from past lessons and fully carried out the Three People's Principles. Modern democracy has prevailed and has brought profound changes to Taiwan. On the mainland, the party abandoned the Three People's Principles and practiced Marxism for twenty-eight years but failed at every level. Although only very few people in China believe that Marxism represents the future of

China, the CPC retains Marxism as the state ideology. Moreover, the party has posed as the sole representative of Marxism in the Chinese context in order to preserve its monopolistic power. Marxism and the party are two sides of the same coin. Therefore, removing Marxism from the state's official ideological position and ending the one-party system are dual tasks involved in remaking China's public philosophy.

In chapter 4, we will explore the relationship between economy and public philosophy. I will argue that modernity is not an economic conception but an integrated notion of social development. The current official Chinese philosophy behind the economic reform movement, the theory of the four modernizations—the initial socialist stage, gradual reform, pragmatism, and the open-door policy—inhibits further reforms in China, fails to sustain Chinese economic growth for the long term, and blocks the process of democratization. The Chinese economy has already slowed down and will slow down more if changes in the official philosophy are not made. The central requirement for economic reform to be successful is to push the Chinese economy fully to a market system and make China a capitalist society. Capitalism is the entryway to China's democratization. To make China a capitalist society, the party must withdraw from China's economic activities and remake China's official philosophy behind the economic reform movement.

In chapter 5, we will examine the role of a new public philosophy's impact on political reform. I will point out the problems in the political arena and offer some suggestions for political reform, focusing on political pluralism, civil society, a multiparty system, and human rights. Some questions will be raised: What is the ultimate obstacle to China's political reform? What caused the failure of the democratic movement in China? Should China be ruled by the party? What is the individual's status in communist China? I will conclude that the fundamental obstacle to an acceptance of democratic principles is not, as Chinese officials have said, China's low level of economy, or the large percentages of the Chinese people who have low levels of education and do not know how to practice human rights, or that China has no democratic tradition, or that the Chinese people today prefer political stability to improved living standards. Rather, the party resists a democratic system, a reform of civil society, and the Chinese people's participation in sharing power with the party. The party is the ultimate obstacle to China's democratization.

In chapter 6, I will present an overview of the development of religion in China, including Confucianism, Buddhism, Daoism, Islam, and Christianity. I will examine the relationship of Chinese traditional culture and religion within the political system, explain the meaning and significance of religion to the Chinese people and to Chinese modernization and democratization, examine characteristics of Confucian religion in the three epochs, show the values of Confucian religion in the global context, and point out the importance of Chinese indigenous religions' and Christianity's working together in the Chinese context. I will also discuss the characteristics of the church-state relationship in China and conclude that state control of religion has been the defining characteristic of church-state relations for more than 2,000 years. The party has never relinquished its control of religion. This state control of religion results in at least two adverse consequences. First, the state oppresses religions, and freedom of religion becomes an empty slogan. Second, there is no separation between church and state, making it impossible for religious pluralism and civil society to develop. Under party control, Chinese religion is unable to act as an independent force to balance the social and political orders. That is why at present Chinese religion plays only a marginal role in Chinese politics. Religious freedom and function in China are thus dependent on political reform. Democratization is not about how to Christianize China but about how to reform the one-party system.

Remaking public educational philosophy is the key to remaking China's overall public philosophy because education directly affects people's outlook and public philosophy, changes value standards, increases the level of culture, and improves the quality of leadership. All those factors, in turn, affect economy, politics, and spiritual life as well as social evolution. In chapter 7, we will study public philosophy from an educational perspective. I will analyze the characteristics of the traditional Chinese educational system, evaluate the educational system under the Communist regime, reveal the inner connections between the present educational system and Confucianism, analyze unsolved educational problems, explore the requirements and characteristics of a new educational system for democratization in the twenty-first century, and set forth four suggestions for the improvement of China's educational system. Those four suggestions are: the highly centralized control of education must be reformed; communist education must be removed from Chinese education; democratic education should be introduced into Chinese education; and the educational system and mechanism must be further reformed.

Finally, in chapter 8, I will examine the issue of remaking China's public philosophy in a global context and predict China's future for the twenty-first century. I will discuss the interrelationships among remaking China's public philosophy and capitalism, globalization, and democratization. I conclude that the first step for China's democratization is to capitalize China. As for the relationship between China and globalization, on the one hand, there can be no integrated globalization without China's full cooperation. On the other hand, China relies heavily on international assistance for its modernization. Therefore, improvement of the Chinese social order is an initial step toward improvement of the global order. To remake China's public philosophy essentially is to rearrange China's social and political order in the global context. China's recent economic progress does not change the nature of the Chinese national identity. Evidence indicates that China is moving away from communism and is no longer a typical totalitarian dictatorship, but China's uncertain future depends on the so-called inside revolution through improvements in the five areas of reform. Therefore, remaking China's public philosophy is extremely important to China's peaceful transition from its current political system to a democratic system.

NOTES

1. Immanuel C. Y. Hsu, *The Rise of Modern China*, 5th ed. (New York: Oxford University Press, 1995), p. 11.

2. Michael J. Mazarr, "Trust: The Social Virtues and the Creation of Prosperity," *Washington Quarterly* 19 (Spring 1996), p. 177.

3. Francis Fukuyama, *Trust: The Social Virtues and the Creation of Prosperity* (New York: Free Press, 1995), pp. 4–5.

4. Samuel P. Huntington, *The Clash of Civilizations and the Remaking of World Order* (New York: Simon & Schuster, 1996).

5. Anthony Giddens, *The Third Way: The Renewal of Social Democracy* (Oxford, England: Polity Press, 1998), p. 24.

6. Ibid., p. 78.

7. See Jurgen Habermas, *Between Facts and Norms: Contributions to a Discourse Theory of Law and Democracy* (Cambridge, Mass.: MIT Press, 1996).

8. Arif Dirlik, "Post-Socialism? Reflections on Socialism with Chinese Characteristics," in *Marxism and Capitalism in the People's Republic of China*, ed. Peter P. Cheng (Lanham, Md.: University Press of America, 1989), p. 13.

9. Hui Wang, *Gradual Revolution* (Beijing: China Planning Publishing House, 1998), pp. 3–5.

10. Robert F. Cuervo, "The Definition of Public Philosophy: Lippmann and Murray," in Richard J. Bishirjian, *A Public Philosophy Reader* (New Rochelle, N.Y.: Arlington House, 1978), p. 47.

11. Quoted in Richard J. Bishirjian, *A Public Philosophy Reader*, p. 47.

12. Quoted in Cuervo, "The Definition of Public Philosophy," p. 98.

13. Walter Lippmann, *Essays in the Public Philosophy* (Boston: Little, Brown and Company, 1955), p. 101.

14. Ibid., pp. 98–99.

15. Ibid.

16. Quoted in Bishirjian, *A Public Philosophy Reader*, p. 32.

17. Bishirjian, *A Public Philosophy Reader*, p. 36.

18. Ibid., p. 55.

19. Ibid., p. 17.

20. Ibid., p. 18.

21. Ibid., p. 22.

22. Ibid., p. 36.

23. Ibid., p. 22.

24. Ibid., p. 23.

25. Ibid., p. 36.

26. Ibid., p. 24.
27. Michael J. Sandel, *Democracy's Discontent: America in Search of a Public Philosophy* (Cambridge, Mass.: Belknap Press, 1996), p. 4.
28. Ibid., p. 5.
29. Ibid., p. 4.
30. Robert N. Bellah, *The Broken Covenant: American Civil Religion in Time of Trial* (Chicago: University of Chicago Press, 1992), p. 139.
31. Ibid., p. xvi.
32. Ibid., p. 3.
33. Ibid., p. 176.
34. Ibid., p. 19.
35. Leroy S. Rouner, ed., *Civil Religion and Political Theology,* 2d ed. (Notre Dame, Ind.: University of Notre Dame Press, 1992), p. 8.
36. Bishirjian, *A Public Philosophy Reader,* p. 51.
37. Ibid., p. 48.
38. Ibid., p. 24.
39. Richard John Neuhaus, "From Civil Religion to Public Philosophy," in *Civil Religion and Political Theology,* ed. Leroy S. Rouner (Notre Dame, Indiana: University of Notre Dame Press, 1986), p. 103.
40. Ibid., p. 104.
41. H. Stephen Gardner, *Comparative Economic Systems* (Fort Worth, Tex.: Dryden Press, 1998), p. 3.

CHAPTER 2

The Historical Basis of China's Public Philosophy

Contemporary China was a long time in the making. The history of China is a mirror that reflects contemporary China. China's public philosophy at present has certain connections with Chinese history. Remaking China's public philosophy must involve changing old Chinese culture and tradition because culture is the DNA of a society's development. Why has the highly centralized political system persisted in its development over 2,000 years in China? Why have many reformists failed to change Chinese political systems in the past 150 years? Why does the Chinese government still regard the modern democratic system as foreign? Why has the one-party system lasted for more than a half-century in China? To fully answer these questions, we must take a historical view and examine the historical roots of present-day China. It is impossible to understand contemporary China's public philosophy and to envision a new Chinese public philosophy without such an examination. As Lucien W. Pye has noted, "No serious analysis of ideology can go far without an examination of historical traditions."[1]

WHY STUDY CHINA'S HISTORY?

Like Egypt, Babylonia, and Greece, China has a very long history. World history began in China,[2] and it moved from the East to the West.[3] China at the least is one of the cradles of world civilization. Based on written records, China developed its own political system, culture, ideology, religion, and educational program over a period of 3,000 years. Although Western countries borrowed from Eastern civilization without realizing it,[4] Western culture arguably imposed itself on Eastern civilization and built a modern age. Western culture flowed into China and Asia beginning in the seventeenth century. Consequently, Chinese culture has been challenged by the West for 300 years and twisted by Marxism for 50 years. Since the first Opium War, which began in 1839, China also has struggled with its political and cultural puzzle: What type of political system is best for China? What is the relationship between Chinese culture and Western culture? What role should Western culture play in Chinese society? These issues have been debated for more than a century in China. Today, communist China still resists modern democratic theory and tries to retain its own political system, so-called socialism with Chinese characteristics. This type of socialism actually ties into the Chinese traditional patriarchal system very clearly. Some scholars observe that China is today "the only giant of the ancient world to survive into the twentieth century."[5] According to Pye, "No culture in the world matches China's in durability. More, it is a culture long under siege. For two hundred years it has staved off a challenge from the West."[6] The fundamental reason that China has lagged behind in modern times is not that China always lacked the resources necessary for daily life. China, before the seventeenth century, was the most advanced country in the world in agriculture, science, and technology, and its resources were rich and plentiful.[7] Rather, China's political system and public philosophy were stagnant for a long time. To understand the roots of the one-party system and the essential characteristics of traditional China's public philosophy and to offer a solution to remake China's public philosophy for the twenty-first century, we must first examine the period of Chinese history that is the most important in affecting China's current public philosophy.

Periodization studies of Chinese history are plentiful. The two-period theory is among many theoretical models for dividing Chinese history. According to this theory, the first cycle of Chinese history is from its beginning to A.D. 383 and is characterized as Classical China. The second cycle is from A.D. 383 until today and is characterized as Tartar-Buddhist China.[8]

A second model is the three-period theory. This theory sees an ancient period lasting from the Xia dynasty (2100–1700 B.C.) to the end of the Warring States period (475–221 B.C.) and might be characterized as the aristocratic political structure and self-development of the Chinese people. Then follows the medieval period from the Qin dynasty (221–206 B.C.) to the middle of the Qing dynasty (A.D. 1795), which was characterized by autocratic government. Finally, the modern period extends from the middle of the Qing dynasty (1795) to contemporary time (1912), an era marked by transformation and modern government.[9]

A third model is the four-period theory: the ancient period from the Xia dynasty to the end of the Warring States period, the medieval period from the Qin dynasty to the last year of the Tang dynasty (A.D. 907), the early modern period from the Five dynasties (907–960) to the Ming dynasty (1368–1644), and the modern period from the Qing dynasty until contemporary time.[10] Miyazaki Ichisada has divided Chinese history into four stages: the establishment of an ancient empire, an aristocratic society, a period of autocratic government, and a period of modernizing progress.[11]

A fourth model is the five-period theory. According to John Meskill, Karl Marx divided history into five main types of relations of production: "primitive communal period, the slave society, the feudal society, the capitalist society, and the socialist society."[12] When Marx's theory is applied to Chinese history, the five periods are as follows: the period of primitive communism from the Xia dynasty to the Shang dynasty (1700–1100 B.C.), the slave society from the Western Zhou dynasty (1100–771 B.C.) to the Spring and Autumn period (770–476 B.C.), the feudal society from the Warring States period (475–221 B.C.) to the first Opium War (A.D. 1840), the semicolonial and semicapitalist society from the first Opium War to the end of the Nationalist government (1912–1949), and the socialist society from the founding of the People's Republic of China to the present time.

In each of the above typologies, the criteria for the division of Chinese history are quite different. The criteria of the two-period theory are type of culture and religion; the criteria of the three- and four-period theories are level of civilization (Chang) and type of political system (Ichisada); and the criteria of the five-period theory is level of production and nature of the superstructure (Marx). Each of the three typologies has its own disadvantages for understanding China's public philosophy. The two-period theory ignores the roots of Chinese history, the significance of its political system, the influence of Western thought, and the differences among stages during the second cycle. The three-period theory in some respects hides the main cultural stream that developed and deeply influenced China for more than 2,000 years. Ichisada's theory does not view religion as an important part of public philosophy. Marx's theory is materialist determinism, and it overemphasizes production and class struggle and ignores the role of culture and belief systems in the evolution of history. According to Marxism, the communist society/socialist society is the highest level of human society. This conclusion evidently contradicts reality.

Whether we use a correct criterion for the divisions of Chinese history is directly related to remaking China's public philosophy. The theory reflecting the political and religious activities as well as the relations of state and church in a given society is called the public philosophy. Understanding the inner connection between politics and religion is especially important for understanding the roots of China's public philosophy and the historical characteristics of its political and belief systems. Through this lens, Chinese history can be seen as divided into three periods: premedieval, medieval, and modern.

First is the premedieval period from the Xia dynasty (2100–1600 B.C.) to the end of the Spring and Autumn period (770–475 B.C.), characterized as the formative stage of public philosophy. During this stage, China's public philosophy began to sprout. Confucius (551–479 B.C.) was born, but his school of thought had not yet become popular. The Four Books (*Confucian Analects, The Great Learning, The Work of Mencius,* and *The Doctrine of Mean*) and the Five Classics (*The Book of Songs, The Book of History, The Book of Changes, The Book of Rites,* and *The Spring and Autumn Annals*), the representative works of traditional Chinese public philosophy, had not been completed. Different schools of thought began to debate, focusing on China's social structure and political system, but Buddhism had not yet entered into China during that period. Thus, in the modern sense, China did not officially form its public philosophy in this stage.

Second is the medieval period from the Warring States period (475–221 B.C.) to the end of the Qing dynasty (A.D. 1644–1911), characterized as the continuation and improvement stage of public philosophy. Beginning in the period of the Warring States, great cultural debates occurred in China among the nine schools of thought—Confucianist, Daoist, Yin Yang, Legalist, Mohist (utilitarianism), Political Strategist, Eclectic, Logician (nominalism), and Agriculturalist. After the debates, Confucianism became the official ideology in the Han dynasty (206 B.C.–A.D. 220). Buddhism entered China in the first century A.D. and gradually became part of Chinese culture. In the development of Confucianism, other schools of thought including Buddhism and Daoism challenged it from time to time, but Confucianism as both religion and ideology was a dominant public philosophy during that period of time. Politically, since the first unified Chinese government—the Qin dynasty—established in 221 B.C., China followed the basic political pattern until 1911.

Third is the modern period from the founding of the Republic of China (1912–1949) to the period of the People's Republic of China (1949 to present), characterized as the reform stage of public philosophy. Confucianism was fiercely attacked for the first time in Chinese history by the May Fourth Movement of 1919, the new cultural movement. However, the Nationalist government continuously defended Confucian tradition to preserve China's traditional family values and patriarchal social structure. Thirty years later, Confucianism was under deadly attack for the second time, by the communist revolution. Before the reform movement began in 1978, Confucianism in China was categorized as the feudal culture and surviver's of feudalism, and only Marxism, Leninism, and Mao Zedong's thought were established as orthodoxy. Marxism and communism have been shaking since the reform movement began, however. China has reached another turning point to change its public philosophy.

The public philosophy in premodern China formed in the second, or medieval, period, but it stemmed from the first stage. John Meskill found that "the history of every culture followed a sequence of epochs toward the fulfillment of the Idea of the Culture, the ideal of primitive culture-form."[13] Although every aspect of China's public philosophy in the first stage was only a preparation for the second stage, Chinese culture, tradition, custom, and social structure in the first stage had an astonishing and remarkable impact on the whole of Chinese history. The main characteristic of Chinese history in the first stage is the patriarchal system. The patriarchal system is the primitive miniature of Chinese history and the base of its highly centralized political system, which lasted more than 2,000 years in China. At this point, the patriarchal system can be considered as the key to understanding China's public philosophy and political system, both past and present.

Nevertheless, contemporary China's public philosophy is directly influenced by the second period of Chinese history. In the beginning of the second period, during the Warring States period, China completed its transition from slave society to feudal society. Due to changes of production relations and production mode, the productive force was liberated from the old social system. In turn, the economic development made it possible for Chinese cultural and ideological fervor to emerge. All classical authors, such as Confucius, Mencius, Lao Zi, Zhuang Zi, Mo Zi, and Hanfei Zi, were enthusiastically devoted to political and cultural debate. This great debate was best described by the Chinese idiom, "a hundred flowers in bloom and a hundred schools of thought contend." Following the Warring States period, the Qin dynasty, which first unified China with a centralized political system, was established. The Qin dynasty set up a social structure and a political system that were rooted in the first period of Chinese history. The following 2,000 years witnessed the continuation and improvement of the social structure and political system. After the Qin dynasty fell, Confucianism prevailed over other schools of thought. Through various channels, especially educational programs, Confucianism continued to develop for more than 2,000 years, taking different forms in different times. Looking back at Chinese history, China's public philosophy in the third period is clearly branded by the basic characters of public philosophy in the second period. Political systems in the Republic era and the Mao era are essentially identical with that of the second period. A Confucian ethical code and family values still dominated the Republic of China and remain in the People's Republic of China at the grassroots level. Some scholars point out that China's culture was very conservative and that political institutions and thought went unchanged from antiquity to modern times. It is widely accepted, as F. W. Mote writes, that in the period of 1,589 years from the Qin dynasty to the Yuan dynasty (1279–1368), the Chinese political system only "conformed to late Zhou models."[14]

THE CHARACTERISTICS OF HISTORIC CHINA

Chinese written history can be traced back 4,700 years, through archaeological discoveries. Haung Di, the head of a tribe in southwestern China, established the Xia dynasty. Over the following 2,000 years, China gradually became a Hua-Xia nation (Chinese nation) through the Shang dynasty and the Western Zhou dynasty. Tan Wang led the revolution to overthrow the Xia dynasty and established the Shang dynasty (about 1766–1059 B.C.), which marked the beginning of authentic Chinese history.[15] According to the Oracle inscriptions (scripts carved on tortoise shells by the elders of the Shang dynasty and considered to be the earliest written Chinese language), production in the Shang dynasty reached the Bronze Age and moved into the stage of agriculture. Although it is debatable whether the Western Zhou dynasty was a feudal system, the social productive forces in the Western Zhou definitely were much more developed. The Western Zhou dynasty already had become a prosperous agricultural society.[16] Politically, the Western Zhou dynasty began forming the primary political structure, and the state was a well-organized hierarchy that emerged as a political system in the second stage of Chinese history. Because of its centralized government, the Zhou dynasty was the longest dynasty in Chinese history, extending from about 1100 to 221 B.C. In the Zhou dynasty, the king of China, the symbol of the Son of Heaven, was at the top of the pyramidal political structure. Under the king, officials were divided into five ranks: duke, marquis, earl, viscount, and baron.[17] During this period, "Local government officials were appointed by the court to serve limited terms in a succession of different places as opposed to the system of hereditary posts."[18] This political system was "closely connected with the patriarchal system."[19] There is ample evidence to show that the highly centralized Chinese political system actually began in the Western Zhou. Then, in 770 B.C. China entered into the Eastern Zhou (including the Spring and Autumn and the Warring States periods), under which the emperor lost his sole authority and China was divided into many local kingdoms. Finally, after many crucial battles, six states survived. By 221 B.C., Ying Zheng, one of the six local kings, united all six states and established the first great empire in Chinese history, the Qin dynasty. He called himself "the First Emperor." The Qin dynasty laid down the foundations for Chinese feudal society, including ideological censorship. The Qin maintained its highly centralized political system by ruthless means and military force.

In the 2,000 years between the Qin and the Qing dynasties, China changed little, especially from a political perspective. What was the main characteristic of Chinese feudal society, and how did the characteristics of Chinese feudal society affect China's public philosophy for the ensuing 2,000 years? To answer these questions, one must look into the Chinese economy first, because the economy is the base of a society, and it indirectly influences the nature of public philosophy. In other words, a public philosophy always reflects the level of a society's economy in some respects. Old China's public philosophy and political system fit its agricultural economy. China's economy was agricultural before its doors were opened to Western countries in the nineteenth century.[20] Jacques Gernet has classified Chinese culture as an agricultural culture. The Chinese people lived "with a highly developed agriculture which forms their predominant activity."[21] Chinese civilization was closely tied to "a highly developed agriculture which confined itself almost exclusively to the plains and valleys."[22]

China became an agricultural society 4,000 years ago. By the thirteenth century A.D., China was the most sophisticated agricultural country in the world.[23] The general characteristic of an agricultural society is a backward mode of production and low efficiency of production. The thinking and behavior of peasants were very conservative and irrational. Consequently, the Chinese people concentrated their efforts on agriculture and neglected commerce. They concentrated on reality and ignored imagination; they concentrated on the present situation and neglected the future; and they concentrated on human relationships and social order and neglected metaphysics and spiritual life. Due to the weak economy and the lack of education, heavy physical labor, and isolated lifestyle of the agricultural society, the Chinese peasants were forced to maintain their simple daily life of "got up to work at sunrise and retired at sunset." They were virtually caged in the farm and home. As a common Chinese saying puts it, they were "born there, grew up there, and died there." They knew little of outside of the world, and ancestor worship was very popular because it had the easiest rites for farmers to ask blessings. Under these circumstances, no other religion, indigenous or foreign, significantly affected the way of Chinese life. Certainly, the nonreligious inclination of the Chinese people was based not on science and technology but on the unique experiences of Chinese agricultural society. Confucianism, Daoism, and other schools reflected this historical characteristic. Even Buddhism, an imported religion, made accommodations to fit the agricultural soil.

The peasants' need for reasonable living conditions and a peaceful daily life was the basic precondition for keeping the agricultural society stable. If peasants lost their essential need, it would lead to rebellion—either to overthrowing the government or to forcing the government to reform its economic policy. Confucius was wise enough to persuade China's rulers to establish a benevolent government in order to keep central government functioning and lasting longer. Some rulers in China long ago realized the truth that "common people are like water in the river, and the emperor is like a boat. The water could carry the boat and it could overturn the boat as well." The traditional idea in the agricultural society was that the consensus of the people was the foundation of an ideal government. The ideas of a benevolent government and the policy of the benevolent ruler resulted from this Chinese tradition. According to Confucianism, a benevolent government must first meet the basic living needs of the common people. Good governments and good emperors encouraged officials to treat the common people as their own children. Accordingly, good officials were honorably called "parent officials." In Chinese history, however, only a few emperors practiced the true model of a good parent, and few governments were benevolent. But, to be sure, the function of every top leader of the Chinese government from ancient times to the present has been to act as the father and exercise his absolute authority over the Chinese people.

Although European countries went through the stage of an agricultural society's coordinating with a monarchical political system, many Western societies abandoned their historic burdens and established democratic systems after the Industrial Revolution. To be sure, Biblical and Graeco-Roman traditions played a critical role in the transition from agricultural society to industrial society and, correspondingly, from a monarchical system to a democratic system. In contrast with the Biblical tradition, Confucianism is more philosophical and sociological and emphasizes *jen* (love) and *li* (propriety) from a humanist perspective. Confucian political theory is based not on political theory and theology but on family ethical codes. According to Confucianism, the state should be a moral product of social evolution, and the emperor should be a good example for the common people. If a leader sets a good example, it will be followed by his subordinates. Ironically, the ruling class never put this idea into practice; it only encouraged the common people to follow Confucian teachings to obey their rulers unilaterally. Two other traditional religions, Daoism and Buddhism, also significantly differ from Christianity. A monolithic and divine God is not central to Daoism or Buddhism. Traditional Chinese religions emphasized "self-cultivation" and "deny self and return to propriety," no matter how the government treated the people. Within this cultural and ideological framework, a dictatorial political system was easily developed.

In the old agricultural society, the Chinese family was not only a basic social cell to produce population and keep the society continuing, but it also was a basic work unit to keep gigantic political machines running. Two thousand years ago, China of course lacked modes of communication, and huge numbers of peasants were scattered over the vast areas of land. When the Chinese government organized massive projects such as a water-control system, water channels, and a national road system, it became necessary in some respects for China to establish a corresponding centralized government in order to make connections among families, villages, and counties; create an environment for agriculture to develop;

and efficiently control the entire country from top to bottom. Chao-ting Chi put it in this way, "The premodern Chinese empire was an agricultural one in which the decisive factor of political control was based on control over the key economic areas."[24] The Qin dynasty, the first highly centralized government, successfully organized a number of public projects, the Great Wall being the most famous. At that point, a centralized government was the necessary form of political system, but after that, no Chinese government, including the current Chinese one, has been willing to give up this model.

There is no unified opinion on the characteristics of the Chinese political system in the second period of Chinese history. At least five models are described as exhibiting the characteristics of the Chinese political system during this second stage: aristocratic government, autocratic government, constitutional monarchical government, absolute monarchical government, and the authoritarian imperial system. Aristocratic government refers to rule by a hereditary ruling class. Autocratic government refers to government by a member of a ruling family; this type of government is despotism. Monarchical government takes at least two forms: constitutional monarchical government and absolute monarchical government. Constitutional monarchical government refers to government power exercised by a single person, by his power checked by the constitution and other branches of the government. In contrast, in an absolute monarchial government, the monarch is ultimately the sole ruler of the country and is accountable only to God. The absolute monarchial right to rule is generally hereditary and lifelong. Authoritarian government is characterized by the people's obedience to authority. The term *centralized government* describes only a form of government, not the nature of the government. An aristocratic government, an autocratic government, an absolute monarchical government, and an authoritarian government could all be highly centralized, but centralization does not describe the essential distinctions among these four types of government. Therefore, an absolute monarchical government best describes Chinese politics in the second period of Chinese history. The Western Zhou dynasty had begun putting the centralized government in shape. Then the Qing dynasty formed the first absolute monarchical government. Under this system, the emperor Qin Shi-huang began to build the Great Wall and introduced standard weights and measures, the length of cart axles, the calendar, currency, national laws, and a uniform script. He concentrated all power in his own hands and proceeded to establish a huge bureaucracy. To keep absolute power, Qin Shi-huang campaigned against Confucian scholars and other Chinese intellectuals, burned hundreds of thousands of books, and buried alive more than 400 Confucian scholars. His great contribution to Chinese history was to establish the provincial and county system, which was adopted and improved upon later by every feudal dynasty and became "a permanent institution in the Chinese body politic."[25] To justify his cruel persecution of intellectuals, he promoted and practiced legalism. Based on Legalism, one of nine schools of thought, human nature was selfish and depraved, and the only tool to check human selfishness and depravity was laws. Legalists employed the three basic principles: *fa* (law), *shi* (situation), and *shu* (strategy). Hence severe punishment was the basic way for the Qin dynasty to govern Chinese society.

This severe punishment produced great hatred and dissatisfaction among Chinese society. In addition, extremely high taxes, conscript labor, and severe persecution contributed largely to the peasants' rebellion at the end of the Qin dynasty, by which the Qin dynasty was replaced by the Han dynasty (206 B.C.–A.D. 220). The first emperor of the Han dynasty learned the lesson of the Qin dynasty and carried out more flexible policies in regard to Chinese peasants. Correspondingly, China's public philosophy departed from that of the Qin by gradually accepting Confucianism. Although the Han dynasty's political structure continued its predecessor's centralized system with an absolute monarchical government, it improved upon and stabilized the system. In order to improve the relationship between the ruling class and the ruled class, the Han dynasty began to follow Confucian political philosophy, departing from legalism. Confucianism became the official ideology in the Han dynasty. Having followed a benevolent pattern, the Chinese people enthusiastically devoted themselves to social production and greatly promoted the development of society. The Han dynasty became the first golden age in Chinese history, lasting more than 200 years. The brief Sui dynasty (A.D. 581–618) continued the political model of the Qin dynasty and officially started the civil service examination system, which guaranteed to recruit those officials who were educated by Confucianism and who were loyal to and supported the absolute monarchical government. The Chinese centralized empire reached its most glorious height in the Tang dynasty (618–917). The Tang dynasty perfected the civil service examination system, and its political system was the "most elaborate and complete in the long monarchical age."[26] As China's territory expanded and its population grew, the Chinese political system became more and more centralized. After the Tang dynasty, the emperors of the Song dynasty (960–1279) went to an extreme and concentrated all civil and military powers in their own hands. The founder of the Ming dynasty (1368–1644) regarded the nation as his private property and appointed his twenty-three sons to govern twenty-three principalities of China. The Qing dynasty (1644–1911) was the last absolute monarchical system, and its government structure was largely inherited from the system of the Ming "but was more highly centralized."[27] Obviously, the Chinese political system had become more and more centralized with the passage of time, and there is no doubt that behind this highly centralized political system must be a public philosophy that favored it.

Due to the fact that the civil service examination system was the main channel to recruit Chinese officials from the Sui and Qing dynasties, the ruling class and the ruled class were quite distinct from each other in theory and in practice. Those who were educated and had moral integrity exercised political authority; those who were not educated and lacked moral integrity were subjects. However, it was not necessary that the structure of political authority of the Chinese empire in the second period be elitist. Theoretically, Chinese political power during that period consisted of two classes: the elite and the common people.[28] In premodern China, the Chinese elite included two groups: the members of one group held their official position based on hereditary relationships, either to the royal family or to a noble family; the other group was formed by Confucians who were selected through the civil service examination. The former constituted the main part of Chinese officialdom in Chinese feudal society. The Chinese civil service examination system, which officially started in the Sui dynasty, was gradually improved through several dynasties. It was ultimately completed in the Song dynasty,[29] and finally reached its height in the Qing dynasty. Clearly, few Confucian scholars were selected to be officials through the civil service examination before the Sui dynasty. Compared with individuals of noble origin, Confucian scholars were the last to be considered for official positions. In addition, those selected through the civil service examination were not necessarily elite because the content of the examination did not serve the goal of nurturing the political elite. To the contrary, many Confucian officials were bookish and blindly loyal to political authority. As one writer says, "Because the examination had degenerated into a mere contest of skill in the composition of a type of mechanical 'eight-legged' essay, the Chinese creative genius was impaired."[30] Moreover, the civil service examination system suppressed many talented Chinese people. In an agricultural society, only wealthy families could afford to support their children until they completed the examination because it required long study. As a result, "the bureaucracy was limited to the wealthy landlord class, meaning that this after all was a kind of aristocracy."[31] Also, it cannot be denied that the percentage of Confucian officials was increasing until the civil service examination system was established, and "as the competitive examination system became one of the major channels for recruiting government officials, the scholar-officials became the main body of bureaucracy and the main part of the ruling class" in the Ming and the Qing dynasties.[32] In Chinese feudal society, money could buy both official positions and diplomas. Chinese political corruption was a popular phenomenon and greatly decreased the quality of officialdom. More importantly, emperors were at the top of the ruling class and held absolute power over all citizens and officials, including the elite. Even if every official was one of the elite, it was no way to change the nature of the Chinese political system—the absolute monarchical system—because Confucian scholars and the elite became part of the political machine after they became officials.

Although Western culture has influenced China for centuries, the Chinese political system has retained its traditional character. Western societies had had contact with China since the seventh century, but they largely brought Western culture into China through Western missionaries in the Qing dynasty, starting the process of reshaping China's public philosophy. Surprisingly, the Chinese political system was not swayed by Western public philosophy and artillery. The modern nation-state emerged in Europe in the eighteenth century, and it was "several centuries ahead of the same development in China."[33] China did not accept and practice the theory of the modern nation-state until the beginning of the twentieth century. The modern reform movement in China began after the second Opium War. The political reform movement of 1898, led by Kang Youwei, Liang Qichao, Tan Sitong, and Yan Fu, was supported by Emperor Guang Xu. During the reform movement, the Chinese government reformed the civil service examination system; established Westernized schools; opened modern banks; developed mines, railways, and other industrial enterprises; and sent students abroad. The reform movement still was not tolerated by the Chinese government, even though all reform measures were implemented within the old political framework. Empress Dowager Ci Xi oppressed the movement. Some reformers were killed, and the others fled China for Japan. The reform movement only lasted 100 days without advocating the theory of the modern nation-state. The causes of the failure of the reform movement obviously were not "the inexperience of the reformers" and "ill-considered strategy."[34] Rather, the reform movement failed because it was limited to a small group of Confucian scholars and politicians and did not touch the core of the political system and the public philosophy. The failure of the reform movement of 1898 led some reformers to organize a violent revolution and, finally, led to the revolution of 1911, which overthrew the last absolute monarchical system and established the first modern government, the Republic of China. According to F. W. Mote, the modern nation-state possesses at least four characteristics: "political power is established through national self-determination"; "there is recognition of the coexistence of other nations and the maintenance of reciprocal diplomatic relations"; "law is respected and political institutions are stressed"; and there is "wider popular participation in political power."[35] According to Mote, "China totally lacked all four of these characteristics throughout the period of the authoritarian world empire."[36] Based on this criterion, the Republic of China theoretically started the history of the modern state-nation in China. Yet the transition from the traditional Chinese political system to a modern democratic system still has not been completed.

THE ROOTS OF THE CHINESE POLITICAL SYSTEM

Looking at China's centralized political structure, its influence, and its development, the patriarchal system is the starting point to constitute an absolute monarchical government and social order. The patriarchal system became well developed in the Western Zhou dynasty. Under the patriarchal system, the clan became the tie of genetic relations and was closely connected with the government. The government and the political system in the Western Zhou dynasty began to carry out the *fen-feng* (enfiefment system) based on genetic relations. The government was mainly composed of the royal family as the main body and collateral noble families as its supplement. The term *fen-feng* refers to a system of enfiefing vassals to build a loose structure of decentralized authority, but Chinese feudalism was significantly different from Western "true" feudalism.[37] Eventually, tribal society, the Western Zhou, and patriarchal organizations disappeared, but the patriarchal culture has never disappeared in China. In the second period of Chinese history, patriarchal culture and religion permeated every aspect of society. The continuation of the patriarchal tradition was the basic principle supporting the existence and development of Chinese feudal politics. Moreover, signs of the patriarchal system are evident in modern Chinese society and contemporary time. The typical example is nepotism, such as the son of Jiang Jieshi's being appointed president of the Nationalist Party. In communist China, it is extremely common for family members of higher-level officials to have been appointed officials or to run official businesses (*guan-dao*) for private purposes by using political powers. The model of party rule in essence is family rule. Thus the communist system is a new patriarchal system by its nature.

The basic patriarchal principle places the father at the center of family and society. The government is an enlarged family; the emperor was the father of the nation and the high priest of religion. The emperor/father held both secular and divine power to rule the entire society. The main characteristic of the patriarchal system is that government power combines with clan power, divine power, and the authority of the husband. Thus in China the family was the basic social unit, which was not limited to the family circle but also extended to public life and political relations. The ruler-subject relationship was exactly the same as the relationship between fathers and sons. As Cho-yun Hsu says, "The familial network embraced all of China with the feudal structure as the political counterpart of the family structure."[38] It is no wonder that some scholars view Chinese culture as family spirit. The keys to this family spirit were the three cardinal guides (ruler guides subject, father guides son, and husband guides wife) and the five constant virtues (benevolence, righteousness, propriety, knowledge, and sincerity). In order to justify the emperor's power, the emperor was posed as the son of heaven; he thus embodied the will of heaven. In the name of heaven, Chinese emperors did everything that they wanted. The heavenly mandate was the orthodox theoretical foundation for premodern China to be recognized as an orthodox government, and it was also the core of the theory of the union of heaven and humanity used by the Chinese ruling class to control the Chinese people. In a Chinese parable, heaven and earth originally were inextricably joined in a chaotic mass. About a hundred thousand years ago, Pan-gu split the mass into two parts, heaven and earth, which gradually came to be separated by their present distance. To keep the patriarchal system running forever, the Chinese ruling class modified the Pan-gu creation story and put heaven, nature, and humankind together in a social and political context. However, deep inside the Chinese emperor and the ruling class, heaven and earth were but an empty shell, while the emperor's power was supreme.

In the patriarchal ideology, the human being is an integral part of nature under heaven. Everything on earth, including Chinese people and their property, belonged to the emperor.[39] In an old Chinese saying, "under the wide heaven all is the king's land; within the sea-boundaries of the land, all are the king's servants."[40] The emperor was the sole source of power, final authority, and all laws. All in all, only one person, the "emperor himself [held] the power of handing down the final decision: however powerful the ministers, they [were] not given the slightest right to make decisions for the emperor."[41] Common people were expected to unconditionally respect the emperor's power in order to follow the law and nature. When authoritarianism was taken to an extreme, family ethics, human feeling, social organization, the political system, economic activity, and daily life were controlled by the emperor's power. Therefore, centralized power, autocracy, and dictatorship became a historical necessity in Chinese feudal society; arbitrary rule became the political style. Only one person laid down the law and put into practice the statement, What I say counts. There were no distinctions between law and policy and the leader's speech. This patriarchal tradition is easily found in present-day China, where the top leader's speech is above the law, and where the law has remained a tool of policy rather than an impartial and independent arbiter.

In historic China's patriarchal society, filial piety was required in the family and in social life. Extending the principle of filial piety into the political system, loyalty and obedience became the first criteria to recruit officials. According to Confucianism, all under heaven are of one family, and all nations are of one people. No one was permitted to violate the "emperor's teachings of the deceased" and the "forefathers' discipline exercised by the head of a feudal household." Dong Zhongshu (179–104

B.C.), chief minister to Wu Di of the Han dynasty and the first Chinese imperial scholar who proposed to canonize Confucian learning into the state, established the theory of the interaction between heaven and humanity. Dong's teachings, such as "Heaven changeth not, likewise the Way changeth not," and "the imitation of the ancients," became a moral code and the principle of conduct for every feudal dynasty. Any reform or other effort that strayed from tradition and custom was regarded as an abandonment of orthodoxy. The emperor always tested officials' loyalty using the strategy, "point to a deer, call it a horse." In Chinese feudal society, a person had to die if the emperor wanted him or her dead. In periods ruled by wise and open-minded emperors, philosophers might rebuke rulers with impunity, "but in the unified empire one might be put to death." This explains why in the past the minds of the Chinese people were "not very creative."[42] Therefore, the absolute monarchical system—based on ignorance and blind obedience and highly conservative—was entwined in the Chinese ethos. Gilbert Rozman points out that one of the important reasons for China's failing to complete reforms in the nineteenth century was that the Chinese people were unwilling to abandon their old traditions and customs, such as Dao, Way, and heaven.[43]

The patriarchal system deeply affected the Chinese feudal political system. Under the patriarchal system, the patriarchal clan relation and blood lineage were the basic criteria to determine a person's social status. The Chinese palace hired only eunuchs to serve prince and queen in order to keep the blood of the royal family and royal lineage pure and retain power within the royal family. In the feudal society, the eldest son had the exclusive right to inherit his father's legacy. The eldest son of an emperor was legally the heir to the throne. Political capability, administrative skill, and knowledge of the position were not the main criteria used to select and evaluate officials. Naturally, nepotism derived from these patriarchal relations. Political figures, their family members, and relatives were interrelated in the social and political network. The rise and decline of any political figure would affect others. "Whenever a main family collapsed," Hsu says, "the relationships that had existed through it came to an end."[44] When a man became powerful, those near him rode his coattails to success. Conversely, when a man was in violation of the law, all of his relatives and friends were punished. This nepotism inevitably resulted in antirationalism. Wisdom and rationality became dim and dark in Chinese feudal society. The legitimacy of an absolute monarchical government was based on the unconditional obedience of the common people. Confucian ethics provided the theoretical foundation for antirationalism, because Confucianism required that everyone follow the principles of loyalty, filial piety, kindness, ritual, propriety, and trustworthiness. Therefore, Confucian principles required the Chinese people "not to do things which do not conform to the rites," to "look at nothing that is not consistent with propriety," "not to listen to things which do not conform to the rites," and "not to say things which do not conform to the rites." The Chinese communist politics today is still based on nepotism and familism. Nepotism and *guanxi* (connections) are the most important tools to practice business and politics. The party sets very similar principles for the Chinese people using a different vocabulary: "be loyal to the party" and "follow the party unconditionally."

The patriarchal system supported a rigid hierarchical system to fit its political structure. Under this system, the Chinese people were divided into different ranks: farmer, soldier, merchant, artist, politician, official, and Confucian. This tradition discouraged people from going into business because the rank of merchant in the social structure was of a very low status, below that of a peasant. Even a successful merchant was not highly regarded, but was merely a "small man." This partly explains why China gradually became a backward country; the development of commercial activity might lead to social changes, such as "the emergence of commercial centers, increased division of labor, regional inter-dependency."[45] Officialdom was divided into more than twenty ranks in the Qin dynasty and reduced to less than twenty ranks in later dynasties. Under the emperor, the order of ranks was as follows: "chief minister, great officer, upper scholar, middle scholar, and lower scholar."[46] Different ranks of officials received different salaries, wore different types of clothes, possessed different carriages, and enjoyed different privileges. The hierarchical system was pyramidal. Everyone had to follow the social ethical code of "letting the king be a king, the minister a minister, the father a father, and the son a son."

The patriarchal culture contributed to China's adoption of a closed-door policy. In an agricultural society, the family, as a basic work unit, is concerned only about the harvest from its own farm. Chinese peasants did not communicate with one another throughout their lives, though the crowing of their cocks and the barking of their dogs were within earshot. In addition, much of China was inland, and the Chinese people knew little of the outside world. The imperial government regarded its territory as the principal body of the world and the center of the world. The term *China* in Chinese, *Zhong-Guo,* literally refers to the center of the world, the so-called Middle Kingdom. Based on this fantasy, Chinese emperors required every official visitor from abroad to pay tribute and to obey Chinese tradition by *kowtowing* before the emperor. Even when Lord Macartney, an English ambassador, came to China in 1793, "he was forced to kneel in obeisance."[47] However, China was not born to isolation, despite its difficult seas, lofty mountains, massive barren lands, rocky shores, and a lack of good harbors.[48] Looking back on Chinese history, China did not maintain a closed-door policy before the Qing dynasty. For example, Zheng He sailed from China to many places in his seven epic voyages, including the South Pacific, the Indian Ocean, Taiwan, the Persian Gulf, and distant Africa. His final expedition, from 1405 to 1433, was at least some sixty years before Columbus's voyages. There is no evidence to prove that China was absolutely isolated before the eighteenth century. The first contact between China and foreign countries can be traced to the Han dynasty, in which Buddhism systematically entered China and inspired and enlightened whole Chinese cultures. In the Tang dynasty, there were a large number of foreign residents in China, especially in Chang-An, the Tang capital. Many official embassies came from all over Asia.[49] Indian monks and Persian priests also flowed into China. The Nestorian monument was erected in Changan in 628. The monument recorded the first Christian missionary group from abroad and commemorates the coming of missionaries from Palestine bringing the "Luminous Religion." Some foreigners even settled in China, and foreigners and Chinese lived together unsegregated in some areas. In the Tang dynasty, foreign sea trade increased. At that time, the Indian Ocean was safe, and most of China's foreign trade operated there as well as in the South China Sea. All these activities brought exotic cultures to China, including material goods and ideas.[50] Therefore, the aphorism regarding the "nonpluralistic nature of early Chinese culture," is not true.[51] China today comprises the Han people and more than fifty-six ethnic minorities. The ethnic minorities are about 90 million in population and inhabit 50 to 60 percent of the country's total area. From a historical perspective, Chinese culture absorbed good elements from every Chinese minority and gradually formed its Hua-Xia culture, that is, its Chinese culture. In addition, the dominant ideology of Confucianism as philosophy and religion—even of Taoism and Buddhism—is not an exclusive belief system. On the contrary, China assimilated many foreign cultures before the eighteenth century, including Persian culture, Indian Buddhist culture, and Arab culture.

In the sixteenth century, the Renaissance reached a peak and brought Europe into a new era of philosophy, art, literature, and natural science. The Renaissance was followed by the Industrial Revolution and the bourgeois revolution. Europe accumulated huge industrial power in the middle of the eighteenth century, colonized other regions in the nineteenth century, and brought China into a semicolonial period. Some Western scholars call this period the "ruin of Asia."[52] Although Europe began to surpass China from this time onward, the Manchu (Qing dynasty) aristocrat was not prejudiced against Western science and technology at the beginning of the Qing dynasty. In 1697, the emperor Kangxi sent a delegation to France to hire scientists for China. He often called missionaries to his palace to lecture on the sciences, including geometry, physics, optics, and astronomy. At the end of the eighteenth century, the Manchu ruling class became very corrupt, however, and lost its appetite for learning about foreign cultures and science. In addition, China was never willing to change its public philosophy and political system, and it feared a confrontation with modern Western civilization. Gradually, China completely cut off any cultural and commercial exchange with Western countries, closed its doors, resisted advanced culture and technology, and blindly enjoyed its parochial arrogance to deceive the Chinese people. As a result, China was defeated by the challenges of Western countries and culture. After the Communist Party came to power, the Chinese government continuously carried out the closed-door policy for twenty-eight years. The history of Chinese foreign policy clearly indicates that its closed-door policy was related to the weakness of Chinese society. A strong and highly civilized nation opens its doors to the rest of the world. Following this logic, the difference between Chinese culture and Western culture essentially involves time. In other words, the difference between Chinese culture and Western culture is basically the difference between an ancient and a modern culture: China resisted adapting to new culture and stagnated in Eastern feudal society until Western countries forced open its doors using gunboats and artillery.

CHINESE SOCIETY AND CHINESE PATRIARCHAL RELIGION

The Chinese patriarchal system was supported by Chinese patriarchal religion. Precisely, patriarchal religion is part of China's patriarchal system. Traditional patriarchal religion was a clan-based religion that derived from the primitive clan and formed in the Xia dynasty. The basis of the patriarchal religion was the worship of ancestors as well as of the land, sun, moon, mountain, river, and ghosts. China's patriarchal religion classified four types of god: heavenly god, earthly god, manly ghost, and material god. Correspondingly, there were four types of worship: heaven worship, land worship, ancestor worship, and grain worship. The patriarchal religion was not only the product of the patriarchal system but was one of the ideological pillars in Chinese feudal society to sustain the continual development of the absolute monarchical system.

The traditional patriarchal religion had a profound impact on other Chinese religions, daily life, culture, and politics. It is acknowledged worldwide that China has three traditional religions: Confucianism, Daoism, and Buddhism. Few scholars, however, are aware that Chinese traditional religion and foreign religions in China were deeply influenced by Chinese patriarchal religion. The traditional Chinese patriarchal religion had the most popular believers of any religion in the world before the twentieth century and was an important base for the fifty-six nations in China to reach a common recognition. This strengthened rather than destroyed some aspects of the clan religious system after China entered the second period of Chinese history. Compared with the rest of the world, China was the only country in which ancient patriarchal religion continued to develop systematically; thus, it became more powerful in Chinese feudal society. The rise and decline of dynasties did not shake the orthodox position of the patriarchal religion. The entrance of Buddhism and the rise of Daoism also did not change the position of patriarchal religion as an established religion. For most Chinese people, including both the nobility and the common people, ancestor worship is first, and the belief in other religions is second. As a matter of fact, all other religions have been only marginally relevant for most Chinese people from ancient times to the present.

The patriarchal religion was unified with the king and with government tradition. It both demonstrated the power of the king and was controlled by him. Important sacrificial rites were national events and were presided over by the king or emperor, thereby indicating that the king's power was endowed by heavenly power. Therefore, the traditional patriarchal religion actually dominated other religions and became an established religion, although it did not have a formal religious structure. Other religions were not permitted to contradict the patriarchal religion in idea, moral code, belief, or rites. It is not difficult to find an inner connection between Daoism and patriarchal religion through a look at witchcraft, which is a primary religion and one type of patriarchal religion. Many basic Daoist ideas, rites, and ghosts came from witchcraft. Some indigenous Buddhist priests tried to compromise the patriarchal religion by emphasizing the conformity between the two religions and making the distinction between their content and their form. Nestorians came to China in the seventh century, but their mission was not successful because the Nestorians did not coordinate with traditional Chinese culture. This is also one of reasons why some later Christian missionaries failed in China. To the Christian missionary Matteo Ricci's credit, therefore, when he came to China in the sixteenth century, he changed the missionary style and applied the concepts of heavenly God, or *Shang Di* in Chinese, based on Confucian classics, and compromised with some Chinese traditional customs and rites, such as the worship of Confucius and ancestors. Therefore, the Christian missionary movement in the sixteenth century represented by Ricci was successful. The development of Islam in China essentially was a process by which Muslims learned to compromise with the patriarchal religion and the Chinese moral code.

The patriarchal religion also impacted the daily life of the Chinese nation. Compared with other types of Chinese culture, the patriarchal religion was easier to develop among common Chinese people by religious rites, prayer, festivals, and ceremony. The common Chinese people were more difficult to teach and less likely to accept formal Chinese culture due to their limited education. Therefore, the basic ideas of Chinese culture and tradition came from the patriarchal religion. Ethically, the patriarchal religion maintained human moral behavior and social order by ancestor worship, so that the mode of human relationships kept going generation after generation. Economically, the patriarchal religion—through grain worship, land worship, and nature worship—sacralized the periodization of agricultural production and the natural environment required for agricultural production. Because the patriarchal religion was the easiest and most useful belief system, it became the most popular religion, especially in premodern China. Hopefully, with the development of Chinese economy and education, other types of religion, especially Christianity, will grow faster in contemporary China.

Likewise, the patriarchal religion impacted Chinese culture. The Four Books and the Five Classics came out in the periods of Spring and Autumn and the Warring States. The Four Books and the Five Classics represent traditional Chinese culture. In the process of improvement, Confucianism became the spiritual pillar of patriarchal society. The important reasons why Confucianism had such a profound influence on Chinese society and culture were that the central principles of Confucianism preserved traditional Chinese familial values, which conformed to the core of the patriarchal religion. In the development of Confucianism, the disciples of Confucianism protected Chinese traditional culture, coordinated with the government, participated in politics, were devoted to those kings who had high moral behavior, emphasized propriety (*li*) and the harmony of social relationships, insisted on the "mandate of heaven," and proved the legitimacy of the emperor's power in morality and religion. Dong Chongshu, the first scholar and politician in the Han dynasty, made Confucianism a religion and made the most important contribution to the theory of correspondence between humankind and universe: the principle of "heaven changeth not, likewise the Way changeth not." He also confirmed the divine nature of heaven, the divine nature of "three cardinals and the five constant virtues," and proved the divine nature of the emperor's power. The aim of all these theories was to prove that heaven determined the social relationship between ruled and ruler, son and father, wife and husband, female and male, and brothers and sisters. The law of social life was in conformity with the law of nature. The union of moral behavior, nature, and society was based on the law of the universe. Therefore, the first important responsibility for the individual was to follow the universal law and promote social and universal harmony. Clearly, this central idea extended patriarchal religion to Chinese culture.

Finally, the patriarchal religion impacted Chinese politics. The development of ancestor worship in traditional Chinese society generally synchronized with the evolution of the patriarchal political system. Under many circumstances, the Chinese political system and ancestor worship coordinated with each other. Patriarchal religion maintained the emperor's power through the rite of heaven worship. When the patriarchal religion unified with the political system, the king or the head of the clan presided over the ceremony of ancestor worship. After the family separated from the state, the clan and the family held the rituals of ancestor worship at the family level; the emperor held the rituals of ancestor worship in national services. The political system provided the social value for ancestor worship and regulated the activities of ancestor worship; ancestor worship, in turn, sustained the political system. As Benjamin Schwartz notes, "Ancestor worship may have greatly influenced the political system of early China."[53] The combination of ancestor worship and the patriarchal system produced the teaching of loyalty and filial piety. In premodern China, filial piety was not merely an ethical value, but had a "religious resonance."[54] Therefore, the Chinese political system was very similar to the familial system. Since the Qin dynasty, the typical patriarchal system has been gradually destroyed and is no longer a unified political system for the whole country. Correspondingly, ancestor worship is no longer a unified political activity sponsored by the state, although clan and familial religious activity are still present. However, the family is still the basic element of society; clan law and the regulation of ancestor worship became more systematic over time, especially the ideas of genetic relations and the tradition of ancestor worship. In the later feudal societies of the Ming and Qing dynasties, ancestor worship was more popular and was completely dispersed into every family as one of the basic familial functions. According to the regulations of ancestor worship, people were permitted to worship only the father before the Ming dynasty, but there was freedom to worship both parents during the Ming dynasty, and all grandparents during the Qing. Patriarchal religion and politics did not disappear after the feudal system was abolished. The politics in the Republic of China era clearly reflected ancestor worship. Worship of Mao under the Mao regime, especially during the Cultural Revolution, was a typical mixture of communist politics and ancestor worship. By using patriarchal religion, Jiang has held his highest power after having retired from his position as president of China. This clearly shows that Chinese patriarchal tradition is the base of the Chinese communist regime.

CONCLUSION

Due to the fact that China has a long history, its characteristics are twofold: China possesses great cultural wealth, but it also has a heavy historic burden that suffocates its democratic development. China's highly centralized political system inherited a strong patriarchal tradition from its predecessors. While Western societies rose rapidly and stepped into democratic systems in the nineteenth century, China slept under the traditional concept of the "Middle Kingdom" and gradually became a weak country colonized by Western interests. Under these circumstances, it was impossible for China to fully develop into a capitalist society. Therefore, modern

China was significantly deficient in a modern political and economic sense.

The distinguishing characteristics of premodern China were its backward economy (an agricultural economy with a primitive mode of production), despotic dictatorship (a highly centralized system ruled by a single person without the regulation of law for more than 2,000 years), and spiritual emptiness (a patriarchal religion dominating the mind of the Chinese people). Unlike Western societies, premodern China did not have a constitutional tradition and a full religious tradition. In contrast with Western societies, it is more difficult for China to reform its old public philosophy and start a democratic society. Thus premodern China lacked the concept of the modern nation-state. Even Liang Qi-chao, the first and most prominent pioneer of democracy in modern Chinese history, did not believe that China was ready for a democratic system, because the Chinese people owed personal allegiance to the ruler but not to the state. Moreover, he claimed that "the republican form of government is not as good as constitutional monarchy, which has fewer flaws and functions more efficiently,"[55] and "constitutional government is in essence government by public opinion."[56]

An agricultural economy provides the best soil for despotic dictatorship. In some respects, the two are twins. At this point in time, economic modernization is very important to political reform. Ninety years after the last Chinese emperor was overthrown, China is growing rapidly toward economic modernization, the first step for Chinese democratization. However, the communist system essentially is still ruled by a single person, the general secretary of the Communist Party; patriarchal religion is very influential; patriarchal culture remains; and nepotism is a common phenomenon. The only answer to explain the uneven development between China's economy and its politics is that the political system is a relatively independent force. Even if the economy reaches a high level, Chinese political power can resist political changes. China is at a crossroads: It must accept a democratic system, or keep its authoritarian system. There are only two types of governance, regardless of form: good government and bad government. Two hundred years of history have proven that the democratic system offers the best opportunity for good government. History has likewise proven that dictatorial government is bad government.[57] When classical political theory insists that political institutions produce the best type of society and individuals, we should remember that public philosophy affects the design of political institutions and, finally, regulates a social and political order. Without doubt, great efforts are needed to change the traditional Chinese patriarchal culture—the root of the one-party system.

NOTES

1. Lucian W. Pye, *The Mandarin and the Cadre: China's Political Cultures* (Ann Arbor: University of Michigan, 1988), p. 21.

2. John Meskill, ed., *The Pattern of Chinese History: Cycles, Development, or Stagnation?* (Westport, Conn.: Greenwood Press, 1965), p. ix.

3. G.W.F. Hegel, "The Childhood of History," in *The Pattern of Chinese History: Cycles, Development, or Stagnation?*, p. 13.

4. Jacques Gernet, *A History of Chinese Civilization* (New York: Cambridge University Press, 1982), p. 3.

5. H. Stephen Gardner, *Comparative Economic Systems* (New York: The Dryden Press, 1998), p. 654.

6. Pye, *The Mandarin and the Cadre,*" p. ix.

7. Gernet, *A History of Chinese Civilization*, p. 20.

8. Quoted in Meskill, *The Pattern of Chinese History,*" p. xx.

9. Chun-shu Chang, ed., *The Making of China: Main Themes in Premodern Chinese History* (Englewood Cliffs, N.J.: Prentice-Hall, 1975), p. 4.

10. Ibid., p. 4.

11. Miyazaki Ichisada, "The Four Ages of Chinese History," in *The Pattern of Chinese History*, p. 53.

12. Quoted in Meskill, *The Pattern of Chinese History*, p. x.

13. Ibid., p. xi.

14. F. W. Mote, *A History of Chinese Political Thought* (Princeton, N.J.: Princeton University Press, 1979), p. 13.

15. Mousheng Lin, *Men and Ideas: An Informal History of Chinese Political Thought* (New York: Hohn Day, 1942), p. 18.

16. Bozan Jian, Shao Xunzheng, and Hu Hua, *A Concise History of China* (Beijing: Foreign Languages Press, 1981), p. 12.

17. Lin, *Men and Ideas*, p. 18.

18. Shouyi Bai, ed., *An Outline History of China* (Beijing: Foreign Languages Press, 1976), p. 19.

19. Bozan, Shao, and Hu, *A Concise History of China*, p. 13.

20. Tse-tsung Chow, *The May Fourth Movement: Intellectual Revolution in Modern China* (Stanford, Calif.: Stanford University Press, 1967), p. 8.

21. Gernet, *A History of Chinese Civilization*, p. 14.

22. Ibid., p. 26.

23. Mark Elvin, *The Pattern of the Chinese Past* (Stanford, Calif.: Stanford University Press, 1973), p. 129.

24. Chao-ting Chi, "Key Economic Areas in Chinese History: From the Huangho Basin to the Yangtze Valley," in *The Making of China: Main Themes in Premodern Chinese History*, p. 230.

25. Lin, *Men and Ideas*, p. 124.

26. Ibid., p. 128.

27. Bozan, Shao, and Hu, *A Concise History of China*, p. 81.

28. James R. Thomas, *Chinese Politics* (Jiangsu, China: People's Publishing House of Jiangsu, 1992), p. 34.

29. Ichisada, "The Four Ages of Chinese History," p. 55.

30. Ping-Ti Ho, "Social Composition of Ming-Qing Ruling Class," in *The Making of China: Main Themes in Premodern Chinese History,* p. 298.

31. Ichisada, "The Four Ages of Chinese History," p. 56.

32. Ho, "Social Composition of Ming-Qing Ruling Class," p. 298.

33. Mote, *A History of Chinese Political Thought,* p. 25

34. Immanuel C. Y. Hsu, *The Rise of Modern China,* 5th ed. (New York: Oxford University Press, 1995), p. 380.

35. Mote, *A History of Chinese Political Thought,* p. 25.

36. Ibid., p. 26.

37. Ibid., p. 5.

38. Cho-yun Hsu, "The Transition of Ancient Chinese Society," in *The Making of China: Main Themes in Premodern Chinese History,* p. 64.

39. Gilbert Rozman, ed., *China's Modernization* (Jiangsu Province: China: People's Publishing House, 1998), p. 63.

40. Mote, *A History of Chinese Political Thought,* p. 23.

41. Ichisada, "The Four Ages of Chinese History," p. 55.

42. H. G. Greel, "The Eclectics of Han Thought," in *The Making of China: Main Themes in Premodern Chinese History,* p. 141.

43. Rozman, *China's Modernization,* p. 63.

44. Hsu, "The Transition of Ancient Chinese Society," p. 6.

45. Ibid., p. 71.

46. Lin, *Men and Ideas,* p. 19.

47. Mote, *A History of Chinese Political Thought,* p. 24.

48. Paul S. Ropp, ed., *Heritage of China: Contemporary Perspectives on Chinese Civilization* (Berkeley: University of California Press, 1990), p. 49.

49. Edward H. Schafer, "The Glory of the Tang Empire," in *The Making of China: Main Themes in Premodern Chinese History,* p. 170.

50. Ibid., p. 174.

51. Ropp, *Heritage of China,"* p. 49.

52. Ichisada, "The Four Ages of Chinese History," p. 6.

53. Benjamin Schwartz, *China's Cultural Values* (Arizona: Lionheart Press, 1993), p. 10.

54. Ibid., p. 8.

55. Quoted in Andrew J. Nathan, *Chinese Democracy* (Berkeley: University of California Press, 1986), p. 60.

56. Quoted in John Fitzgerald, *Awakening China: Politics, Culture, and Class in the Nationalist Revolution* (Stanford, Calif.: Stanford University Press, 1996), p. 207.

57. Robert E. Goodin and Hans-Dieter Klingemann, eds., *A New Handbook of Political Science* (Oxford, England: Oxford University Press, 1996), p. 134.

CHAPTER 3

Ideological Battles through Centuries

Public philosophy has never separated from ideology, especially in communist China. There is little doubt that communist China is an ideological country. It is generally accepted that ideological propaganda is the most important vehicle with which the Communist Party of China (CPC) drives the communist revolution. After communism prevailed over China, the party relied heavily on ideology to mobilize socialist campaigns to retain its power. According to China's Constitution, Marxism is the official ideology of China. The party requires that the Chinese people accept and practice Marxism, think what the party thinks, say what the party says, and do what the party wants. The party wants to brainwash the Chinese people through political education. To terminate the one-party system, Chinese ideology must be remade. From a global perspective, with the development of communications and technology, the role of ideology has become increasingly important in the international economy and international politics. Ideology has become the source of social development and the channel of international cooperation. The contemporary world is becoming smaller and smaller. The terms *globalization* and *global village* are sometimes employed to describe this great modern phenomenon. Although modern democracy is the mainstream in the process of globalization, the world is full of conflict, including military wars, religious conflicts, and terrorist attacks. All conflicts, including those between communist China and democratic societies, ultimately derive from ideological conflicts. In this sense, to achieve international peace, one must first make ideological peace.

CHINA'S IDEOLOGY AND THE GLOBAL SOCIAL ORDER

Every country is a basic unit of the global village; a global order actually is a country's social order writ large. Improvement of the social order in every country is the initial step toward improvement of the global order. Before China opened its doors to the world, the Chinese government was extremely hostile to Western countries. China began merging into the global economy when the reform movement began. China's admission to the World Trade Organization (WTO) is a big step toward globalization, but ideological conflicts among China and democratic countries remain critical as the Chinese government continues to carry out a socialist system with Chinese characteristics under the leadership of the party. However, the Western concept of globalization means that the world is dominated by "transnational capitalist operations."[1] In other words, the global order and globalization should be aligned by a capitalist economy and democratic politics. At this point, China cannot become a good member of the global village without solving these ideological conflicts. A good social order is produced by a good government and ultimately is determined by a good public philosophy. In 1943, Walter Lippmann wrote a book, *An Inquiry into the Principles of the Good Society*, in which he revealed the connections between democratic principles and a good society. He pointed out that communism, socialism, and fascism are the principles of totalitarian regimes. Of course, this statement should be reevaluated today because traditional communism is disappearing and socialism has entered into the postsocialism stage. However, Lippmann's conclusion is valid in China because totalitarianism is the basic characteristic of the Chinese government. So it is reasonable to doubt that, even though China is now a member of the WTO, the Chinese communist government is willing to produce a good social order to contribute to the global order.

A social order is sustained by certain support systems that, basically, include an ideological system, an economic system, a political system, a religious system, plus an educational program. A democratic social order is generally supported by a liberal ideology, a market economy, democratic politics, and plural religion. Eric Carlton lists four important aspects of social control: law to enforce social conduct, custom to institutionalize behavior, moral precepts to promote social harmony, and religious precepts to interpret the will of the gods.[2] However, each of these four aspects requires a theoretical foundation, that is, an ideology. In contrast with the Western support system, in China, Marxism-Maoism is the established ideology; the planned economy is the dominant economy; the discussion of the separation of three powers is not allowed; and independent religious organization is strictly prohibited. More and more Chinese people have realized that Marxism and communism are no longer a remedy for

China and the Chinese people, but the party still tries to hold Marxism and communism for ideological control. President Jiang Zemin, in his speech at the meeting to celebrate the eightieth anniversary of the founding of the CPC, insisted that Marxism is the guiding principle of the party. Guided by Marxism, how can China sincerely cooperate with democratic countries? It is necessary to reform the official ideology in order to rearrange China's social and political order along the global order.

Strictly speaking, modern ideology has only about 200 years of history. It is the product of the Industrial Revolution and the democratic movement. Central to modern ideology is the idea that "since we have made the world, we can also remake it."[3] The term *ideology* derived from the French Enlightenment and brought with it political questions about a new direction for the world.[4] Hence, ideology at its beginning was political rather than philosophical. French ideology emphasizes that "truth is a correspondence with reality."[5] In Germany, Georg Wilhelm Friedrich Hegel applied this French ideology to intellectual and philosophical pursuits. German ideology emphasizes making truth rather than making observations.[6] Karl Marx synthesized French and German ideas and emphasized the political meaning of ideology to explain social and political changes.[7] Evidently, ideology in communist countries is basically used for political campaigns only. In the United States, Americans did not fully realize the importance of ideology until the cold war in the mid-twentieth century, but ideology became a serious and scholarly subject when the U.S. competed with the Soviet Union in the arms race.[8] The United States even overemphasized ideology and campaigned against communism for more than twenty years during the cold war.

Although the term *ideology* is frequently used today, the meaning of ideology remains uncertain. At its inception, ideology referred to "any visionary and grandiose scheme of social reform."[9] Now, most scholars agree that ideology is "a system of beliefs about the economic, political, and social arrangements of a society,"[10] "the body of ideas reflecting the social needs and aspirations of an individual, group, class, or culture,"[11] and "a phenomenon particularly characteristic of a certain stage of political and economic growth."[12] Ideology has three image models of society: a countermodel to examine social problems, a utopian model to design a new social structure, and an action-oriented model to explain the way of "destroying the old society and realizing the ideal."[13] According to the Chinese official definition, ideology is the dominant social public opinion and belief, which is supported by the ruling class and which, in turn, serves the ruling class. China's ideology from ancient times to the present is established ideology. Confucianism was decreed by the Han emperor; Sun Yat-senism was supported by the nationalist government; and Marxism is the official ideology under the Constitution of the People's Republic of China. Therefore, in the Chinese context only one voice represents ideology; that is, official ideology. "Self-consciousness" and individual voices under the communist regime are oppressed. The party's voice is the voice of Chinese ideology.

Because the CPC tightly controls the media to propagate ideology, it is unavoidable that contemporary Chinese ideology is very political. The central functions of Chinese ideology are to serve the party's political campaigns, provide theoretical foundation to justify the communist system, identify the entire cultural system, unify the Chinese people and the party members working for the party and the socialist country, encourage political enthusiasm among the Chinese people to follow in the party's footsteps, propagandize Marxism and Maoism, and specify new social goals and values to guide the Chinese people and society toward the communist society.[14] In the post-Mao era, the Chinese official ideology has been declining. Zhiling Lin and Thomas W. Robinson observe that current Chinese ideology actually is a hybrid that mixes three components: "orthodox Marxist doctrine as the dominant state-sanctioned 'correct' philosophy," "the Confucian tradition as the ideological foundation of China's cultural identity," and "contemporary cultural nationalism as a rallying call for the rejuvenation of China."[15] Although Chinese ideology began generating from different sources, under the highly centralized government, Chinese official ideology is composed from the top to the bottom and transforms the top leader's will into the will of the common people.[16] In other words, the common people must obey any Chinese official's will, no matter what it is. This characteristic of Chinese ideology obviously inherits from and reflects the patriarchal tradition. However, some new cultural forms and thoughts cannot be blocked in China as the reform expands. In addition, the government cannot control whether the Chinese people are able to learn a different ideology at present, but the conflict between official ideology and the trend toward a new culture will not end until the Chinese government is elected by the people. Therefore, Chinese modernization and democratization can also be seen as ideological reconstruction.

Contemporary China's ideology has deep historical roots. As Benjamin Schwartz has noted, "In a fundamental way the millennial culture of China on the deepest level is still very much there."[17] In postrevolutionary society, Chinese ideology is mixed with traditional culture.[18] From a historical perspective, the development of Chinese ideology can be divided into three periods: Confucianism, which dominated Chinese ideology from the Han dynasty to the end of the Qing dynasty; Sun Yat-sen's Three People's Principles, which were established as official ideology after the Republic of China was founded in 1912; and Marxism, which became the orthodox ideology of the People's Republic of China after the CPC came to power in 1949. Strictly speaking, however, the saying that only the three "isms" dominated China successively is not precisely accurate. In ancient China, there were *san jiao* (three religions: Confucianism, Daoism, and

Buddhism) and *jiu liu* (nine schools of thought: those of the Confucians, the Daoists, the Yin Yang, the Legalists, the Mohists, the Political Strategists, the Eclectics, the Logicians, and the Agriculturists). In modern China, traditional Chinese ideology was attacked, nationalism arose, and Western ideas flowed in, including pragmatism, utilitarianism, anarchism, socialism, and various foreign religions. Today, more than fifty years after the party's ideology began to rule China, concepts of either "Confucian China" or "nationalist China" are extremely misleading.[19] However, since Confucianism dominated China for over two thousand years, we certainly must take the influence of Confucianism on contemporary Chinese ideology into account in order to remake China's public philosophy.

CONFUCIANISM AS THE DOMINANT IDEOLOGY IN PREMODERN CHINA

Chinese ideology in premodern China was characterized as humanism. In Western societies, humanism is a movement advocating individual value and capabilities while respecting scientific knowledge and cultivating classics. Unlike Western humanism, heaven and family are the two cornerstones of an integrated Chinese humanism. The theory of the union of heaven and the individual is the foundation of Chinese humanism. *Tian* (heaven) is the superior power beyond human control. The Chinese emperor was the mediator between heaven and society. The Chinese people had no choice but to obey the will of the emperor/heaven. Therefore, traditional Chinese humanism did not encourage individual initiative but taught the Chinese people that being tame and docile preserved the collective values—the family's authority and political authority. Confucianism was the most influential school of thought, and has "created the national myth—actually a cultural myth—in traditional China."[20] Although some scholars avoid using the word *ideology* to describe Confucianism, Confucian doctrine has traditionally functioned as an ideology to serve political life in China.[21] Like Marxism, Confucianism also became a state ideology in response to "the changing political needs of its believers."[22] Confucius was born in 551 B.C. during the Warring States period in which Chinese emperors lost their absolute power over local governments and China was divided into hundreds of feudalistic states. Every local lord tried to conquer all the other states to take over the throne. During the Warring States period, wars and violence were spread over all the land, and the old social order was broken (*li beng*). In Confucius's eyes, the old social order was the best social order because it was compatible with *li* (propriety). Confucius was determined to bring the society back to the traditional system (*fu li*). In the *Analects*, Confucius said "to conquer yourself and return to propriety is humanity." This was the core of Confucian humanism and reflected the characteristics of his political ambition.

To promote his teaching, Confucius established schools and traveled around China to persuade local lords to set good examples and run benevolent governments. Therefore, Confucianism at its inception was a political and ethical philosophy with little metaphysical speculation.[23] In this sense, Confucianism was "a strongly conservative governing ideology."[24] Obviously, his teaching was not welcomed by most local lords in his time. According to historical records, Confucius and his disciples were always driven out by local lords and ran away like "homeless dogs" because Confucian humanism had no reference to plundering, killing, and cheating.

The basic concept of Confucianism is based on the five constant virtues: *jen* (benevolence), *yi* (righteousness), *li* (propriety), *zhi* (knowledge/wisdom), and *xin* (sincerity). The main Confucian teaching is the three cardinal guides: ruler guides subject, father guides son, and husband guides wife. All these Confucian principles deal with human relationships and the social order. According to Confucius, the regulation of human relations is the basis of social order. Confucianism's social utopia is the harmony of the individual, the group, and the country. In order to fulfill his idea, Confucius emphasized the individual, the family, and participation. First, the individual is the basic element of a family and society. Confucius "realized that the character of a society itself essentially depended upon the character of the moral ideas."[25] Hence, Confucius was most concerned with the human heart, emphasized self, and developed educational programs to train *jun-zi* (gentlemen). To be a *jun-zi* is the precondition to regulate the family and to serve the country. The key to becoming a *jun-zi* is self-cultivation through knowledge. For Confucius, mind, will, and character were the three most important aspects in developing self.[26] A *jun-zi* is supposed to possess a righteous mind, a strong will, and moral character. Second, the family is a basic social institution and the first school to nurture *jun-zi*. Confucius set forth a series of principles that became a feudal ethical code for regulating individual behavior, familial relations, and social conduct, including the five relationships (ruled is subject to ruler; son is subject to father; wife is subject to husband; younger is subject to elder; and friends must trust each other); the three obediences (in ancient China a woman was required to obey her father before marriage, her husband during married life, and her sons in widowhood), the four virtues (fidelity, physical charm, propriety in speech, and efficiency in needlework), the three cardinal guides, and the five constant virtues. All these Confucian principles worked together as a net to maintain Chinese social order and political structure and to restrain the human nature of the Chinese people. To be sure, Chinese women suffered the most from Confucian humanism. Third, according to Confucianism, the individual is only an element of family, group, and society. Individual value was embodied in collective value, and group and collective value were above individual value. A *jun-zi* must devote himself to the country and build a new society. This requirement was called "regulating family and ruling the state." Therefore, the ultimate goal of Confucian teaching was to maintain traditional social order. Confucius said, "Those who strive to bring about the Golden Rule in a world society must first put their nation in order." However, a good society "is impossible unless the families within it are well managed." "To manage the family well requires a sound character. Sound character implies the presence of mind and the earnestness of will."[27]

Some scholars argue that Confucianism did not dominate China until the Song dynasty. Even in the Tang dynasty, "China was still largely a Buddhist society." What interested the Chinese people during the period before the Song dynasty was not Confucianism but other schools of thought.[28] This argument ignores the simple fact that the civil service examination system had been carried out for a long time before the Song dynasty. The civil service examination system had a close connection with Confucianism because Confucius was the founder of Chinese education; four Confucian books were the basic content of the examination; and Confucian scholars became the basic resources for Chinese officialdom before the Song dynasty. It is unimaginable that the Confucian government would let other schools of thought dominate the Chinese society. The truth is that since Confucianism was established as an official ideology in the Han dynasty, it never lost its dominant ideological position in Chinese history until the Chinese feudal system was replaced by the Republic of China, though there were many battles among Confucianism and other schools of thought during this period. It is also true that Confucianism was not popular or accepted by the ruling class or the common people in Confucius's time. The first emperor, Qin Shi Huang, appreciated only legalism and took strong measures to persecute Confucian scholars, because Confucius believed that people are educable and the government should rule by example. Because Qin Shi Huang took the throne by military force, he had to use violent punishment to suppress local rebels and dissidents. One might have taken power by military force, but one could hardly maintain power by military force. That was why the Qin dynasty existed for only a short period of time and was replaced by the Han dynasty after fifteen years. Drawing the lesson from the fall of the Qin dynasty, Dong Zhongshu, Confucian scholar and chief minister to Wu Di of the Han dynasty, suggested that the emperor Han Wu Di follow Confucianism only and abolish all other schools of thought, in order to establish a benevolent government. Han Wu Di realized that only the *wen-zhi* (benevolent government) could keep his rule alive. Soon after the emperor Han Wu Di reviewed Dong's suggestion to the throne, he issued the edict to put Dong's suggestions into practice[29] and dismissed all non-Confucian scholars from government. Based on Han's regulation, only those who excelled in the Confucian classics were qualified as rulers of the realm. Thus Confucianism "did not come to dominate Chinese life by accident."[30]

First, compared with other schools of thought, Confucianism was the best school by which the ruling class might maintain its power over the long term. Confucian cosmological theory of the union of nature and human beings was compatible with agricultural society, patriarchal social structure, and the needs of the ruling class. Based on this theory, the emperor had absolute power and exercised his authority on the earth in the name of heaven. Confucius also viewed the state as one large family and the emperor as its father. All officials and the common people were the emperor's children, who must obey their father unconditionally. In turn, the ruler should not neglect his parental obligations. He had to expend love and care on his subjects.[31] Thus this theory of the relationship between ruler and ruled was completely compatible with the needs of an absolute monarchical government.

The philosophy of Lao Zi and Zhuang Zi was generally recognized as the basic source of Daoism. *Dao* (Way) is the central concept of the philosophy of Lao Zhuang. Dao is the mysterious principle of the universe and the infinite way of the universe, beginningless and endless, characterized as "normalcy, naturalness, selflessness, and nothingness."[32] In contrast with Confucianism, Lao-Zhuang emphasized the contradiction between human society and the natural world. According to Lao-Zhuang, human beings created civilization but lost their morality. In order to avoid evil one must be willing "either to flee from civilized society or to destroy it."[33] Therefore, Lao-Zhuang advocated a negative philosophy and preached "do-nothing-ism" and nihilism. In practice, this negative theory neither pleased the ruling class nor fit the needs of the Chinese people.

Mocianism was founded by Mo Zi and adopted later by legalists. It is characterized as Chinese unitarianism. According to Wang, Mocianism was "committed to transforming ideals into realities"[34] and judged useful based solely on beneficial effects. For Confucius, the moral qualities of the ruler were the decisive factors for the state. Unlike Confucianism, Mo Zi claimed that the state was the highest value and humans were only the instrument. "Governing is a trade similar to that of a butcher."[35] This naked unitarianism and political theory were not compatible with the style of Eastern humanism and the hypocritical face of the *ren zheng* (benevolent government).

Legalists viewed human nature as wicked and self-seeking and advocated that a centralized government exercise absolute power and impose harsh punishments. Law and regulation were the only instruments for the complete control of the country and all citizens.[36] Legalism was limited to only a narrow area—law, which had no philosophical and universal value. More importantly, the harsh governance of legalist theory would not help the ruling class to gain the Chinese people's support. Legalism could be used for a short time and for special needs, but it could not be used for the state ideology over a long term.

Sun Zi was the founder of the strategist or militarist school and spent all his life studying the techniques of war and the strategies to win wars.[37] His book *Sun Zi on Military Strategies* has been widely relied on in military battles from ancient times to the present. His military strategy is recognized and applied in business and administration worldwide. Although his strategy contained rich philosophical ideas, it was not comprehensive enough to achieve recognition as an official ideology to regulate the Chinese society.

Second, Confucianism kept expanding its influence and strengthening its dominant position through its educational program. Confucius was the greatest teacher in Chinese history, and he made tremendous efforts to develop educational programs. His disciples did the same thing for more than 2,000 years. The Han dynasty began to select officials from Confucian scholars, and the Sui dynasty institutionalized the civil service examination system. At the beginning, whether or not the Confucian scholar had an opportunity to serve his emperor depended on the recommendation from his family head and the village elders. From the time of the Sui dynasty, the civil service examination was open to all Confucian scholars and became the most important channel for recruiting officials. This system offered hope for those who were not of noble origin but who wanted to have a bright future, if they could pass the examination. The content of the examination was the Confucian text. Anyone who wanted to be an official was required to study Confucianism and pass the examination. The main concern of most Chinese families was to learn Confucianism and prepare their children for the examinations. This trend created a huge demand for Confucian books and became the stimulus for the development of printing techniques.[38] In turn, the printing techniques promoted Confucianism's spread over the country. Therefore, in ancient China, Confucianism became the tool of the Chinese people to fulfill their political dreams, the bridge to cross the gap from the status of common people to official positions, the only source of moral behavior, and the sole standard of social and political values. Under pervasive Confucian influence, "the Chinese respect for scholarship is perhaps more serious than the Western respect for the clergy."[39] Moreover, "The influx of Western civilization during the last one hundred years has affected but little the scholars' traditional position of leadership."[40]

Third, Confucianism constantly strengthened itself by assimilating good ideas from other schools of thought for more than 2,000 years. Confucianism went through two epochs in premodern China after it was established as an official ideology in the Han dynasty. The first epoch was the period from the Han dynasty to the Tang dynasty, characterized as traditional Confucianism. In this stage, Confucian scholars established some connections with neighboring countries and learned from other schools. During the Song dynasty, Confucianism entered into the second epoch and is characterized as neo-Confucianism (*li xue*). Neo-Confucianism assimilated Buddhist cosmology, modified its theoretical system, and made Confucian ethics and political theory more metaphysical.[41] The most significant neo-Confucianist scholars, such as Wang Yangmin, Zhu Xi, Cheng Hao, and Cheng Yi, introduced important conceptions of *qi* and *li* to reconstruct Confucian theory. Neo-Confucianism fostered the concepts of the "ethic of thrift, honesty, and effort" from Daoism and promoted productive activities;[42] reinterpreted the meaning of learning, human freedom, and law; and further developed educational programs. Following the Song dynasty, traditional Confucian values began to move in a modern, liberal direction and became more vigorous.[43] Therefore Confucianism is not an exclusive system. Although Confucian scholars were proud of traditional Confucian thought, they worked with other schools of thoughts.

Confucianism also has had a considerable negative impact on China. First, according to Confucianism, the individual is not the center of society. Instead, the state dominates and shapes society, and the emperor holds absolute power over government.[44] Confucius viewed the state as a moral product of social evolution,[45] an expression of social harmony between the ruling and the ruled, and a hierarchy of the ruling and ruled classes. According to Confucius, "men are not born equal in intelligence, although all people can become moral men." Also, "Some are endowed with superior intelligence, others with inferior."[46] The ruled must obey the ruler, and the emperor is on the top of the ruling class. Hence Confucianism as ideology "valued hierarchy in both political and social spheres."[47] Second, according to Confucianism, a good society is maintained by a moral obligation, not by an obligatory law.[48] This tradition of the neglect of law was derived from the concept of the state as one great family. A good ruler is the most important thing for a country.[49] In the ancient Chinese context, punishment came from the will of heaven, not from common law. According to Confucius, "Lead the people by laws and regulate them by punishments, and the people will try to avoid wrongdoing but will have no sense of shame. Lead the people by virtue and regulate them by the rules of propriety, and the people will have a sense of shame, and moreover will become good."[50] Third, Confucianism has religious functions but does not have full religious characteristics such as a formal religious text, ritual, and independent religious organizations to influence the social and political order. In the ancient West, the church had sufficient autonomous power to affect government, and in most of the early modern European states, the church had become subordinated to secular authority but still had considerable autonomous power. In China there have been no separate organizations, powerful religious bodies, or spiritual leaders to challenge the authority of monarchs.[51] Correspondingly, from ancient times to the present day, Confucianism has been treated as a school of thought; the Confucian institution has been categorized as an academic institution; and Confucian scholars and disciples have been called intellectuals.

The core of Confucianism intentionally preserved traditional Chinese family values and protected the patriarchal system, namely, the harmonious society. Confucianism helped to build up a unique hierarchical and centralized political system in China. Thus the confrontation between Confucianism and the great challenge of the modern nation-state was unavoidable when the traditional Chinese political system reached its height. It is understandable that Confucianism as a state-sponsored ideology was fiercely attacked by reformists in the beginning of the twentieth century. Theoretically, after the civil service examination was abolished in 1905, Confucianism lost its position as China's state ideology. Beginning with the first intellectual movement in modern China, the May Fourth Movement, many Chinese intellectuals and Western scholars blamed Confucianism for China's inhumane ethics and patriarchal system. Interestingly, the nationalist government held onto the basic Confucian values in the schools and social life. Confucian tradition has fairly strongly influenced East Asian countries including Japan and the four "Mini Dragons" (Taiwan, South Korea, Hong Kong, and Singapore, so named because their economies developed quickly in the last quarter of the twentieth century). These East Asian countries have shared Confucian values with China and faced a similar challenge from Western ideas and practices. Peter R. Moody asserts that "Eastern Asian societies are characterized by personalism, familism, and political moralism."[52] Taiwan's government—the nationalist government—has taken a positive attitude toward Confucianism in order to preserve traditional family values and harmonious social relations. The vast majority of Taiwanese do not view Confucianism as an old tradition. Both South Korea and Singapore in the 1970s used Confucian ideology to support their authoritarian government and to promote a national economy. Even in modern Japanese politics, nepotism is a popular phenomenon, "the relationship between the leader and his followers is based on loyalty, favor, and seniority," and more than 35 percent of Diet members are sons of past and present Diet members. Ho describes the characteristic of Japanese society as "Japan Inc."[53] At present, Eastern democratic countries have neither found Confucianism an obstacle to the acceptance of democracy and practice of human rights or incompatible with their own traditional values. On the contrary, in East Asian countries Confucianism is a primary means of keeping social and political stability, promoting different educational programs, and encouraging people to work hard and discipline themselves.

In mainland China, the Chinese government before 1978 regarded Confucianism as old ideology, old tradition, and old culture. In the Cultural Revolution, Mao followed the first Chinese emperor and burned Confucian books and exiled Confucian scholars and other intellectuals. But that did not help China become a strong nation. On the contrary, it turned out to be a disaster for the country. The reform movement makes Chinese people rethink Confucian values and the relation of Confucianism to modernization. In examining Confucianism, it is undeniable that Confucianism has tended to advocate unlimited authority for the monarchical government, neglect the individual,[54] emphasize individual loyalty to the ruler without providing individual rights, uphold a caste system and patriarchal family values, demand one-sided (female) chastity, and make the Chinese people too meek to survive in the modern world.[55] Confucianism as an embodiment of traditional Chinese values carries an emphasis on family life rather than individual life and is concerned with social and cosmic harmony rather than individual rights. Elders should be respected, scholarship should emphasize the study of Chinese tradition, superiority should be pursued through self-cultivation, *jun-zi* should be recruited to hold public office, government should be benevolent, family loyalty is to be observed, men should work to support their families, and women should stay home and take care of household duties.[56] However, Confucianism is a very rich school of thought including political, religious, ethical, and educational areas. It is hard to imagine that China in its modernization and democratization can simply sever the connections with Confucianism. Thus it is not fair to simply conclude that Confucianism is incompatible with modernization and democracy. The statement that Confucianism should be held responsible for the failures of modernization and democratization is false. Such a statement would mislead the Chinese people and international society because it actually offers an excuse for the CPC to suppress Chinese democratic movements.

At present, quite a few Western scholars hold a negative view of Confucianism concerning individual freedom and liberty. Although Chinese social and familial relations remain stable, post-Mao China shows a radical departure from traditional Chinese culture. It is very visible that in China materialism is increasing, social relations are becoming superficial, submission to authority is weakening, and adventurism and risk are on the rise.[57] As Godwin Chu and Yanan Ju put it, "The Chinese people no longer endorse the Confucian precepts of harmony and tolerance, nor do they submit compliantly to the authority that previous generations did."[58] The question raised here is why the Chinese political system has not been changed after Confucian values have been reevaluated. There are at least two possible answers: First, the theoretical foundation of the current political system does not derive from Confucianism. And, second, the changes to China's public philosophy are limited to the grassroots level, and Chinese official ideology and top officials still resist these changes.

THE THREE PEOPLE'S PRINCIPLES IN THEORY AND PRACTICE

The first modern nation-state government in Chinese history was the Republic of China. Sun Yat-sen was the founder of the Republic of China, and his Three People's Principles are the framework of the Republic of China's political and social structure. So the key to understanding modern China is to understand Sun Yat-sen and the Three People's Principles. Preceding Sun Yat-sen, some pioneers made great theoretical contributions to modern Chinese ideology. The first Opium War was the watershed event dividing ancient China and modern China, during which British gunboats forced China to open its doors to the rest of the world. China for the second time was confronted with Western countries. Unlike the first time, before the fourteenth century, Western countries possessed strong economic and political power. Western countries affected China in the nineteenth century in two ways: military forces threatened China, and cultural thoughts impacted Chinese tradition.[59] Because of the failure of the Opium Wars, the Chinese people began to seek a new way to build a new China. The awakening of the Chinese people went through three stages: technological reform, institutional reform, and, finally, ideological revolution. The ideological revolution was the most difficult because its task was to wake up the Chinese people; in Chinese, *juexing*, "to undergo an awakening."[60] The ideological revolution awakened the Chinese people from the illusion of parochial arrogance and moved the political philosophy from "one world" to the idea of one nation, and to the idea of a powerful state.[61]

The first great political theorist in modern China was Kang Youwei (1858–1927). He promoted radical change in China, advocated the abolition of private property and families, and proclaimed a constitutional monarchy. For Kang, societal change was inevitable according to heavenly law. Hence, he promoted the reform movement and called for institutional and traditional philosophical changes. His political blueprint was "completely antithetical to orthodox Confucian teachings,"[62] but his basic political thought was in the frame of Confucianism, and his ethical ideas and social values remained in Confucianism.[63] Lin Mousheng called him "the last of the Confucians."[64] As the forerunner of democracy, Kang's theory could be considered the ideological bridge between modern China and premodern China.

Liang Qichao (1873–1929), a follower of Kang, was a more influential political scholar who inspired Chinese intellectuals for a generation with his writing. He introduced Western thought into China, including that of Francis Bacon, René Descartes, Charles Darwin, Aristotle, Adam Smith, Immanuel Kant, and Jean-Jacques Rousseau. He advocated radical change and constitutional republicanism. With other revolutionaries, he led the political reform movement of 1898 and plotted to overthrow the Qing dynasty. After the reform movement was suppressed by Ci Xi, Liang fled to Japan. In 1903, he dramatically changed his political attitude and began supporting constitutional monarchy. According to Liang, the Chinese people were not ready for a constitutional republic and the political infrastructure of a republic, and constitutional monarchy was a necessary transitional period to the constitutional republic.[65]

Sun Yat-sen (1866–1925) was born into a farm-owning family and attended an Anglican boy's school in Honolulu, where he was influenced by Christianity and gradually became a revolutionary. It took a long time for Sun to form the Three People's Principles. In his search for a new China, he was deeply influenced by Western cultures, spending a lot of time in foreign countries and becoming one of the most westernized Chinese. He studied at a Christian boarding school, received a diploma from a Hong Kong medical school, practiced medicine in Hong Kong, raised funds in the United States, formed friendships with British and American scholars and politicians including Bertrand Russell and John Dewey, and visited many European countries. Sun envisioned a very different future for a new China and sought the institutionalization of a Western form of democracy in it.

After China was defeated in the Sino-French War in 1885, Sun was determined to devote himself to overthrowing the Qing dynasty and establishing the Republic of China. Because of persecution, he left China for Japan in 1895. There he received a westernized education and organized the Tong Meng Hui, the former Nationalist Party. Although he was not a great strategist or a profound ideologist,[66] Sun was the first man in Chinese history to systematically advocate democratic principles, arguing that it was not enough to acknowledge the sovereignty of the country and that the end of the revolution could not be attained without a democracy.[67] All his political efforts were made to establish a capitalist-based country. In reality, the nature of the nationalist government is not democratic, though the form of the government was based on the Three People's Principles. The Revolution of 1911 was not a bourgeois revolution because most of its revolutionaries were high-ranking officials, landowners, military officers, the heads of secret societies, and armed bands.[68] On 12 March 1925, when Sun died of liver cancer, U.S. news media reported the event.[69] His legacy has influenced generations of Chinese and has become the most important source of democracy in the Chinese context. The history of Chinese democracy cannot be understood without studying his Three People's Principles.

The Three People's Principles (*San Min Zhu Yi*)—the Principle of Nationalism, the Principle of Democracy, and the Principle of People's Livelihood—represented Sun's political blueprint for a new China. The Principle of Nationalism showed that the Chinese nation was a glorious nation with a rich culture, but the Qing dynasty humiliated the country, forfeited its sovereignty, and destroyed its national spirit. Sun strongly condemned imperialism, criticized contemporary capitalism, and sought a better world that could be achieved by proper policies. He favored tariff protection, reacting against the free trade policy that had been forced upon China by Western powers. Sun called for the unity of China and maintained its independence in the family of nations. Confronted with Western imperialism, Sun said, China did not have any choice but to turn to nationalism. In order to fulfill the great unity, he promoted four urgent tasks: restoring China's national status, studying China's knowledge, enhancing China's national position, and learning Western thought.

In examining Chinese history, Sun pointed out that the Chinese people only had ideas about popular rights but that no democratic system had evolved. He analyzed why some countries became republics and others adopted constitutional monarchism and reached the conclusion that China must become a republic because the Chinese people had suffered from the Manchu's (Qing dynasty) oppression for more than 260 years and there were no grounds for preserving the monarchical form of government. Sun's Principle of Democracy borrowed the two basic concepts of liberty and equality from the Declaration of Independence of the United Sates and the French Declaration of Human Rights. On a tour of Europe and the United States, Sun made a close study of their governments and laws and pointed out that China's examinative and censorial powers should be placed on the same level with the U.S. legislative, judicial, and executive branches, thereby resulting in a five-fold separation of powers. The traditional Chinese government was organized on a three-power basis: "the power to rule, including the executive, legislative, judicial functional, the power to recruit officials, and the power to censor,"[70] but a new central government would have five *yuan,* or boards: the executive yuan, the legislative yuan, the judicial yuan, the examination yuan, and the censor yuan. The nationalist government formally practiced the separation of the five powers in 1928 after the Organic Law of the Republic of China was ratified. In his *Outline of National Reconstruction,* published in 1924, Sun proposed three stages of revolution: first, the rule of the military, the period of destruction in which military rule would be installed; second, the rule of a provisional constitution, the transitional period in which a provisional constitution would be promulgated; and third, the rule of a permanent constitution, which would see the completion of national reconstruction and usher in the constitutional government.[71]

The Principle of People's Livelihood is the most important of the three principles. It refers generally to the idea of the service state and seeks to gradually improve the living standards of the common people. In his time, Sun personally saw the instability of economic structures in Western societies. To avoid economic crisis, Sun realized that the principle of state ownership was the most profound, reliable, and practical system in China. Sun sympathized with the common Chinese people, who had substandard living conditions, and he fought for them. In order to improve the living standards of the Chinese people, he promoted two programs in the Principle of the People's Livelihood: equalization of land ownership, and regulation of capital. Sun also reversed the order of the Three People's Principles, putting the Principle of People's Livelihood first and the Principle of Nationalism last. The new order of the Three People's Principles is: the Principle of People's Livelihood, the Principle of Democracy, and the Principle of Nationalism. His central idea was the same as Abraham Lincoln's "government of the people, by the people, and for the people."[72]

It is worth noting that Sun's vision of a new society was influenced by the old formula of Great Harmony, although Sun clearly saw that the old political system was totalitarian. Thus, in proposing a democratic system for a new China, Sun did not realize the importance of remaking China's ideology and moral code. To the contrary, Sun very much appreciated certain Chinese traditional values and drew on the humanist traditions of Confucianism, for instance, the Chinese family value "First comes Loyalty and Filial Devotion, then Kindness and Love, then Faithfulness and Justice, then Harmony and Peace." But his selectivity—his rejection of some values and acceptance of others—was why Sun was misunderstood by both traditional Chinese intellectuals and communist revolutionaries. Heirs of Confucian scholars were skeptical of Sun, and some Chinese intellectuals had a hard time accepting his leadership.[73] Communist revolutionaries said his theory had limitations and was influenced by Confucianism and capitalism.

The subjects of Sun Yat-senism and communism are the two great ideologies in China in the twentieth century. The two ideologies have flourished together and have influenced all Chinese leaders.[74] It should be noted that Sun's political scheme had not been fulfilled by his death in 1925. His will, stated from his deathbed, was "the revolution is not successful; comrades must keep going on." The ideological conflicts continued after Sun died. One side was represented by Chang Chunmai, Hu Shi, Liang Shuming, and Jiang Jieshi. The other side was represented by Li Dachao, Chen Duxiu, and Mao Zedong. The two sides went in opposite directions, resulting in opposite societies: a democratic society and a dictatorial society. Jiang declared that he was the true heir to Sun. Of course, it is debatable whether or not, as his successor, Jiang carried out the Three People's Principles on the mainland. To be sure, Jiang betrayed Sun's principle of the alliance of the Nationalist Party and the Communist Party and killed tens of thousands of communists, workers, and peasants in 1927.

Jiang then brought China to civil war for more than twenty years. It is widely believed that the Three People's Principles were never fully put into practice under the nationalist government on the mainland.

The Communist Party denounced Jiang Jieshi for betraying Sun's Three People's Principles and claimed that the CPC was Sun's true heir. Actually, there is an uncrossed bridge between Sun Yat-senism and communism that derives from their fundamentally divergent ideological bases. Sun Yat-senism is based on Western democracy, Confucianism, and some self-developed theories. Sun had an unshakable faith in China's traditional culture and derived many of his ideas from Confucianism. Chinese communism is based on Marxism and rejects Confucianism, Western democracy, traditional Chinese culture, and Christianity. It is very clear that, when the People's Republic of China established a dictatorial form of government, the Chinese government went in the opposite direction of Sun Yat-senism.

Actually, after Jiang Jieshi died in 1975, his son, Jiang Jingguo, began pursuing Sun Yat-sen's goal, which Sun had not fulfilled during his time. The Taiwan government finally made an important step forward and abandoned martial law in favor of democracy. In 1985, Jiang Jingguo agreed to hold free elections and led Taiwan formally into a democratic society. The Three People's Principles, the theoretical foundation of the Nationalist Party, undoubtedly have contributed to the "Taiwanese miracle." At this point, Sun's ideology is working better than Marxism and Maoism. Taiwan is now the fourteenth-largest trader in the world, with foreign reserves topping those of the United States by $86 billion and a per capita annual income that, at U.S. $8,813, is more than twenty-five times that of the mainland. Truly, writes Wen-shun Chi, "Taiwan's achievement in the field of the people's livelihood is so extraordinary."[75] Taiwan's great achievements make it difficult for the government of the People's Republic to unite with Taiwan, because the economic gulf between Taiwan and the mainland is based on intense ideological conflicts. The policy of "one country and two systems" is only good for the transition period. For the long term, it is impossible to establish a greater China without a unified public philosophy.

What is the nature of ideological conflict in China? Chi noted in 1986 that "ideological conflicts between capitalism and socialism in the strict sense did not exist in China at all."[76] The real ideological conflict was "the conflict between democracy and despotism" and "between the ruling and the ruled, between the government and the people."[77] Politically, Chi's conclusion can still be applied to China today; yet, economically, his conclusion is no longer valid because the ideological conflict between capitalism and socialism is evident. Capitalism is developing in China, but the party resists it because the party fears that capitalism undermines the one-party system fundamentally. Inevitably, the

Chinese ideology has changed significantly since the reform movement began. A. James Gregor has observed that "what remained of Marxism in the mainland was the hegemonic rule of the Communist party."[78] But in looking at the reality in China, the Constitution of China states that the Four Cardinal Principles (the socialist road, dictatorship of the proletariat, leadership of the Communist Party, and Marxism-Leninism-Mao Zedong Thought) are the guiding principles for the Chinese people and society. According to the party, the Four Cardinal Principles are the cornerstones of contemporary Chinese politics, and Marxism is the foundation of Chinese ideology.

MARXISM IN CONTEMPORARY CHINA

Karl Marx (1818–1883), with the help and support of Friedrich Engels (1820–1895), founded Marxism, modern communism, and socialism. Marxism combines three types of theory—philosophy, political economics, and socialism—but the core of Marxism is political science in response to the Industrial Revolution and the capitalist system. The goal of Marxism is to overthrow the capitalist society and establish the communist society. *The Communist Manifesto,* written by Marx and Engels, was published in 1848 and marked the birth of Marxism. The *Manifesto* declared that capitalist society would inevitably collapse and that socialist society would inevitably emerge, based on the theory of the contradiction between production and productive relations in capitalist societies. In the 1860s, Marx in *Das Kapital* once again tried to systematically present his declaration from an economic perspective, in which he advocated materialism, economic determinism, public ownership, violent revolution, class struggle, a one-party system, proletarian dictatorship, and the communist society. Marx predicted that the communist revolution would break out soon, but in fact there were only some minor revolutions during Marx's lifetime, such as the German Revolution of 1848 and the Paris Commune of 1871. Marx and Engels never saw a proletarian dictatorship come to power, and thus they did not prove the hypothesis of their theory.

After Marx and Engels passed away, their followers became increasingly uneasy about the materialist theory of the "superstructure,"that is, a system of cultural, religious, political, and philosophical beliefs, which provides explanations for capitalist society, the misery of the oppressed, and the welfare of the oppressors.[79] Some socialists and Marxist scholars suspected Marxist theory, some reinterpreted Marxism, and some pushed Marxism to an extreme. Marxism spawned several varieties after Marx died, according to David McLellan, because Marx left a lot of manuscripts to be explained, and his thinking was sometimes ambivalent.[80] In addition, the different stages of a capitalist society and the special situations of different countries must also be taken into account. According to Marx, socialist revolutions would take place in the advanced industrial countries. Marx and Engels both believed that the economic systems of the most advanced industrial countries had already reached revolutionary maturity, but revolutions never took place in developed countries. It may be that the revolution will never happen. Therefore, wise disciples of Marxism in Western countries wanted to reinterpret Marxism to fit the reality of capitalist societies. Chinese Marxists call these neo-Marxists revisionists.

Marxism moved from Germany to other countries after Marx died. The Russian Revolution of 1917 led to the formation of the Soviet Union, the first socialist country in the world. Vladimir Ilich Lenin (1870–1924) represented the second generation of Marxism, and his interpretation of Marxism was the orthodox Marxism during his time. After Lenin died, Joseph Stalin (1879–1953) replaced Lenin as the leader of the international Marxist movement. Thus the Soviet Union became the headquarters of the international communist movement. The Soviet Union required every communist party to follow the Soviet model, and Marxist movements flourished in many countries after World War II. Lenin and Stalin pushed Marxism to an extreme. They attacked capitalist democracy and assisted proletariat dictatorships. According to Lenin and Stalin, in capitalist societies everyone has equal rights, but everyone does not have equal power. Capitalist democracy is a façade masking class dictatorship. It is clear that "Neo-Marxism in the West, and Marxism-Leninism in the under-developed countries, play different roles. In the former case, Neo-Marxism acts as a dissolver of the existing order. In the latter case, Marxism-Leninism is at least a potential basis and justification for the establishment of varying degrees of despotic and totalitarian regimes."[81]

Just as Confucianism did not become a dominant ideology in premodern China by accident, it was necessary for Marxism to become an official ideology in communist China. The introduction of Marxism in China was promoted by two important events: the Russian Revolution of 1917 and the May Fourth Movement of 1919. The former was like a hurricane in the way its effects swept across China and brought Marxism into China. The latter was the first intellectual and ideological revolution in response to Western democracy, attacking old Chinese culture and political institutions, introducing Western ideas of science and democracy to China, and propagandizing Marxism. It contributed to the Marxist movement and the birth of the Communist Party of China. When Mao attended the party's first conference, as one of twelve delegates, he was a young assistant librarian at Beijing University. Fourteen years later, Mao consolidated his dominant position in the party at the Zun Yi Conference in 1935 and held the sole right to interpret Marxism. Since then, Maoism has become Marxism in the Chinese context. Unlike Sun, Mao did not receive formal higher education and never believed in Western education, but he read a lot of Chinese classic books. He undoubtedly was deeply influenced by Chinese tradition. Mao spent all his life in China. For many reasons, Mao could be considered a traditionalist. Caimu Cui argues that Mao's encounter with Marxism did not fundamentally change his traditional frame of reference.[82] He rejected the idea that developed industrial capitalism was a prerequisite for socialist revolution because China was a poor agricultural country. He denied that the industrial proletariat were the bearer of the socialist future because 90 percent of China's population were peasants.

After the People's Republic of China was founded in 1949, Marxism became the state ideology. Mao, representing the third generation of Marxism, called his theory Marxism with Chinese characteristics. Although China broke off formal ties with the Soviet Union following the introduction of de-Stalinization in the 1960s, Mao inherited Leninism-Stalinism and encouraged the entire nation to worship him, proclaiming Maoism to be the sole universal truth. His little red book became the revolutionary bible. However, Mao actually was not a theorist, but a traditional Chinese strategist. Some Western scholars call him a romantic revolutionist. He only succeeded in power struggles by using political strategy and violence. His theory was very simple: "fight against whatever Western countries support; support whatever Western countries fight against." According to Mao, poor socialism is better than rich capitalism. Thus he defended his socialism and attacked capitalist economy and democracy. His sole purposes in interpreting Marxism were to eliminate political dissidents, perfect his God/father image, and strengthen his power. Therefore, Marxism in China, the modern political ideology, "is very much a civil religion."[83] That is, "Marxism is a civil religion, both in theory and in the actual role that it plays in those countries unfortunate enough to be governed by Communist parties."[84]

Mao believed that he could do everything that he wanted, and that China could catch up with Britain and the United States under his leadership because he was able to defeat the Guomintang. However, his failure became inevitable when he continued to rely on Chinese tradition to govern China. During Mao's time, he kept all power in his own hands, including power over the party, executive power, military power, and power over the National People's Congress. The centralized government had reached its highest point in Chinese history, and Mao became the absolute dictator of China. Internationally, China was isolated and enjoyed a self-sufficient and self-reliant economy free from foreign capital and foreign control. Economically, China overemphasized agriculture and heavy industry and made the structure of the Chinese economy unbalanced. The Great Leap Forward and the Cultural Revolution as well as other class-struggle campaigns brought poverty, persecution, bloodshed, dictatorship, and ignorance to China. In every respect, Marxism and Maoism failed to reach their goals in ideology, economics, culture, religion, and politics. The history of the Marxist movement has proven that "Marxism is a utopian ideology,"[85] because Marx's ideas were divorced from historical realities.[86] The Chinese people have awakened to this reality, and they realize that China has a long way to go to catch up with more advanced countries.

After Mao died, Deng Xiaoping regained his power and ruled the most populous nation in the world. Deng, a general designer of the reform movement, also made great efforts in promoting this reform movement—the second revolution of the CPC. However, Deng was a pragmatist, and his ideology was very clear: to keep the party in power but make the Chinese people rich. Thus, the purpose of this reform movement was to develop the Chinese economy and improve the living standards of the Chinese people. Deng said that "the purpose of socialism is to make the country rich and strong."[87] This implied that the socialist system and the party system could not be reformed. When the Chinese people called for democracy, he suppressed the democratic movement with no hesitation. The Tiananmen Square Incident is the typical example reflecting the nature of Deng's ideology. As long as the CPC is in power, China will keep Marxism as the state ideology. Marxism and the party are the necessary tools for the top leaders to control China. Marxism and the party work together and constitute the main obstacle to China's democratization. Although the highest power of the party has been switched from Jiang Zemin to Hu Jingtao in the Sixteenth National Congress of the Communist Party of China in 2002, and even though some analysts have observed that China's official ideology is eroding, a fundamental ideological change is not to be expected soon. There is no point for the party's existence without Marxism. Reforming the one-party system is the key to reforming Marxism and remaking China's public philosophy.

CONCLUSION

China's ideology has presented a perplexing situation throughout Chinese written history. Confucianism, Sun Yat-senism, and Marxism have played different roles in different periods of Chinese history. During the Han dynasty, Confucianism was established as the Chinese ideology, because Confucianism was more compatible with the needs of the Chinese ruling class and the centralized Chinese government. Confucianism is a very complicated system that has had both positive and negative impacts on China. As a whole, Confucianism does not fit Chinese democratization and the new global order. Confucius legitimized an absolute monarchical government, but he also advocated a benevolent government, although he did not realize that a truly benevolent government was impossible within the absolute monarchical system. We should not expect that Confucius, limited by his time, could have solved this theoretical dilemma. However, Confucianism contains many good elements, including educational, social, and cultural ideas, that can serve Chinese modernization as well as international civil society. Its good features enable Confucianism to continue to have a great influence worldwide. To be sure, the important thing is to reinterpret Confucianism and incorporate it within a new public philosophy for China. Remaking China's public philosophy will be a long process because the roots of Confucian culture and politics run very deep. Sun Yat-sen laid a foundation of democratic principles and the basic structure of democratic government, but he could not escape the influence of the old Chinese culture. He labored hard for a new China, but his attempts failed. His failure came about not because he lacked political ability and vision but because his antagonists—old public philosophy, cultural background, and political tradition—were too strong to conquer. The Taiwanese government has learned lessons from the past and fully carries out the Three People's Principles; today it enjoys political democracy and economic prosperity. On the mainland, the Communist Party of China practiced Marxism for more than fifty years as a ruling party and has proven that Marxism is not a remedy for a new China, but a monster. The decline of the state ideology "is bound to weaken the regime's ability to govern."[88]However, the CPC retains Marxism as the state ideology in order to preserve its monopolistic power. Therefore, remaking China's public philosophy and reforming the Chinese political system, from a historical perspective, must involve reworking Confucianism and the Three People's Principles and removing Marxism from its position as official ideology.

NOTES

1. Aihwa Ong and Donald M. Nonini, eds., *Ungrounded Empires: The Cultural Politics of Modern Chinese Transnationalism* (New York: Routledge, 1997), p. 196.
2. Eric Carlton, *Ideology and Social Order* (London: Routledge & Kegan Paul, 1977), p. 13.
3. David McLellan, *Ideology: Concepts in Social Thought* (Minneapolis: University of Minnesota Press, 1986), p. 2.
4. Ibid., pp. 3–4.
5. Ibid., p. 8.
6. Quoted in McLellan, *Ideology: Concepts in Social Thought*, p. 9.
7. Ibid., p. 8.
8. Judith N. Shklar, *Political Theory and Ideology* (London: Macmillan, 1970), p. 1.
9. Ibid.
10. John Bryan Starr, *Ideology and Culture: An Introduction to the Dialectic of Contemporary Chinese Politics* (New York: Harper & Row, 1973), p. 10.
11. *The American Heritage Dictionary of the English Language*, 3d ed. (New York: Dell Publishing, 1994), s.v. "ideology."
12. Starr, *Ideology and Culture*, p. 10.
13. Ibid., p. 10.
14. Richard H. Solomon, "From Commitment to Giant: The Evolving Func-

tions of Ideology in the Revolutionary Process," in *Ideology and Politics in Contemporary China*, ed. Chalmers Johnson (Seattle: University of Washington Press, 1973), p. 161.

15. Zhiling Lin and Thomas W. Robinson, eds., *The Chinese and Their Future: Beijing, Taipei, and Hong Kong* (Washington, D.C. : AEI Press, 1994), p. 7.

16. Johnson, ed., *Ideology and Politics in Contemporary China*, p. 23.

17. Benjamin Isadore Schwartz, *China's Cultural Values* (Mesa, Ariz.: Lionheart Press, 1993), p. 22.

18. Starr, *Ideology and Culture*, p. 20.

19. Richard W. Wilson, Sidney L. Greenblatt, and Amy Auerbacher Wilson, eds., *Value Change in Chinese Society* (New York: Praeger, 1979), p. 40.

20. Starr, *Ideology and Culture*, p. 35.

21. John W. Dardess, *Confucianism and Autocracy: Professional Elites in the Founding of the Ming Dynasty* (Berkeley: University of California Press, 1983), p. 7.

22. Kenneth Lieberthal, *Governing China: From Revolution through Reform* (New York: W.W. Norton & Company, 1995), p. 7.

23. Lin Mousheng, *Men and Ideas: An Informal History of Chinese Political Thought* (New York: John Day Company, 1942), p. 3.

24. Lieberthal, *Governing China*, p. 7.

25. Paul Myron Anthony Linebarger, *The Political Doctrines of Sun Yat-sen: An Exposition of the San Min Chu I* (Westport, Conn.: Hyperion Press, 1936), p. 29.

26. Gung-hsing Wang, *The Chinese Mind* (New York: John Day Company, 1946), p. 18.

27. Quoted in Wang, *The Chinese Mind*, p. 21.

28. John E. Ho, *East Asian Philosophy: With Historical Background and Present Influence* (New York: Peter Lang, 1992), p. 2.

29. Wang, *The Chinese Mind*, p. 114.

30. Ibid.

31. Vitaly A. Rubin, *Individual and State in Ancient China: Essays on Four Chinese Philosophers* (New York: Columbia University Press, 1976), p. 116.

32. Quoted in Wang, *The Chinese Mind*, p. 62.

33. Rubin, *Individual and State in Ancient China*, p. 119.

34. Wang, *The Chinese Mind*, p. 82.

35. Rubin, *Individual and State in Ancient China*, , p. 117.

36. Herrlee Glessner Creel, *Chinese Thought, from Confucius to Mao Tse-tung* (Chicago: University of Chicago Press, 1953), p. 152.

37. Wang, *The Chinese Mind*, p. 92.

38. Ho, *East Asian Philosophy*, p. 3.

39. Wang, *The Chinese Mind*, p. 118.

40. Ibid., p. 115.

41. Creel, *Chinese Thought, from Confucius to Mao Tse-tung*, p. 204.

42. Timothy Brook and Hy V. Luong, eds., *Culture and Economy: The Shaping of Capitalism in Eastern Asia* (Ann Arbor: University of Michigan Press, 1997), p. 24.

43. William Theodore De Bary, *The Liberal Tradition in China* (New York: Columbia University Press, 1983), p. 43.

44. Peter R. Moody, *Political Opposition in Post-Confucian Society* (New York: Praeger, 1988), p. 251.

45. Lin, *Men and Ideas*, p. 35.

46. Ibid., p. 36.
47. Lieberthal, *Governing China*, p. 7.
48. Schwartz, *China's Cultural Values*, p. 32.
49. Rubin, *Individual and State in Ancient China*, p. 117.
50. Quoted in Richard W. Wilson, Sidney L. Greenblatt, and Amy Auerbacher Wilson, eds., *Moral Behavior in Chinese Society* (New York: Praeger, 1981), p. 104.
51. Paul S. Ropp, ed., *Heritage of China: Contemporary Perspectives on Chinese Civilization* (Berkeley: University of California Press, 1990), p. 262.
52. Moody, *Political Opposition in Post-Confucian Society*, p. 250.
53. Ho, *East Asian Philosophy*, p. 183.
54. Tse-tsung Chow, *The May Fourth Movement: Intellectual Revolution in Modern China* (Stanford, Calif.: Stanford University Press, 1967), p. 301.
55. Ibid., p. 303.
56. Wilson, Greenblatt, and Wilson, *Value Change in Chinese Society*, p. 14.
57. Godwin Chu and Yanan Ju, *The Great Wall in Ruins: Communication and Cultural Change in China* (Albany: State University of New York Press, 1993), p. 296.
58. Ibid.
59. Linebarger, *The Political Doctrines of Sun Yat-sen*, p. 52.
60. John Fitzgerald, *Awakening China: Politics, Culture, and Class in the Nationalist Revolution* (Stanford, Calif.: Stanford University Press, 1996), p. 5.
61. Ibid., pp. 6–7.
62. Wen-shun Chi, *Ideological Conflicts in Modern China: Democracy and Authoritarianism* (New Brunswick, N.J.: Transaction Books, 1986), p. 15.
63. Kung-chuan Hsiao, *A Modern China and a New World* (Seattle: University of Washington Press, 1957), p. 95.
64. Lin, *Men and Ideas*, p. 215.
65. Chi, *Ideological Conflicts in Modern China*, p. 53.
66. Harold Z. Shiffrin, *Sun Yat-sen, Reluctant Revolutionary* (Boston: Little, Brown and Company, 1980), p. 4.
67. A. James Gregor, *Marxism, China, and Development: Reflections on Theory and Reality* (New Brunswick, N.J.: Transaction Publishers, 1995), 233.
68. Spence, Jonathan D., *Chinese Roundabout: Essays in History and Culture* (New York: W.W. Norton & Company, 1993), p. 269.
69. Linebarger, *The Political Doctrines of Sun Yat-sen*, p. 1.
70. Wang, *The Chinese Mind*, p. 180.
71. Quoted in Shao Chuan Leng and Norman D. Palmer, *Sun Yat-sen and Communism* (Westport, Conn.: Greenwood Press, 1976), p. 20.
72. Ibid., p. 84.
73. Shiffrin, *Sun Yat-sen, Reluctant Revolutionary*, p. 5.
74. Leng and Palmer, *Sun Yat-sen and Communism*, p. 171.
75. Chi, *Ideological Conflicts in Modern China*, p. 92.
76. Ibid., p. 325.
77. Ibid.
78. Gregor, *Marxism, China, and Development*, p. 259.
79. Shklar, *Political Theory and Ideology*, p. 6.
80. See David McLellan, *Marxism after Marx: An Introduction* (New York: Harper & Row, 1980).

81. Milorad M. Drachkovitch, ed., *Marxist Ideology in the Contemporary World: Its Appeals and Paradoxes* (New York: Pall Mall Press, 1966), p. xiv.

82. Caimu Cui, "Mao Zedong's Traditionalism" (Ph.D. diss. University of Tennessee, 1997); available on-line at http://wwwlib.umi.com/dissertation/fullcit/9809934.

83. Richard J. Bishirjian, *A Public Philosophy Reader* (New Rochelle, N.Y.: Arlington House, 1978), p. 25.

84. Ibid., p. 26.

85. Maurice J. Meisner, *Marxism, Maoism, and Utopianism: Eight Essays* (Madison: University of Wisconsin Press, 1982), p. 7.

86. Ibid., p. 10.

87. Gregor, *Marxism, China, and Development*, p. 238.

88. Shiping Zheng, *Party vs. State in Post-1949 China: The Institutional Dilemma* (New York: Cambridge University Press, 1997), p. 4.

CHAPTER 4

The Real Dangers behind Chinese Economic Prosperity

The market mechanism drives economic development. In turn, economic growth opens the way for political change. Although economic prosperity does not necessarily deliver a society a vibrant democracy, a capitalist economy is the entryway to a democratic society. A democratic society is based on and supported by a market economy. The Chinese economy in the Mao era was in the traditional socialist box. While Mao enjoyed absolute power, China, correspondingly, strictly carried out a planned economy. Without a doubt, this economic system was directly responsible for the failures of China's economy. Following a long debate on the implementation of a market economy after Mao's death, the CPC partially lifted the ban on a market economy. Since then, the Chinese economy has gradually expanded outside the traditional socialist box. However, the market economy in China is still restricted within the socialist system, which is called the "socialist market economy" with Chinese characteristics. The core of a capitalist economy is privatization. The party understands that a capitalist market economy will inevitably undermine China's one-party system and result in democratization; therefore, it has persistently resisted implementing a capitalist economic system. Over the past two decades, the Chinese economy has steadily developed. The further improvement of China's economic performance is not only an economic issue but a political issue. In the years to come, what economic system will China adopt—a socialist economic system, or a capitalist economic system? This issue will significantly affect the process of China's democratization in the twenty-first century. Reforming the official ideas behind the economic reform movement is part of remaking China's public philosophy.

THE THEORETICAL ROOTS OF CHINA'S ECONOMY

Generally, economic theory and political systems guide the direction of economic development. In modern Western history, early economists such as Adam Smith and John Stuart Mill founded the classical school of economics in the eighteenth century, emphasizing the role of a market economy in the evolution of capitalist society and believing that a laissez-faire economy and the impulse of self-interest would enhance the public welfare. By the mid-twentieth century, John Maynard Keynes departed from the principle of state noninterference in economic affairs and developed a new economic theory that placed more emphasis on government interference in economic activities, which "[has] led to governmental attempts to control business cycles."[1] His theory became the most influential economic formulation of capitalist society. Communist China's economy has been deeply guided by Marxist political economics. Karl Marx believed that economics was the primary driving force of history and paid little attention to the role of politics and culture in the development of a society. His political theory emphasized that industrial capitalism is a prerequisite for socialist revolution, and the industrial proletariat is the builder of the socialist society. Friedrich Engels made efforts to modify Marx's prejudice and pointed out that government and politics are not negative factors. Instead, government and politics react positively on economic development. Since the Communist Party came to power in 1949, the Chinese government has been guided by Marxism, Maoism, and political determinism. However, Engels's "reaction theory" was taken to an extreme in China. The party overemphasized the role of politics and class struggle and believed that Marxist revolutionary theory could be used not only in politics but also in economic activities. When the reaction theory was put in practice, a planned economy became the dominant principle of the Chinese economy. Guided by Mao's slogan "promote social production while campaigning revolutionary mobilization," class struggle was regarded as the sole driving force for socialist China to develop its economy. From the first day of the founding of the People's Republic of China, Mao never stopped campaigning class struggles. In the 1950s, through the Great Leap Forward, the People's Commune, and the Socialist Education Campaigns, Mao called for the Chinese people to catch up with the economic levels of Britain and the United States within twenty years. As a consequence, 30 million Chinese people died of hunger. In the 1960s and 1970s, Mao encouraged the Chinese people to promote the economy through the Great Cultural Revolution and declared that the spiritual atom bomb surpassed the material atom bomb. As a result, the Chinese economy collapsed, but the Chinese government ignored reality and kept operating the economy by implementing revolutionary ideas, including the mass line (Mao's idea that the people are the force making world history), frequent political campaigns, egalitarianism, and anti-intellectualism. These ideas produced only failure, however, for the Chinese economy. During this period, Western countries heavily criticized the utopian nature of Maoism. The Chinese government, however, completely ignored Western criticism and suggestions, and it kept up its fantasy until Mao died in 1976. Before the reform movement, China was on the verge of economic bankruptcy and greatly lacked material goods. The Chinese people lived in poverty.

It is not difficult to imagine what the Chinese people really wanted when they woke up from the nightmare after Mao's death. They wanted money, material goods, and a normal human life. There is no doubt that the Maoist Chinese politics must be discarded to reach these goals. In this context, Deng Xiaoping sold his pragmatic philosophy—"the cat is good only as long as it catches a mouse." The reform program has acted as the cat catching the mouse of economic growth. At the time, this philosophy obviously met the needs of the Chinese people and got unprecedented support from the majority of them. When Deng announced the four modernizations—of industry, agriculture, national defense, and science and technology—the Four Modernizations became a slogan used by the Chinese government to inspire the Chinese people to develop the Chinese economy. The party promulgates the idea that the sole purpose of economic reform is to make China rich and improve the living standard of the Chinese people. In this sense, the Chinese government actually returned to the traditional track of Marxist economic theory—economic determinism. It was not an unconscious theoretical deviation but a deliberate political departure, because the CPC has no intention of making China into a democratic society. Although the Chinese government "shift[ed] toward weaker central leadership overall" after Deng passed away in 1997,[2] the government today remains unwilling to depart from the old social and political path. The popular philosophy propagandized by the party that developing economy is the first priority and the sole purpose of the reform movement is a misunderstanding, because this idea at least failed to address the question: How can China ultimately fulfill both economic and political goals? Many observers do not believe that China can transform itself and become democratic based on Marxism.[3] A society is a system. Economic growth is determined not only by market mechanisms but also by other factors, including politics and public philosophy. Public philosophy plays an important role in making economic policy, inspiring people's initiative, guiding the direction of societal development, and regulating the social and political order. It is a naïve idea that China will become a developed country as long as it concentrates only on its economy.

China has made conspicuous economic achievements in the past two decades. It has developed its economy dramatically in agriculture, industry, railways, highways, energy, the automotive industry, telecommunications, advertising, education, and foreign trade. According to Bangguo Wu, Chinese vice premier, China's GNP grew about 9.7 percent per year from 1979 through 1998. Its GDP increased by 7.8 percent in 1998 and 7.1 percent in 1999.[4] In 2000, China's GDP continuously grew about 8 percent, and for the first time in Chinese history it exceeded 1 trillion U.S. dollars (equal to 8.8 trillion Ren Min Bi). While the world economy has been slowing down, China's economy in 2001 kept growing, at a GDP growth rate of about 7 percent. It is expected that the Chinese economy in 2003 will continue to grow. Undisputedly, China has achieved the world's highest growth rate since it began its economic reform. As Wu notes, "China is now among the largest producers of many major products in the world, such as cotton, grain, electricity, iron and steel, coal, chemical fertilizer, cement, and household electronic appliances. China became the seventh largest economy in the world in terms of its economic aggregates and the tenth largest trading nation. And its foreign exchange reserve is the second largest in the world."[5] China may reach the level of a developed country in the second half of the twenty-first century. China is not only becoming an economic giant since its unification with Hong Kong and Macao, but it will achieve still greater growth if it is unified with Taiwan. Now, China stands on the verge of becoming a political giant. Harry J. Waters, in his book *China's Economic Development Strategies for the 21st Century,* predicts that reunification with Taiwan will become a reality in the twenty-first century, even though China faces serious political and ideological challenges.[6]

A superpower in contemporary times should possess four attributes, according to Francis A. Lees: "large diversified national economy; major conventional military force; nuclear weapon capability; and strategic geographic location."[7] China will fully obtain these characteristics in this century if the reform movement continues. Over the next several decades, China will challenge Japan as the second-ranked economy in the world. Since 1994, some Western scholars, such as Bryce Harland, have predicted that China could become an economic and political threat to the United Sates if the Chinese economy keeps growing at its present rate.[8] Some scholars and politicians questioned the rush to favor China. They suggested that the U.S. government not renew China's most-favored-nation trading status, but the Clinton administration decided to divorce the issue of human rights from the issue of granting China such status.[9] Consequently, the U.S. Congress granted permanent most-favored-nation trading status to China in September 2000. Finally, China was admitted to the WTO in November 2001 following difficult negotiations between China and the WTO. China's accession to the WTO will further strengthen its position in international society.

The achievements of China's reform movement have caught the world's attention. In recent years, unlike their harsh criticism before the reform movement, Western scholars have developed a new theme—that China is flirting with capitalism and rapidly becoming a capitalist society.[10] The Chinese planned economy and socialist system, so they say, are shrinking and dying.[11] Moreover, perhaps "China's rush to a market economy is also a rush towards individual liberty."[12] Many scholars have claimed that "China is no longer a Communist country in any meaningful sense."[13] Some China specialists even believe that it is a misconception that post-Mao China is still a communist state, because political change is inseparable from economic and social changes.[14] Therefore, Western scholars have raised the question of whether there is any meaning to applying the term *socialist* to China in the 1990s.[15] Generally, because of China's economic achievements, many Western scholars hold very optimistic viewpoints on the reform movement and China's future. However, it will be impossible for China to make a breakthrough in both economic and political areas within the socialist and communist framework. At present, the party repeatedly declares that China still upholds the Four Cardinal Principles—the socialist road, the people's democratic dictatorship, Marxism-Leninism and Mao Zedong Thought, and the leadership of the CPC—and firmly walks the socialist road with Chinese characteristics, and that some compromises with capitalism are only "necessary to 'take one step back' so as to take 'one step forward towards socialism' at a later date."[16] Jiang Zemin in July 2001 confidently declared that the Communist Party represents China's advanced productive forces, advanced culture, and the fundamental interests of the overwhelming majority of the Chinese people.[17] Hence the party will continue to hold the leadership of and direct the Chinese economy in the twenty-first century.

THE HISTORICAL INQUIRY: CHINA'S ECONOMIC REFORM MOVEMENT

The Chinese economy had a glorious history, but China's economic fall began several centuries ago. It is acknowledged worldwide that China was the most developed country in the world before the fourteenth century, but that it gradually lost its leading position. An analysis of the causes behind China's falling economy in the past would be very helpful in specifying the role of public philosophy in the economic development and the reform movement. According to Mark Elvin, after the Qin dynasty (221–206 B.C.), China made considerable progress in the improvement of transportation, communications, and military techniques. China's economy and its technology also made significant progress during the period A.D. 800 to 1300. China had the world's earliest mechanized industry by the tenth century,[18] and it was the most sophisticated agricultural country by the thirteenth century.[19] But the Chinese medieval economic revolution fell into decline about the fourteenth century. Although there was "a renewal of economic growth between 1500 and 1800, technological invention was almost entirely absent."[20]

Why did China lose its leading position in economy and technology? Chinese scholars have discussed the issue frequently, to inspire the Chinese people to solve similar problems and to promote the contemporary Chinese economy. In sum, economically, agriculture of a non-Western character was the base of the Chinese economy in premodern times. Chinese agriculture was family based, small-scale, and scattered over China's huge land mass. This type of inland agriculture made Chinese farmers easily satisfied with their harvest and their daily life, and it was easier for them to lose the stimulation to seek something new. The Chinese people were subjected to harsh taxation and slavelike servitude.[21] Politically, a highly centralized government acted as both political agent and economic agent and tightly controlled the Chinese economy. Thus local governments and basic economic units lacked the incentive to increase productivity by improving production and technology. Derk Bodde has observed that such centralism may have been harmful to science.[22] Ideologically, China emphasized oneness, together with the bureaucratic form of government that maintained this oneness.[23] In the seventeenth century, *wen zi yu* (execution of an author for writing something against the government) became an important tool by which the ruling class sought to control the soul of the Chinese people. No one dared go one step beyond the limit. The creative role and thought of the individual were suffocated in premodern China. Educationally, China institutionalized the civil service examination beginning with the Sui dynasty, but this educational system did not serve the development of the Chinese economy. When Justin Yifu Lin analyzed why the Industrial Revolution did not originate in China, he pointed out one of reasons was that "the systems of admission, evaluation, and promotion provided little opportunity or incentive for scientific research."[24] Culturally, science was separated from technology in ancient China.[25] The sciences and technology were pursued by two groups. Science was pursued by the Confucian scholars, who obtained knowledge only from books and criticized technology. Technology was pursued by artisans, who generally were less-educated people. Because artisans made their living by their skills, Confucian scholars treated them as "the small men," the ruled class. Therefore, the development of technology was not encouraged in ancient China. Yet science was divorced from the needs of society. Bodde notes that "Han mathematicians, unlike their Greek and Hellenistic opposites, showed little interest in explaining their techniques."[26] Geographically, mountains and desert covered many areas in China. In ancient times, the Chinese people lived inland and were stimulated little by the outside world. A wall was built around every city, which separated the people from the countryside. Because of the registration system, Chinese peasants were not free to move from the countryside to the city. Hence the cities did not function as the centers of finance, politics, and commerce. According to Elvin, "It is possible that this was in part the cause, as well as the effect, of the spate of inventions in the medieval age and the relative stagnation which followed."[27] Finally, the Chinese economy was also disrupted by the Mongol domination during the period from 1234 to 1368. In addition, Western countries invaded China, plundered its property, forced China to accept many unfair treaties, and developed the dirty trade with China—the opium business. At the end of the Qing dynasty, China's economy was burdened by horrible drug addiction, population pressures, and political corruption.[28] All these factors together finally caused the dynastic system to collapse in the Qing dynasty.

During the period of the Republic of China, from 1912 to 1949, the republic was a so-called sovereign and independent country, but the nationalist government seldom exercised its sovereign rights to develop its home economy. The Republic of China certainly had a double burden in economic affairs. First, it was very difficult to reconstruct the traditional economy and build a new economic system in such a short period of time. Second, under imperialist pressures and competition, China found it difficult to establish its own national industry. Under the nationalist government, the Chinese economy neither grew in size nor altered in structure to any significant degree.[29] The economy was still overwhelmingly agricultural, with a backward means of production.[30] Chinese national industries and traditional industries occupied a small percentage of the country's economy. Modern factory production was dominated by handicraft manufacturing. China remained stagnant under the nationalist government on the mainland because the government was more weak and corrupt than before despite its highly centralized and dictatorial system. The ruling class only took care of its own interests and was never concerned for the nation and the common people. Jiang Jieshi, the top leader of the nationalist party and government, was not accused of corruption, but he did nothing to prevent it. He spent most of the time launching three civil wars, trying to eliminate the CPC. The top priority on his government agenda was to rule all of China, not to promote economic development. Because of his military background, Jiang never was "capable of pushing the Chinese economy off the dead center of stagnation."[31] In addition, in the years of the nationalist government on the mainland, war with the Japanese interrupted the normal development of China's economy. Wang Wei, Jiang's royal disciple, pointed out that Jiang was a hero, but that he ruled China by despotic dictatorship. That was why the nationalist government lost the support of the people and was defeated by the Communist Party.[32] Jiang left an awful mess when the nationalist government departed the mainland for Taiwan. The Chinese people were excited and put new hope in the new government when Chairman Mao declared the establishment of the People's Republic of China in October 1949. The new China became an independent country and truly exercised its sovereignty. Mao profoundly transformed the ownership system, the kinship structure, the class structure, and the political culture. His main achievements were laying the foundations for heavy industry, eliminating foreign control of Chinese industry, eliminating all major property-based inequalities, and providing for the basic needs of the people.[33]

However, the Chinese political and economic system as a whole followed the Lenin-Stalin model. It stressed centralized government within a large bureaucratic system, utilized ideology to legitimize the communist systems, and maximized party control over the government and the economy. In the economic arena, Mao destroyed the market system, implemented a socialist planned economy, and abolished private ownership. In industry, Mao borrowed the heavy-industry-oriented development strategy of the Soviet Union and destroyed the balance between heavy industry and light industry. While 45 percent of government investment went to heavy industry, Chinese agriculture received less than 10 percent of state investment between 1950 and 1979. In agriculture, Mao organized the commune system and virtually destroyed the peasants' incentive to work. Mao also prohibited all commodity economic activities in order to pursue a pure communist system, and he closed China's door to the outside world to carry out a self-reliant and self-sufficient policy. All these economic policies resulted in economic failures. Most China specialists agree that the main obstacle to developing the economy was Mao's insistence on a highly centralized planned economy and CPC leadership of all economic activities. During his tenure, the "party exercised a monopoly of power" over every area.[34] Instead of controlling the functions of government and enterprise, the party controlled and managed everything through vertical and horizontal leadership. The main tools for the party to tightly control enterprise were political control, administrative command, and ideological education. State-owned enterprises did not have any rights to handle their own affairs. Consequently, the enterprises passively implemented the party's commands and lost their initiative. Thus the main problem of the Chinese economy before the reform movement "was low economic efficiency arising from structural imbalance and incentive problems."[35] Mao's extreme revolutionary-centered model brought the Chinese economy to the verge of collapse and made Chinese people live in a miserable situation before the reform movement.

After Mao died in 1976, the Chinese people began calling for political and economic changes. This background provided a stage for Deng Xiaoping to open a new chapter of Chinese history. At this historical moment, the only choice for the party was to promote a reform movement and improve the living standard of the Chinese people. Deng conformed to the historical trend of the times and started the Second Long March toward Socialist Modernization—the economic reform movement.[36] Through the reform movement, Deng ended the history of China's poverty, opened up China's doors to the world, and made China a part of the global village. In this sense, Deng's impact on China was no less profound than Mao's, because he brought China to a new economic stage. China is becoming an economic power in the world.

Theoretically, there is an inner relationship between economic wealth and democracy, because the market economy is associated with the capitalist system and weakens the state's vertical controls.[37] Economic growth is a precondition of democracy[38] because it provides more opportunities for people to receive an education, enlarges the middle class, enables people to live in a comfortable environment, softens social conflict, reduces the boundaries between the state and society,[39] makes the mass media more popular, and provides the common people more opportunities to participate in democratic politics. Therefore, economic prosperity is compatible with liberal democracy, but, according to Francis Fukuyama, there does not appear to be a necessary connection between the two.[40] The economy as a relatively independent system has its own inner law. It may take time for economic booms to shatter the political blocks. Deng's reform program lubricated the rusted machine—the Chinese economic system—but his communist mind prevented him from making China into a democracy. His economic reform only indicated that China is departing from the typical socialist system.

SIGNIFICANCE AND SHORTCOMINGS OF THE REFORM MOVEMENT

Before the reform movement, the image of Mao was sacred in China. Maoism was recognized as the absolute correct interpretation of Marxism in the Chinese context. After Mao died, the greatest obstacle to reform became the "two whatevers": "We must resolutely support whatever decision Chairman Mao made and follow whatever directives Chairman Mao issued." Radical change in policy first required change in the theoretical foundations of that policy.[41] In order to smash the two whatevers, Deng campaigned for a new Marxist movement and focused on two slogans: "To seek truth from facts" and "Practice is the sole criterion to test truth." He implied that the economy was the sole criterion by which to judge the party's policy and the socialist system, and that the living standard of the Chinese people was the basic criterion for evaluating the level of the socialist system. Deng successfully reinterpreted Marxism/Maoism by using Marxism. This ideological campaign paved the way for the economic reform movement and provided a new theoretical foundation for the party to shift its emphasis from the class struggle to economic development.

The Chinese reform movement began with agricultural reform in the rural regions. In order to create a stable social environment for the reform movement, Deng reversed the emphasis from heavy industry to agriculture, greatly increasing agricultural productivity and producing enough grain to feed the Chinese people. After reform-minded Hu Yaobang was appointed as a general secretary of the CPC in 1981, the government officially promoted a household responsibility system that "covered 98 percent of the rural population" within three years.[42] Under the new party policy, land was distributed to single households, each of which became a basic work unit that contracted with its production team. The nature of household responsibility is to separate ownership from management and make a connection between the quantity of work and profits. With land distribution and better policy, farmers gained much more incentive to work hard and showed less need for supervision.[43] The household responsibility system experienced great success, and the experiment was later extended to urban families and industry. Soon large numbers of small, family-based businesses were growing dramatically in urban areas. Traditional thinking in the Mao regime had held that the Chinese family constituted an obstacle to economic development, but the reform experiences have demonstrated that the family economy has played a positive role in China's recent economic surge.[44] Most family-run businesses in urban areas are administrated by rural migrants, rather than by urbanites, however. At present, the Chinese family remains the cornerstone of Chinese society, and Confucian family values such as fidelity, piety, and loyalty help family-run businesses to be successful.

Because the main obstacle to economic growth during the Mao regime was the party's control and the planned economic system, a dual-track system, "growing out of the plan," became the main vehicle to take China out of the planned economic system and constituted the fundamental characteristic of the transition period.[45] The dual-track system "refers to the coexistence of two coordination mechanisms and not to the coexistence of two ownership systems."[46] During the transitional period, China remains an authoritarian political system with state ownership, and the party remains at the center of the economy in order to regulate the economy, facilitates a financial system, and provides a stable environment to attract foreign investment.[47] The party has cautiously carried out the dual-track system and ensured the leading role of the planned economy supplemented by market regulation. The party also has emphasized that the introduction of a market economy is not meant as the introduction of a capitalist system but is intended to introduce market-based competition into the development of the Chinese economy and to build a market-oriented economy with Chinese characteristics.[48]

The planned economic system is essentially determined by state ownership. State ownership, according to Marxism, is the unshakable foundation of the socialist system. Two types of ownership—state ownership and collective ownership—were the dominant forms of ownership in the Chinese economy before China's reform. China had more than 100,000 state-owned enterprises that occupied about 78 percent of China's total enterprises during Mao's regime. "Ownership" is the right to utilize the assets and the right to transfer this right to another agent through gift or sale.[49] Under the Constitution of the People's Republic of China, state-owned enterprises are owned by the Chinese people. Certainly, it is impossible for 1.3 billion Chinese people to own the firms and exercise the right of control over state-owned enterprises directly. Therefore, the central government and local governments inevitably own the real control rights. State-owned enterprises are subject to the most restrictions and intervention by the government. The state enterprises are like puppets and have no autonomy in the employment of workers, the use of profits, the planning of production, the supply of inputs, or the marketing of their products. According to a World Bank report, about half of industrial state-owned enterprises experienced losses in 1996. The state-owned enterprises' total industrial output fell from 77.6 percent in 1980 to 28.5 percent in 1996 and declined further, to 25 percent, in 2000.[50] It is evident that this iron rice bowl must be smashed if China wants to be modernized.[51] However, reforming ownership in China probably is the most difficult task because public ownership, based on traditional Marxism, is the basic symbol of the socialist system. China had a great debate on how it fundamentally reforms state-owned enterprises and ultimately smashes its planned economic system. There are at least three different viewpoints. First, privatization is a fundamental means to reform the planned economic system and achieve economic reform. Second, it is not necessary to alter ownership in the early stage of the reform; instead, China should take a step-by-step approach, moving forward for the foreseeable future. Third, marketization, not privatization, is the key for China to reform its old institutions and consolidate its socialist economy. Because ownership reform is the most sensitive area, it has been a very slow process. The Third Plenary Session of the Twelfth Central Committee of the Chinese Communist Party adopted the Decision on Restructuring the Economic System in 1984, signaling that industrial reform had begun. The Fourteenth Party Congress in 1992 officially introduced the socialist market-economy system in China. In 1997, the Fifteenth Party Congress recognized that the non-public-ownership sector is an important component of China's socialist economy.

The Chinese government exercised a variety of measures to reform state-owned enterprises in order to improve the performance of public ownership. First, the government allowed the entrance of massive nonstate enterprises, largely without privatization of state enterprise but through new setups and reorganizing. China now has six types of ownership systems: state-owned enterprises, collective enterprises, private enterprises, stock-share enterprises, foreign-invested enterprises, and joint-venture enterprises. State-owned enterprises, accounting for 77.6 percent of the gross industrial product in 1978, dropped to 45.1 percent in 1999. The importance of the emergence of the nonstate sector is not its outstanding performance but rather that it "introduced a competitive market environment to China."[52] Second, the Chinese government restructured state-owned enterprises. Jean Oi believes that the entry of new firms is a powerful force for systemic transformation, but that state-owned enterprise performance can be improved by adjusting internal relations.[53] Others suggest that a state-owned enterprise restructuring can be achieved by stressing enterprise autonomy and that incentives are the way to improve enterprise performance without formal privatization.[54] Therefore, instead of privatizing state-owned enterprises, the Chinese government restructured enterprises by consolidating enterprise property rights and adopting a new form of governance to give enterprises the needed autonomy to generate incentives. Third, the government allowed some state-owned enterprises to separate ownership from management, giving them some degree of commercial freedom and independence, including insuring their rights to lay off workers. The government also leased some small- and medium-sized state-owned enterprises to individuals. Fourth, it provided opportunities and led state-owned enterprises to merge in joint ventures and shareholding companies.[55] The Chinese government also passed the Bankruptcy Law, which allowed more state-owned enterprises to be dissolved, and sold some state-owned enterprises to domestic- or foreign-owned companies. The government has concentrated on 1,000 state-owned enterprises and allowed others to become candidates for bankruptcy, merger, and management buyout.

State-owned enterprise performance has been gradually improved in different ways. In 1999, the state-owned enterprises and state holding companies managed to reap profits amounting to U.S.$11.68 billion, the highest level in the previous five years. Thus, while some scholars suggest that China's economy has already moved decisively toward privatization,[56] most surveys indicate that the state continues to play an important role in the commercial sphere.[57] Other China scholars hold different viewpoints. Louis Putterman has noted that ownership reform in China has indeed been much less radical than the changes in the role of markets.[58] He adds, "Limited reform in the ownership of enterprises is a key element of the evolutionary reform model that is associated with China."[59] To sustain Chinese economic development toward democracy, China must continue to reform state ownership to ensure economic growth.[60] Without a doubt, the nature of public ownership reform is the process of decentralizing power. Precisely, it is the most profound revolution to shift power from the party and the central government to local governments and economic entities, from the government to individuals, but the CPC is not ready to give up its positions of governance and ownership. Instead, the party has tried to postpone the most difficult task of ownership reform.[61] There are clear signs that the party has already moved back several steps to bring about ownership reform. *The Decision on State-Owned Enterprise Reform and Development*, which was promulgated by the Fourth Plenary Session of the Central Committee of the Communist Party in September 1999, tends to be conservative and repeatedly affirms that state ownership must take a dominant position in the socialist economy, emphasizing the leadership of the party in enterprises. One reform measure, issued by the Fourth Plenary Session, is that enterprises are allowed to switch debts to stocks in the name of the market economy.[62] In fact, this means that the party/state continues to invest in state-owned enterprises, resists fundamental public ownership reform, and continues to interfere with the economy. Premier Zhu Rongji's speech given at "The Forum of the Twenty-first Century" on June 4, 2000 in Beijing described the characteristics of the Chinese economy in the twenty-first century but did not mention any reform measures for public ownership.[63]

Accompanied by ownership changes, a market economy has been gradually adopted in China. According to Marxism and Maoism, a market economy is the opposite of a planned economy, which is associated with the socialist system; a market economy is associated with the capitalist system. The acceptance of a market economy is the central symbol of modern capitalism.[64] China went through several stages to move away from a planned economy to a socialist market economy. At the beginning of the 1980s, the government introduced the concept that "the planned economy would be primary and the market economy would be secondary." Then, the CPC decided to take another step and implemented a socialist commodity economy in 1984. Finally, Deng persuaded the Fourteenth National Congress of the CPC to accept a socialist market economy in 1992.[65] A year later, *Issues Concerning the Establishment of a Socialist Market Economy* was promulgated. The most important measures were that the government lifted some restrictions on nonstate industries, gradually liberalized the state material allocation system, further expanded the household production responsibility system, established Sino-foreign joint ventures, decentralized the administrative system (especially the fiscal system), and enabled local governments to retain and allocate more of the tax revenues they collected. The emergence of financial markets in China is another important vehicle driving the Chinese economy. A shareholder system and bond market made it possible for companies to distribute their profits equitably and raise adequate capital to sustain their growth. This in turn helps the government to finance vital infrastructure programs, control capital expenditures, and allocate them efficiently.[66] Chinese government bonds were first issued in 1981. Since then, many enterprises have begun issuing their own bonds to the public. China started to participate in international bond markets in the mid-1980s, was briefly shut out of foreign bond markets after the Tiananmen Square Incident in 1989, and reentered the markets on a large scale in 1991.

The reform movement and the development of the economy produced two important trends: urbanization and migration. During the Mao regime, more than 80 percent of the Chinese population lived in the countryside, and 90 percent of rural residents were employed in agriculture. Economic development has greatly accelerated the urbanization rate. The urban population expanded from 172 million in 1978 to 379 million in 1997. By 2000, the urban population made up about 33 percent of China's nearly 1.3 billion people. It reached 400 million in 2000 and will reach 500 million by 2020.[67] The urbanization level in China was 30.4 percent in 1999 and is expected to hit 50 percent during the next twenty years.[68] The process of urbanization is part of the development of industrialization. Both are necessary for China to be transformed into a capitalist system and democracy. The great expansion of the urban population in past years was caused by the country's economic growth and the reform policy, including the rapid development of rural and local industries, flexible government policy toward internal migration, large state construction projects in cities, an increase in foreign investment, and the growth of satellite cities around metropolises. Urbanization has created a large floating population, counted at 80 million in 1994[69] and 100 million in 1998, with 70 percent of the floating population coming from rural areas. Demographers have estimated that about 130 million persons made up this floating population in 2001.

The general migratory trend is from the western part of China to the eastern part, from the northern part of China to the southern part, and from undeveloped areas to developed areas. At present, 94 percent of the population inhabits 46 percent of China's territory in the eastern and southeastern parts of China.[70] The ongoing internal migration is both a cause and a consequence of the reform movement:[71] (1) the development of industrialization has gradually taken over arable lands, creating surplus laborers; (2) the household responsibility system saves laborers, and farmers are legally permitted to leave their land for cities; (3) many construction projects in cities need to recruit less-educated laborers from the countryside; (4) the nonstate sectors in urban areas are allowed to hire employees who are not urban residents;[72] and (5) better policies and regulation make it possible for migrants to live legally in cities and freely buy what they want. It is worth noting that migrants make a great contribution to the reform movement and democratization. They have brought advanced technologies, experiences, and new ways of thinking to their native hometowns.[73] For more than 2,000 years of China's history, the Chinese people were prohibited from moving freely from one place to another. Under Mao's regime, *hukou* (registration), *dangan* (personnel dossiers), and *danwei* (work units) made it impossible for peasants to move from the countryside to the city. Urban residents were also restricted from moving from one city to another. The increasing numbers of internal migrants indicate that individual rights in China have been increasing, too.

THE OFFICIAL PHILOSOPHY BEHIND CHINA'S ECONOMIC REFORM MOVEMENT

It seems that China's economic prospects are very promising if China maintains its current growth rates. However, it is questionable whether China's economic progress is sustainable. Penelope B. Prime examines the Chinese economy from economic and political perspectives and concludes that "China faces many serious problems in its quest for sustained development." China's achievements have made it harder for the Chinese government leaders to "balance their socialist self-reliant political goals with the increasing marketization and globalization of their economy."[74] Herein lies another perspective from which to examine the real danger to the Chinese economy. A great movement always comes from deep philosophical thinking. What is the philosophy driving China's reform movement, and what keeps it going forward? Can the official philosophy behind the economic reform movement be the theoretical seeds of democracy, which will sustain the reform movement and allow it to continue on the right path toward its ultimate goal—true democratization? Five official principles behind China's economic reform movement are real dangers to China's democratization and the future of China's economy and, therefore, need to be remade.

First is the slogan of the Four Modernizations. The Chinese people suffered from poverty before the reform movement began and were eager to transform China into a powerful country. In 1964, Premier Zhou Enlai formally proposed for the first time to the whole nation a magnificent program for modernizing industry, agriculture, national defense, and science and technology, but under Mao's regime the economy-centered model of socialist construction was viewed as a rightist line. Two years later, the Cultural Revolution interrupted the process of the Four Modernizations for ten years. After Deng regained power, he shifted the emphasis of the nation's work from class struggle to socialist modernization. At the Third Plenum of the Eleventh Central Committee of the Communist Party in 1978, the Four Modernizations were officially proclaimed again.

It was a watershed year in Chinese history that marked China's second liberation. The slogan of the Four Modernizations has awakened the Chinese people and has generated in them a great enthusiasm for the economic reform movement and reconstruction of the socialist economy. The people have benefited from the reform movement and recent economic growth. However, each of the four modernizations relates to economics, not politics. A market economy is always the first step toward a capitalist society, but economic wealth and the market system do not automatically bring a society to democratization. Taiwan and South Korea each took more than thirty years to step into a democratic system after their economies boomed with a market system. Western countries took 200 years to establish democratic systems after the Industrial Revolution. The Four Modernizations is the vehicle to drive China from poverty to economic prosperity, but it is not the vehicle for the second step—moving from an authoritarian system to a democratic one. The Tiananmen Square Incident showed that the Chinese people were ready to practice the fifth modernization—democracy—in 1989. The Four Modernizations alone cannot unite the Chinese people in the twenty-first century. China's political system must be reformed and coordinated with a market economy. Otherwise, the slogan of the Four Modernizations could become an excuse to block the process of democratization.

Second is the theory of the primary stage of socialism. China was a poor country, but Mao never admitted that it would take a long time to transform China into an economic power. On the contrary, Mao declared that China's economy was on the upswing. In order to smash Mao's fantasy and promote the economy, former premier Zhao Ziyang in 1987 set forth the theory of the primary stage of socialism at the Thirteenth Party Congress. According to this theory, China has already established a socialist society, which must be preserved. However, Chinese socialism is at only the initial stage of development, in which China will operate a socialist system at a primary stage until at least 2050. During this stage, productivity forces are at a low level, and elements of capitalism exist, such as a commodities economy, commodities relationships, and a market economy. Thus, because China's economy is at the primary stage of socialism, a capitalist economy should be allowed to develop. This theory provides the foundation for the party to focus on economic growth and to develop a market economy. It is why the party declares that its central task is to develop the economy; all other work must be subordinated to and serve this central task. The theory of the primary stage of socialism basically addresses economic issues within an economic framework, and can meet only the economic needs of the Chinese people. What is the integrated development blueprint for China's future? What are the full needs of the Chinese people while China is getting rich? What will guarantee that China will sustain its economic growth rates over the long term? What is the relationship between economic prosperity and political democracy? The primary-stage theory does not address these questions. Moreover, this theory confirms the leadership of the Communist Party, leaving room for the hard-liners to return to the traditional socialist system. Stephen Gardner observes that "[t]he primary stage thesis provided an ideological basis for economic liberalization, but, at the same time, the Communist Party leadership strengthened its opposition to democratic reform."[75] At this point, even if the primary-stage theory has helped the Chinese people in opening a market economy, it will not serve the process of China's integrated development—economic prosperity and democratization.

Third comes pragmatic theory. Modern China has never had a systematic economic theory to guide economic growth, from the Republic of China to the People's Republic of China and from Mao's regime to the present. Deng, as the general designer of the reform movement, was neither a theorist nor an economist but a typical political pragmatist. The economic reform was successful because "Chinese leaders were flexible and pragmatic."[76] When Deng came to power, China's economic situation was at its worst in the period of the Chinese communist regime. In order to keep the socialist system running, as one scholar has noted, "The question is no longer whether a particular policy is consistent with socialism, the question is whether it works."[77] Deng promoted the Cat Theory, and the theory "cross the river by feeling stones." Deng took many pragmatic measures to reform the economic system and aid the Chinese economic boom; for example, he implemented new policies to attract foreign investment, opened up special economic zones, set forth the proposal "one country, two systems," and made over China's foreign policy to normalize relationships with Western capitalist countries. The answers as to why he restricted human rights and political dissent; suppressed the student movement in 1989; and rejected two successors of his own choice, Hu Yaobang in 1987 and Zhao Ziyan in 1989, can also be found in his pragmatism. Its aim was to keep the Communist Party in power and allow economic reform only. It is true that Deng's pragmatism generated the great energy devoted to economic activity in the beginning of the reform movement, but China could not maintain its economic growth on the strength of his pragmatic ideas alone. Pragmatism is only a painkiller aiding Chinese society through the transitional period. Deng died several years ago, but his theory has been retained by his successor.

Fourth is the theory of gradual reform. Reform movements are characteristic of socialist countries, but different countries take different reform approaches based on different theories. A "rationalizing reform" was adopted by Eastern European countries in the 1960s to make their planned economy work smoothly. The "big bang" reform approach was adopted by Poland and Russia in the 1990s to bring about a radical change of society and to destroy the planned economy.[78] China has taken a gradual reform approach; it is a less-than-radical departure from the socialist system. The gradual approach shares something in common with rationalizing reforms, and both types of reform retain the dominance of the Communist Party and the traditional political system.[79] The Chinese government exaggerated the extent to which its gradual approach achieved the positive effects of the big bang approach but avoided its costs.[80] Some scholars suggest that the reasons for the reform's success are mainly that China allows only a partial reform and leaves the most difficult reform task—political reform—for an uncertain future. Unlike the former Soviet Union, China "allows the Party to survive as an instrument of economic development."[81] The CPC has had a financial incentive to push the reforms along, has made use of preexisting institutions to organize financial and human resources, and has facilitated market production. Lin believes that China's gradual approach "may be both theoretically and empirically preferable to the big bang approach."[82] Although gradual reform has been successful over the past two decades, the gradual approach is not necessarily good for China's democratization if it leads to only partial reform. If the gradual approach continues, it must be understood that a reform movement develops step by step, from economic reform to political reform and democratization. Otherwise, gradual reform will become partial reform and, as such, an obstacle to Chinese democratization. The key to guarantee the success of China's economic reform is not economic but political. The highly centralized political system, a main obstacle to Chinese economic development, has been shaken by the market economy. We have seen that economic reform shifts the power of decision making from the top to the bottom of the hierarchy. The decision-making power of the central government has been gradually reduced; however, decentralizing economic reform did not directly transfer decision-making authority from the central government to economic agents but, rather, to local governments. Local governments expanded their control over business through a variety of informal mechanisms.[83] In the meantime, the CPC continues to play a role not only in directing the central government but also in directing local government and all types of business enterprises.

Fifth is China's partial open-door policy. China during the Middle Kingdom had isolated itself for a long time. Under the Mao regime, the communist government carried out a closed-door policy that caused the Chinese people to live in isolation for twenty-eight years. The post-Mao government realized that China could not become a powerful country without accepting foreign assistance and learning from other countries. The open-door policy became part of Deng's economic reform program. Consequently, three developments ensued. First, China opened its border regions and fourteen coastal cities and built special economic zones, such as the Bohai Rim (which has 18 percent of China's population but 22.8 percent of its GNP); the Yangtze Delta (10.8 percent of the population and 16.9 percent of GNP); and South China, including Guangdong, Fujian, Hainan, and Guangxi (12.6 percent of the population and 14.1 percent of the GNP). Together the three economic zones now constitute 41.4 percent of China's population and 53.8 percent of its GNP.[84] Second, China now accepts foreign investments. By 1994, gross capital inflows to China exceeded U.S.$53 billion, including about U.S.$17 billion in borrowing from commercial banks, international organizations, bilateral development banks, and international bond markets; U.S.$34 billion in direct foreign investment; and about U.S.$2.5 billion in equity investments.[85] By the end of 2000, China had approved 256,354 Sino-foreign equity and contractual enterprises with contractual and paid-in foreign investment standing at U.S.$439.094 billion. In many ways, China is opening up faster to foreign companies than did Japan, South Korea, and Taiwan at similar stages in their economic development. There are several justifications for foreign capital to flow into China: foreign capital needs to expand in order to make profits, China provides a large market for investment by foreign companies, China's new policy attracts foreign capital, and China has maintained political stability after the Tiananmen Square Incident in 1989.[86] Third, China has developed international trade and economic cooperation with other countries. China ranked thirty-second worldwide as an exporting country before 1978. Ten years later, China had jumped to become the thirteenth-largest trading nation in the world. By the mid-1990s, Chinese export goods were worth more than U.S.$100 billion and China was the eighth-largest exporter in the world. China's exports of manufactured goods surpassed the United Kingdom's by the end of 2000.[87] In past years, the pattern of international import and export has taken a basic shape in China. Shi Guangsheng, minister of foreign trade and economic cooperation, stated at a press conference during the Fourth Session of the Ninth National People's Congress (NPC) that China will further expedite the development of foreign trade and economic cooperation, and that the country's import and export trade volume will total U.S.$680 billion by 2005. It should be noted that, in the mid-1990s, state-owned firms' contribution to exports made up only a fifth of the total, although state-owned firms accounted for fully half of all manufactured goods produced. State-owned enterprises "have not participated proportionately in the growth of China's exports."[88] This suggests that it is urgent for China to reform ownership in order to carry out an open-door policy more efficiently. Another problem is that Chinese foreign trade largely depends on foreign-invested firms, and most export business—almost 30 percent of China's total exports—was generated by foreign-funded enterprises. It will be difficult for China to sustain its exports growth rate over the long term.[89]

The practice of an open-door policy has significantly contributed to the transfer of advanced technology and managerial practices to China, has modified the structure of corporate ownership as well as the unfolding of social-class relations, and has gathered capital to promote the Chinese economy and a variety of projects. In particular, foreign investment has increased capital-good imports, stimulated China's economic growth,[90] and influenced the policy-making process considerably.[91] Meanwhile, Western social, cultural, and intellectual values have flowed into China.[92] Nevertheless, the open door is but "half-opened";[93] the Chinese government tightly monitors the influences of Western culture, religion, and politics on China and prohibits the Chinese people from practicing Western democracy. The Chinese government also has made big progress in e-business but does not allow the Chinese people to freely advocate political ideas over the Internet.

The Ninth NPC announced on November 19, 2001 that the Standing Committee of the NPC had approved the motion to join the WTO. Generally speaking, China's entry to the WTO will promote the open-door policy further. China had attempted to become a WTO member ten years earlier, but its membership was not granted until November 2001. The WTO and China had been intensifying their negotiations on China's membership over a long period of time, and China finally decided to make major concessions to meet WTO requirements. According to the agreement between China and the WTO, China will open its telecommunications sector to both services and direct investment; make "a comprehensive commitment on distribution, including wholesaling, direct sales, retailing, and maintenance";[94] and "provide distribution rights in five years for chemical fertilizer, crude oil, and processed petroleum products."[95] China also agreed to lift all restrictions on distribution services and operation of foreign law firms and accounting firms in China. The debate behind the agreement was a serious political one. Because Premier Zhu Rongji strongly supported China's efforts to join the WTO, he was under attack by opposition leaders for "selling out the country." The opposition leaders were very concerned that "joining the WTO will mark another step toward privatizing China's economy and importing even more Western ideas about management and civil society—a headache for those whose job it is to ensure the longevity of the one-party communist state."[96] U.S. trade representative Charlene Barshefsky has pointed out that China's accession to the WTO is "extremely important" to the global society.[97] Without a doubt, China will receive great benefits from the WTO membership in forming stable international economic relationships, deepening its own economic reform, and stimulating China's long-term economic growth. Some scholars have observed that the motivation for economic reform in China is disappearing, but the Chinese government may generate new zeal for reform by means of the WTO membership. However, the economic benefits are the direct products of China's

WTO membership, but the political benefits are by-products. It is difficult to foresee whether China will deepen its own economic and political reform and further improve its record on human rights after joining the WTO, but it is certain that China will face great challenges, including labor pressures and ecological problems. Investment in China's financial markets will be international market risks, because China is lacking in risk-control measures and regulatory systems in its financial market.[98] According to the World Bank, income gaps are increasingly widening in China. All these problems may contribute to political instability and economic crisis. Therefore, the real threat to China's economic growth is the official public philosophy behind the reform movement.

CONCLUSION

The Chinese communist government launched economic reforms two years after Mao died in 1976 in order to keep the CPC in power and meet the basic needs of the Chinese people. Since the early 1980s, the Chinese government has made significant progress in agricultural, industrial, and international trade reform. Basically, China has already fulfilled the first two steps: doubling the GNP to meet the basic needs of the Chinese people by the year 1990, and helping the Chinese people to live a more comfortable life at the end of the twentieth century. Now, the third step is to raise the per-capita GDP up to the level of moderately developed countries by the middle of the twenty-first century.[99] The Chinese government is committed to helping China become an economic giant. Under the leadership of the Communist Party, China has been trying to reform the planned economic system, ownership, and the political system. However, China steadfastly confirms that the Four Cardinal Principles are the foundation for building a new China. At the beginning of the transition period, it was necessary to keep the existing government active based on the experiences of East Asian democratic countries. The governments of Japan, South Korea, and Taiwan, for example, were strong, stable, and fairly authoritarian during their transition period.[100] It takes time to transform a market economy into a fully democratic system because the market economy and political democracy do not necessarily have a connection. Therefore, modernity is not an economic concept, but "an epoch in which a set of contending understandings of self, responsibility, knowledge, rationality, nature, freedom and legitimacy has established sufficient presence to shuffle other possible perspectives out of active consideration."[101] The current official Chinese philosophy behind the reform movement—the theories of the Four Modernizations, the initial socialist stage, and gradual reform; pragmatism; and the partial open-door policy—will not sustain the development of the Chinese economy and the reform movement for the long term but, instead, blocks the process of democratization. The Chinese economy has already slowed down since 1999 and will slow down further without changes in the official philosophy and political system. Obviously, the official Chinese philosophy is the real danger to the future of China's economy and to democracy as well.

Chinese officials explain that the slowdown is caused mainly by internal problems, such as industrial overcapacity and increasing unemployment; China merely needs a period of time to readjust its industry and further reform the financial system.[102] None of those causes of economic downfall are connected to political and cultural factors. It is widely accepted that "political reform is a prerequisite for a full transition to an effective market-oriented economy."[103] As Gordon White notes, "Democratization is an essential precondition for solving the developmental problems of developing countries in general and China in particular."[104] Based on the Chinese official logic, the Chinese government listed a number of priorities for the reform movement for the next decade, such as conducting strategic economic restructuring, continuing the construction of infrastructure, and developing rural industries and small cities and towns.[105] None of these measures involves political reform. Economic problems cannot be solved by economic measures alone. Economic prosperity is not the sole criterion by which to judge a society as good or bad. The central requirement for economic reform to be successful is to push the Chinese economy fully to a market system and to thoroughly reform state ownership. Meanwhile, the CPC must withdraw from Chinese economic activity for this to happen. Therefore, rethinking the philosophy behind China's reform and remaking China's public philosophy are becoming urgent tasks.

NOTES

1. *The Concise Columbia Encyclopedia*, 1995, s.v. "economics."

2. Kenneth Lieberthal, *Governing China: From Revolution through Reform* (New York: W.W. Norton & Company, 1995), p. 230.

3. Benedict Stavis, *China's Political Reform: An Interim Report* (New York: Praeger Publishers, 1987), p. 1.

4. Bangguo Wu, "Chinese Economy in the Twenty-first Century," *Presidents & Prime Ministers* 9 (January 2000), p. 16.

5. Ibid.

6. Harry J. Waters, *China's Economic Development Strategies for the 21st Century* (Westport, Conn.: Quorum Books, 1997).

7. Francis A. Lees, *China Superpower: Requisites for High Growth* (New York: St. Martin's Press, 1997), p. 40.

8. Bryce Harland, "For a Strong China," *Foreign Policy* 94 (Spring 1994), pp. 48–52.

9. Jeffrey E. Garten, "The Rise of the Chinese Economy: The Middle Kingdom Emerges," *Harvard Business Review* 76 (May–June 1998), pp. 167–75.

10. Immanuel C. Hsu, *The Rise of Modern China*, 5th ed. (New York: Oxford University Press, 1995), pp. vii–ix.

11. Andrew Tanzer, "This Time It's for Real," *Forbes* 152 (August 1993): pp. 58–62.

12. Cheng Li, *Rediscovering China: Dynamics and Dilemmas of Reform* (New York: Rowman & Littlefield Publishers, 1997), p. 11.

13. Ibid., p. 54.

14. Ibid.

15. Mark Selden, *The Political Economy of Chinese Development* (Armonk, N.Y.: M.E. Sharpe, 1993), p. 3.

16. Quoted in Michel Chossudovsky, *Towards Capitalist Restoration? Chinese Socialism after Mao* (New York: St. Martin's Press, 1986), p. 214.

17. Jiang Zemin, speech at the meeting to celebrate the eightieth anniversary of the founding of the Chinese Communist Party, July 1, 2001.

18. Mark Elvin, *The Pattern of the Chinese Past* (Stanford, Calif.: Stanford University Press, 1973), p. 180.

19. Ibid., p. 129.

20. Ibid., p. 203.

21. H. Stephen Gardner, *Comparative Economic Systems* (Fort Worth, Tex.: Dryden Press, 1998), p. 656.

22. Derk Bodde, *Chinese Thought, Society, and Science: The Intellectual and Social Background of Science and Technology in Pre-Modern China* (Honolulu: University of Hawaii Press, 1991), p. 363.

23. Ibid., p. 364.

24. Justin Yifu Lin, "The Needham Puzzle: Why the Industrial Revolution Did Not Originate in China," *Economic Development and Cultural Change* 43 (January 1995), pp. 269–92.

25. Bodde, *Chinese Thought, Society, and Science*, p. 3.

26. Ibid., p. 362.

27. Elvin, *The Pattern of the Chinese Past*, p. 178.

28. Gardner, *Comparative Economic Systems*, p. 657.

29. Albert Ferwerker, *The Chinese Economy: 1912–1949* (Ann Arbor, Mich.: Michigan Papers in Chinese Studies, 1968), p. 1.

30. Ibid., p. 25.

31. Ibid., p. 48.

32. *China: A Century of Revolution*, vol. 1, prod. Sue Williams and Kathryn Dietz, dir. Sue Williams, WinStar Home Entertainment, 1997, videocassette.

33. Selden, *The Political Economy of Chinese Development*, p. 17.

34. Ibid., p. 18.

35. Justin Yifu Lin, Fang Cai, and Zhou Li, "The Lessons of China's Transition to a Market Economy," *Cato Journal* 16, no. 2 (Fall 1996), p. 212.

36. Chossudovsky, *Towards Capitalist Restoration?* p. 1.

37. Gordon White, Jude Howell, and Shang Xiaoyuan, *In Search of Civil Society: Market Reform and Social Change in Contemporary China* (Oxford, England: Clarendon Press, 1996), p. 7.

38. Li, *Rediscovering China*, p. 272.

39. Ibid., p. 272.

40. Francis Fukayama, *The End of History and the Last Man* (New York: Maxwell Macmillan International, 1992), p. 125.

41. Gordon White, *Riding the Tiger: The Politics of Economic Reform in Post-Mao China* (Stanford, Calif.: Stanford University Press, 1993), p. 158.

42. Gardner, *Comparative Economic Systems*, p. 680.

43. Ibid., p. 681.

44. Martin King Whyte, "The Social Roots of China's Economic Development," *China Quarterly* 144 (December 1995): pp. 1018–19.

45. See Barry Naughton, *Growing out of Plan: Chinese Economic Reform, 1978–1993* (Cambridge University Press, 1995).

46. Ibid., p. 8.

47. Peter Nolan and Robert F. Ash, "China's Economy on the Eve of Reform," *China Quarterly* 144 (December 1995), pp. 997–98.

48. Shaomin Li, Mingfang Li, and J. Justin Tan, "Understanding Diversification in a Transition Economy: A Theoretical Exploration," *Journal of Applied Management Studies* 7 (June 1998), pp. 77–95.

49. Louis Putterman, "The Role of Ownership and Property Rights in China's Economic Transition," *China Quarterly* 144 (December 1995), p. 1049.

50. Laixiang Sun and Liang Zou, "State-Owned versus Township and Village Enterprises in China," *Comparative Economic Studies* (Summer/Fall 1999), pp. 151–75.

51. Neil C. Hughes, "Smashing the Iron Rice Bowl," *Foreign Affairs* (July/August 1998), p. 71.

52. Naughton, *Growing out of Plan*, p. 169.

53. Jean Oi, "The Role of the Local State in China's Transitional Economy," *China Quarterly* 144 (December 1995), p. 1148.

54. Weil Li, "The Impact of Economic Reform of the Performance of Chinese State Enterprises, 1980–1989," *Journal of Political Economy* 105 (October 1997), p. 1082.

55. Sun and Zou, "State-Owned versus Township and Village Enterprises in China," pp. 151–75.

56. Jeffrey D. Sachs and Wing Thye Woo, "Structural Factors in the Economic Reforms of China, Eastern Europe, and the Former Soviet Union," *Economic Policy* 18, no. 1 (1994), pp. 102–45.

57. Terry Sicular, "Redefining State, Plan and Market: China's Reforms in Agricultural Commerce," *China Quarterly* 144 (December 1995), p. 1020.

58. Putterman, "The Role of Ownership and Property Rights in China's Economic Transition," p. 1053.

59. Ibid., pp. 1058–63.

60. Li, "The Impact of Economic Reform of the Performance of Chinese State Enterprises, 1980–1989," p. 1082.

61. Andrew G. Walder, "China's Transitional Economy: Interpreting Its Significance," *China Quarterly* 144 (December 1995), p. 967.

62. Zhaozhi Shu, " Political Reform Is the Precondition of State-Owned Enterprises," *Zheng Ming* 265 (November 1999), p. 49.

63. "The Four Characteristics of the Chinese Economy in the Next Decade," *Sino-US Evening News* 103 (15 June 2000), p. 1.

64. William H. Overholt, *The Rise of China: How Economic Reform Is Creating a New Superpower* (New York: W.W. Norton & Company, 1994), p. 149.

65. Gardner, *Comparative Economic Systems*, p. 678.

66. Overholt, *The Rise of China*, p. 151.
67. Li, *Rediscovering China*, pp. 152–63.
68. Wu, "Chinese Economy in the Twenty-first Century," pp. 16–23.
69. Li, *Rediscovering China*, p. 130.
70. Ibid., p. 129.
71. Ibid., p. 112.
72. Ibid., p. 129.
73. Ibid., p. 145.
74. Penelope B. Prime, "China's Economic Progress: Is It Sustainable?" in *China Briefing: The Contradictions of Change*, William A. Joseph, ed. (Armonk, N.Y.: M.E. Sharpe, 1997), p. 77.
75. Gardner, *Comparative Economic Systems*, p. 670.
76. Naughton, *Growing out of Plan*, p. 22.
77. Leong Liew, *The Chinese Economy in Transition: From Plan to Market* (Brookfield, Vt.: Edward Ekgar, 1997), p. 4.
78. Naughton, *Growing out of Plan*, pp. 13–17.
79. Ibid., p. 19.
80. Lin, "The Lessons of China's Transition to a Market Economy," p. 225.
81. Walder, "China's Transitional Economy: Interpreting its Significance," p. 972.
82. Lin, "The Lessons of China's Transition to a Market Economy," p. 226.
83. Kang Chen, "The Failure of Recentralization in China: Interplays among Enterprises, Local Governments, and the Center," in *Markets and Politicized Economic Choice*, ed. Arye L. Hillman (Boston: Kluwer Academic Publishers, 1991), pp. 210–11.
84. Susumu Yabuki, *China's New Political Economy: The Giant Awakes* (San Francisco: Westview Press, 1995), p. 191.
85. Nicholas R. Lardy, "The Role of Foreign Trade and Investment in China's Economic Transition," *China Quarterly* 144 (December 1995), p. 1069.
86. Lardy, "The Role of Foreign Trade and Investment in China's Economic Transition," pp. 1066–67.
87. Ibid., p. 1075.
88. Ibid., p. 1078.
89. Ibid., p. 1075.
90. Xiaoyun Wang, "The Debt-Growth Dynamics of Developing Countries: A Case Study of China" (Ph.D. diss., New School for Social Research, 1998); available on-line at http://wwwlib.umi.com/dissertations/fullcit/9900456.
91. Xiaochuan Zhang, "The Political Economy of Foreign Direct Investment in China" (Ph.D. diss., University of Maryland at College Park, 1992); available on-line at http://wwwlib.umi.com/dissertations/fullcit/9234697.
92. Chossudovsky, *Towards Capitalist Restoration?* p. 201.
93. Ibid., p. 213.
94. Office of U.S. Trade Representative, *USTR on China's WTO Accession Market Access Commitments*, released April 8, 2001; available on-line at http://www.usinfo.org/wf/990412/epf103.htm.
95. Ibid.
96. Quoted in *Washington Post*, March 13, 2001, p. A10.
97. Charlene Barshefsky, "China's Entry into WTO Important to Global Community"; available on-line at http://www.china-embassy.org.eng/20478.html.

98. *Xinghua News Agency,* November 25, 2001.

99. Wu, "Chinese Economy in the Twenty-first Century," pp. 16–23.

100. Bruce L. Reynolds, ed. *Chinese Economic Policy: Economic Reform at Midstream* (New York: Paragon House, 1988), pp. 3–4.

101. William E. Connolly, *Political Theory and Modernity* (Ithaca, N.Y.: Cornell University Press, 1993), p. 4.

102. Renhong Wu, "Which Way for the Chinese Economy?" *World and I* 13 (October 1998), pp. 46–52.

103. Kang Chen, Cary H. Jefferson, and Inderjit Singh. "Lessons from China's Economic Reform," *Journal of Comparative Economics* 16 (June 1992), p. 221.

104. White, *Riding the Tiger,* p. 240.

105. Wu, "Chinese Economy in the Twenty-first Century," pp. 16–23.

CHAPTER 5

The Last Fortress of Antidemocratization

Some China specialists predict that China will become the largest economic power in the world during the first half of this century if it maintains its current economic growth rate.[1] In contrast, however, the Chinese political system has lagged very much behind this economic development. The Tiananmen Square Incident of 1989 strongly indicated that the future of the reform movement was at stake. Since that time, the CPC has never stopped suppressing political dissent and resisting modern democracy. It still insists on a one-party system and resists essential political change. Deng Xiaoping has been dead since 1997, but the new leaders of the CPC have no intention of reforming the one-party system. Those who used to hope that China would change its political system in the post-Deng era now place their hopes on Jiang Zemin's successor—Hu Jingtao. Obviously, it is a politically naïve idea to place all democratic hope on a single Chinese leader. It is true that the party's top leader controls all of China, but that does not necessarily mean that a single leader can change the country's political system. In democratic societies, the president is elected by the people, so the authority of the president does, in fact, come from the people. The top leader of the CPC is appointed. Thus the authority of the top Chinese leader is derived not from his personal ability, but from the party system. Therefore, the top leader of the party, as the representative of the party, is hard to change the entire party system. Since the paramount Chinese revolutionary leaders passed away, the party has relied heavily upon political power for governance. Chinese political reform is urgent and pressing. It can be predicted that the greatest challenge of China's future is the political one.[2] China is at a crossroads and must choose a political system and a democratic form of government.[3]

THE ULTIMATE OBSTACLE TO CHINA'S POLITICAL REFORM

An integrated reform movement includes both economic reform and political reform, so why has political change in China lagged far behind the economic reform movement? Tracing back the history of China's reform movement, the call for political reform actually originated as early as 1978, when thousands of Chinese people in Beijing posted written complaints about China's problems on a wall along Chang-An Avenue calling for political reform. That wall is well known as "Democracy Wall." Deng had just regained his political power at that time, and he used the reform movement against his opponents. He slowed down the political reform, however, after he consolidated his power in the beginning of the 1980s. Certainly, Chinese students and intellectuals were not satisfied with Chinese political change, and they began questioning the meaning of communism in the middle of the 1980s for the first time since the Communist Revolution of 1949. The dissatisfaction gradually became a nationwide student movement that reached its height in spring 1989. Deng viewed this movement as a great threat to the Communist regime. As a result, two top Communist leaders, Hu Yaobang and Zhao Ziyang, were ousted from office one after the other, and the Chinese government cracked down on the student movement. It was the first time that the People's Liberation Army opened fire on and killed Chinese citizens since the party took power in 1949. To suppress democracy is to encourage government corruption. As a result, government corruption has become widespread and gone uncurbed since the Tiananmen Square Incident. Political change has lagged far behind economic reform not because the Chinese people have had no desire to promote political reform, but because the party has resisted political reform.

One argument the party has used to resist political reform is that China should balance economic reform with the continuation of the old political structure in order to maintain harmony between the market economy and the socialist system.[4] Of course, this argument conflicts with reality, because a market economy and a socialist system are opposite forces. The development of China's economy and the market system unavoidably and intensively conflicts with the present Chinese political system. On one hand, the market economy, especially the emergence of private ownership, is demanding more and more individual rights and freedoms and is shaking the foundation of the communist system and the Communist Party's power. On the other hand, the Chinese government insists that the Chinese market economy is not a capitalist system but a socialist market economy. Apparently, the continuing dominance of the Chinese political system restrains the economy and all other areas from full development. Theoretically, the market economy is an irresistible force that sooner or later will lead to a democratic society. However, a stronger argument can be made that an authoritarian state is the precondition for rapid economic growth, such as that experienced by Japan, South Korea, Singapore, and Taiwan, yet it is hard to prove a necessary relationship "between marketization and democratization."[5] As Bruce J. Dickson notes, "Democratization is not a natural process but a political one."[6] At this point, the party can resist the natural process of the market economy by using coercive force, even though the implementation of China's market economy generated great enthusiasm to push for political change. Logically, China's future, including its economic and political future, depends on whether the Chinese people remake China's public philosophy and take cautious but firm action to change the Chinese political system. Lance L. P. Gore has predicted that China's future "will have to be fought out on a political battleground."[7]

The core of politics is the relationship between the state and the individual. In democratic societies, private ownership is the foundation of the political system, and the individual is at the center of society. Conversely, public ownership is the foundation of autocratic societies, in which the state shapes the individual. Therefore, societies are fundamentally organized in two basic ways: democratic governments organize society voluntarily through the private interaction of individuals and various organizations; and autocratic governments organize society coercively through a state mandate.[8] The Chinese communist government is an autocracy in which public ownership is the foundation of society. The individual is shaped and controlled by the state. At present, the government wants to retain power by maintaining the system of public ownership. Actually, many Chinese citizens are not ready for privatization.[9] Why? The socialist tradition of public ownership guarantees that everyone has equal rights to the fulfillment of their basic needs. Under the public ownership system, some people feel that they live with a safety net. However, the history of socialist countries has proved that this system nurtured lazy people and destroyed their incentive for social production. There is no doubt that the iron rice bowl must be smashed in order to enhance China's productive force. In the meantime, the disparity between the rich and poor has increased since the reform movement began. Some reports show that China's economy will be gradually dominated by the families of the top party leaders if China does not reform its economic and political systems at the same time. The article "Mysterious Huaneng International," published in the November 24, 2001 issue of *Securities Weekly*, said that Huaneng Power International Inc. actually had become Li Peng's family business. Li is the second most powerful party leader in China. Huaneng was described as being like a ship, with one of Li's sons, Li Xiaopeng, at the tiller and his mother, Zhu Lin, the firm's chairperson, as the captain. This is only one example of how the families of top Chinese leaders control China's economy.[10]

Politics in the Chinese context, rather than being committed to the formation of state-society and state-individuals, is committed to the formation of party/state-society and party/state-individuals. In democratic societies, political parties compete against one another for office and are agents to drive politics forward and keep politics in balance. An elected president represents an entire nation, not a single party. In the Chinese context, the term *Communist Party of China* has a special meaning, which is not of a voluntary political association, but of a political and administrative entity. According to the constitutions of the People's Republic of China and the CPC, the party is the sole leader of the Chinese nation and the Chinese people. The party holds sole power over government and all other organizations. The party's power comes not from the people but is authorized by the constitutions, both of which are written by the party. As an opposition party before 1949, the CPC organized military forces and struggled against the nationalist government for twenty-eight years, finally overthrowing the government and establishing the People's Republic of China by violent revolution in October 1949. In the Chinese peasant's revolutionary tradition, whoever seized the state power sat on the throne. Following this old tradition, Mao Zedong, the head of the party, became the paramount leader of the country after the party took power. The party as the sole ruling party does not lead China through its 64 million party members, but through a small group of leaders. According to Kenneth Lieberthal, the top power elite, comprising about twenty-five to thirty-five individuals, controls China.[11] The party rule represents the interests of only a small group, not of all the people. In a Chinese saying, It is easy to seize power, but difficult to maintain power. The party was supported by the vast majority of the Chinese people in its efforts to seize power before 1949, but it has relied on coercive force to maintain its power. The party is no longer representative of the Chinese people and culture. Jiang's theory of three representatives (the development of China's advanced productive forces, the orientation and development of China's advanced culture, and the fundamental interests of the overwhelming majority of the Chinese people) is completely false. It is true that Deng regained the support of the Chinese people at the beginning of the reform movement, but it did not last. Because of the loss of popular support from Mao to Deng to Jiang, every top party leader has tried to centralize and strengthen his personal authority by making the leadership of the party the first priority for governance. The first of the Four Cardinal Principles is the leadership of the CPC. Deng asserted again and again that the Chinese nation would encounter nationwide disorder and fall apart without the absolute leadership of the party. No one Chinese top leader has considered surrendering power or sharing it with other parties and the people. In premodern China, the Empress Dowager Ci Xi of the Qing dynasty attended to state affairs behind the bamboo curtain for almost forty years. Mao did the same thing. He withdrew from the forefront of Chinese politics twice because of his failures during his tenure, but he never gave up his control of the party. Deng held the position of president of the Central Military Commission in order to control his successor after he retired from the party; it was predicted that Jiang would follow Deng's example and take over the presidency of the Central Military Commission to control his successor, Hu Jingtao, after the Sixteenth National Congress of the Chinese Communist Party in 2002. Given these circumstances, we cannot understand Chinese politics without first understanding the formation of the party-state-society-individual. As Shiping Zheng points out, "Nothing is more crucial than the party's relationship with the state institutions."[12]

The nature of China's party leadership is the party's control of the entire country through its members, its ideology, and its structural system. The leadership, based on Marxism, is a one-party dictatorship—proletariat dictatorship. In other words, party control of the government, the society, and individuals. In order to guarantee the party's monopolistic power, the party did not establish a legitimate government but organized a highly centralized hierarchical government. The relationship of the party and the state was undoubtedly based on the totalitarian model.[13] According to Flemming Christiansen and Shirin Rai, "The totalitarian model was used to describe societies which are totally controlled by one political force, that is, dictatorships and other autocratic regimes."[14] A totalitarian government establishes an official ideology and requires everyone to follow it. The one-party system is headed by a single person who exercises absolute power and control over everything by coercive force, including government, society, voluntary organizations, economic activities, the military and weapons, and mass communications.[15] Clearly, Chinese politics is essentially identical with the characteristics of totalitarian governments, although it is moving toward an authoritarian government. The state in China is the party/state and is a product of the party.[16] The analysis of the relationship between the party and the state is the key to studying Chinese politics. Under the leadership of the party, the state is unable to function as an independent organ; the state is "more dependent on the CCP [Chinese Communist Party]."[17] Theoretically, China also has the three powers of judicial, legislative, and executive branches, but the three powers and all other national organs, including the Chinese People's Political Consultative Conference and the military institution, according to the Constitution of China, are "under the leadership of the Communist Party of China and the guidance of Marxism-Leninism and Mao Zedong

Thought." The party controls the government and permeates governmental affairs thoroughly. All the top leaders at the national level—the National People's Congress, the Judicial Department, the State Council, the Chinese People's Political Consultative Conference, and the Central Military Committee—are the members of the party politburo. Every head of the political and administrative branches at the national level, including the State Planning Commission, the State Education Commission, the State Commission for Reconstructing Economy, the National Economy Commission, propaganda bureaucracies, personnel bureaucracies, and civilian coercive bureaucracies, is overseen by a member of the Political Bureau of the Central Committee of the CPC. Most important government posts from the national to the local level, including legislative, judicial, administrative, and military institutions—even mass organizations such as the Youth League Committee, All-China Women's Federation, and All-China Worker's Federation—are occupied by members of the party leadership. The party tightly controls the government and carries out governmental functions.[18] It should be noted that with about 64 million party members, it is clearly impossible for all party members to be part of the leadership of China. The party system is pyramidal. All of the party's decisions are made by a small group, which is part of the Standing Committee of the Political Bureau. The general secretary of the party is the group's boss.

Many scholars have observed that the party controls the government and the nation through *kou* and *xitong*. *Kou* is the party's gateway and involves the major functional areas organized by the top members of the party. There are four broad *kous:* party affairs, government work, state security, and foreign affairs. The *xitong* is the group of bureaucracies from the national level to the local level that implement broad tasks under party leadership. The *xitongs* include party *xitong,* organizational *xitong,* propaganda and educational *xitong,* political and legal *xitongs,* finance and economic *xitongs,* and the military *xitong.* Different *xitongs* play different roles, but they serve the same goal: to shape Chinese society and regulate the Chinese people. Both *kou* and *xitong* in the configuration of Chinese political power are controlled by the party.[19] In the post-Mao era, the party relaxed some of its controls, giving the government more autonomy and authority. After Deng died in 1997, the position of a single leader over the party is weakening, but the general secretary of the party still plays a central role in the decision-making process. The party absolutely refuses to practice multiparty politics. Only one party, the CPC, rules the entire country. The Clinton administration in 2000 described the nature of China in this way: "The People's Republic of China (PRC) is an authoritarian state in which the Chinese Communist Party (CCP) is the paramount source of power. At the national and regional levels, party members hold almost all top government, police, and military positions. Ultimate authority rests with members of the Politburo."[20] The era of party control is not over,[21] because the party rule does not strongly depend upon a paramount leader but, rather, upon the party's controlling system, or *xitong*, including the organizational system, the military forces, and ideological principles. Although the charismatic leaders Mao and Deng have gone, the party's controlling system remains, and it works. It is impossible to resume the relations of the party and the state that prevailed under Mao, but the top party leader is still able to exercise his personal power over the government and society through the party system. There is no evidence that the party will surrender its position as sole leader in the foreseeable future or reduce its position to the same level as other organizations. Therefore, the CPC has become a major obstacle to governmental affairs in post-1949 China.[22] To fulfill the goal of democratization requires not only separating the party from the state and from mass organizations, but abolishing the party's controlling system. Some reform measures, such as the decentralization of party powers, the separation of the party and government at some levels, the expansion of government authority, and the widening of the government's autonomy, improved the relationship of the party and the government and made them work together more cooperatively. Because all these reform measures worked within the framework of the party's system, however, they could not solve the fundamental problem of party-state-individual relations, that is, abolish the principles of the party and the one-party system.

WHY CHINA'S DEMOCRATIC MOVEMENT FAILED

Modern democracy guarantees individual rights, moderates conflicts, regulates political competition, makes government more legitimate, improves the quality of government, and recruits political leaders from a large pool.[23] According to Samuel P. Huntington, the democratic movement has become global in scope since the third democratic wave began in 1974.[24] Since then, more than thirty countries have "shifted from authoritarianism to democracy."[25] Francis Fukuyama has predicted that "free democratic governments [will] continue to spread to more and more countries around the world."[26] Modern democracy is the best social and political system in the world; it may constitute the "end point of mankind's ideological evolution," the "final form of human government," and the "end of history."[27] For more than 2,000 years, the Chinese people were ruled by absolute monarchical government,[28] and they had no experience with democratic ideas until modern times. No school of thought in premodern China had reference to modern democracy. It is certain that Mencian ideas of *min-ben* (for the people) and Confucian ideas of benevolence completely differ from democratic principles. Kang Youwei (1858–1927) and Liang Qichao (1873–1929), the first and most influential political reformers in modern China, believed that constitutional monarchy was the best form of government. Hence the Hundred-Day-Reform was really "premature and ill-fated" and made only a little progress in educational areas. No significant political progress was achieved during the ten years following that reform. In 1905, the Chinese government, inspired by domestic constitutional voices and political reforms in Japan, sent a constitutional commission to Japan, the United States, and Europe to study their forms of constitutional government. The commission subsequently suggested that the emperor Guangxu adopt a form of constitutional government. An imperial edict was issued in 1906 calling for a constitutional government. It was a good move toward a nation-state, but it was far from democracy. The opening of the National Assembly in 1910 greatly inspired a Chinese democratic spirit.[29] However, the Qing dynasty was reluctant to take further steps along democratic lines, fearing its loss of absolute power. The May Fourth Movement of 1919 was the first public call for modern democracy in Chinese history, but the Nationalist government totally ignored democratic demands of the people and made no effort to improve the internal political system and civil society. For that reason, the Nationalist government lost its popular support and was defeated by the Communist Party. Julia C. Strauss, in *Strong Institutions in Weak Polities: State Building in Republican China*, describes the Nationalist government as strong in institutions but weak in politics.[30] During the thirty-five years after the Nationalist government left the mainland for Taiwan, the Nationalist Party continued to exercise an authoritarian power under a one-party system in Taiwan. Taiwan did not announce a democratic reform package until October 1986, so the Taiwanese never got a chance to enjoy democracy fully during the time of Jiang Jieshi.

In mainland China, Mao, like Jiang Jieshi, never really allowed democracy a chance to succeed. Mao claimed to have implemented a new democratic system, but it was actually an absolute dictatorship. Suzanne Ogden, in *China's Unresolved Issues: Politics, Development, and Culture*, observes that democracy in the Chinese context is "both socialist and Chinese in form," and that democratic centralism is the heart of socialist democracy. Thus, she concludes that socialist democracy bears little resemblance to modern democracy.[31] Deng's economic reform movement promoted economic development, and at the same time it triggered a democratic zeal in the Chinese people. The first wave of the Chinese democratic movement after the reform movement took place in 1979, and the basic democratic principles were addressed in the Chinese Declaration of Human Rights of 1979. Deng actually used this movement to wipe out his political enemies and strengthen his power. Due to serious government corruption, China launched the second wave of democracy in the middle of the 1980s. It clearly set forth slogans demanding political reform: "Reform the political system"; "Abandon the Four Cardinal Principles"; "Fulfill the democratic politics"; and "Eliminate corruption." Unexpectedly, this effort at political reform met with strong resistance from both sides: the hard-liners and the reformers. By that time, Deng had already established and stabilized his power; thus the democratic movement was no longer helpful but was a threat to his power. In order to retain his power, he did not hesitate to sacrifice his previous supporters—Chinese students—and declared the Four Cardinal Principles. Chinese students were greatly enraged by Deng's action. The massive student protest of 1989 finally broke out. Although the Tiananmen Square Incident did not achieve the original goals of the movement, it awakened the Chinese people. Before that incident, most Chinese people, especially Chinese students, believed that Confucianism and Maoism should be held responsible for the failures of the Chinese democratic movement, that Marxism would guide the party to reform the political system, and that the party had ability to reform itself within the party system. Afterward, the Chinese people realized that democracy could not be achieved under the party's leadership.

Besides the party's resistance, other causes of the failure of the democratic movement in China can be summarized as follows: First, China lacked the tradition to practice democracy, and the Chinese people were not sufficiently motivated to promote democratization. Second, democracy was considered a bad thing in China in the nineteenth century because it was related to Western imperialism. Third, the party propagandized for the people's democratic dictatorship, yet the Chinese people indeed suffered from this socialist democracy. Thus the Chinese people hesitate to accept the other type of democracy, although more and more of them have come to realize that modern democracy is a good system for the Chinese society.[32] Fourth, it is much easier for the Chinese people to accept advances in science and technology than to accept democracy, because they can receive benefits from the economic growth derived from those advances without political risk. Actually the CPC has been using this psychology to resist modern democracy.

One of the main arguments for the party to refuse democracy is that China learned its lessons from the reform movement in the former Soviet Union. Unlike the situation in China, at the beginning of economic reform, Mikhail Gorbachev introduced the kind of political reform that would make possible economic reform and shifted authority from the Communist Party to government institutions. However, "the consequences of Gorbachev's bold strategy were political chaos and economic failure."[33] By contrast, Deng "took a more cautious approach of introducing economic reforms without political reforms."[34] From the viewpoint of the CPC, China must follow a gradual reform model, beginning with economic reform so that China can go through the transitional period smoothly. However, the process of introducing market competition and ownership reform is the process of shifting power from the party and the government to the individual. In other words, while the party and government are losing their powers, the individual gains certain rights. At this point, economic reform also has serious political consequences and is a profound revolution. Therefore, the party is trying to slow down the privatization and marketization to keep its own privilege and power. Under the communist regime, the democratic movement inevitably meets great confrontations. Neither nihilism nor radical revolution is the best solution to fulfill democratization in China. An "inside revolution" is the only way to accelerate the process of democratization. The Chinese inside revolution is neither Westernization nor Chinese nationalism, but is an initiative to remake China's public philosophy through educational programs and religious missions to form a democratic consciousness and culture. This program is especially important for the top-to-bottom democratic revolution.

Increasing political participation is part of the process of democratization. The degree of participation is determined by two factors. First, how much political interest do the people have? Second, how much does law permit the people's participation? The political interest of the Chinese people passed through three stages in modern China. Under the Nationalist government, the people generally showed political apathy and ignorance because they wanted to pursue basic needs first under poor economic conditions. Under the Mao regime, influenced by the ideas of class struggle, most people blindly followed Mao and participated in mass politics. Since the reform movement began, the Chinese people have become interested in improving their standard of living, but at the same time, they hate political corruption, which seriously tramples on mass interests.[35] Although the political system has gradually improved over the past years, the Chinese people have only limited opportunities for political participation. In the countryside, Chinese peasants were granted rights to vote for their village leaders several years ago. The Chinese government exaggerated this progress and called this village election democracy with Chinese characteristics. Some American scholars view village elections as a good start for China's future. To them, it is better than none. Even former U.S. president Jimmy Carter made a special trip to China to monitor the village elections in 2001. Unfortunately, the Chinese village, usually composed of twenty to fifty families or less, is not a government authority but a work group. At this point, village elections could be good practice for democracy, but they do not affect Chinese politics at all. In urban areas, residents generally have only the right to participate in politics in their *danwei* (work unit) and to vote for the representatives of the local People's Congress, but they still do not have the right to elect the head of the *danwei*. In contrast with the villages, *danwei* in cities play a more important role in influencing social and governmental affairs, so the party wants to preserve its right to appoint as head of *danwei* those employees who are loyal to the government and the party. Samuel Huntington suggests that the criterion of a democracy is whether power is turned over from one party or group to another through elections.[36] In China, no opposition party is allowed to campaign for office. All mayors, governors, and the president are appointed by the party. To meet the so-called two-turnover test, the one-party system must first be put to an end.

Real participation must be involved in decision making. In China, the decision-making process is divided into three stages: agenda setting, decision making, and policy implementation.[37] Political participation in China is only permitted in the implementation stage, for example, in village elections and *danwei* elections. Multiparty and independent campaigns are prohibited; appeals and adversarial activities are considered dissidents' activities; and political resistance is regarded as an antigovernment activity that must be suppressed. The Chinese common people have no way to influence the first two stages of the decision-making process directly; nor are they allowed to publicize their democratic ideas in public squares. At present, the Internet can be used to indirectly influence the first two stages of the decision-making process, but the Chinese government tightly monitors and regulates electronic communication facilities, including Internet and e-mail, and prohibits Chinese citizens from conducting "abnormal political activities" over the Internet. The government has established special Internet police units to monitor and control Internet content and access. Human rights watchers observe that Chinese authorities have blocked some politically sensitive Web sites provided by certain dissident groups and foreign news organizations, such as the Voice of America, the *Washington Post*, the *New York Times*, and the British Broadcasting Corporation (BBC).[38] It was reported that several Chinese people who posted democratic articles on Web sites were arrested in 2001. In January 2002, the Chinese government issued its most intrusive regulation to control the Internet through screening people's "private e-mail for political content and holding them responsible for subversive postings on their Web sites."[39] This severe censorship is threatening to the normal life of the Chinese people and their individual rights, even though the government's ability to do this is limited.[40] In order to limit political participation within the official framework, the government shapes Chinese political activity by eliminating organizational activities and reshaping "people's psychological orientation" through political education and various punishments.[41] It is no wonder that Andrew J. Nathan asserts that the Chinese people participate in politics without influence.[42] Some scholars even reject the notion of participation in the Chinese Communist regime.[43] The lack of political participation is also an important cause of the increase in political corruption in China, which in turn drives the Chinese people to seek other ways—such as making *guanxi* (connections, or networks) and buying power—to influence Chinese politics or to protect themselves from an oppressive government.

SHOULD CHINA BE RULED BY THE PARTY?

A democratic society is ruled by the people through law, not by a single political party and a single person. Jurgen Habermas, in *Between Facts and Norms: Contributions to a Discourse Theory of Law and Democracy,* argues that democracy and the rule of law are internally related, which means that there is a reciprocal, causal relationship between the rational legitimacy of laws in a democracy and actual practices and procedures because lawmaking is the sum of opinion formation and will formation. Legitimacy is an important characteristic of democratic government. Legitimacy, in the political process, generally refers to the fact that political action takes place within a framework of law and regulation. In medieval society, legitimacy conformed to traditional customs and procedures. In the Renaissance, the new term *consent* was introduced into the meaning of legitimacy. In the Age of Reason, European thinkers added the term *natural law.* The French Revolution interpreted legitimacy by liberty. In democratic societies, legitimacy is what conforms to equality and individual rights. But in Communist China, legitimacy is what conforms to the dictates of the top leader. Chinese society is ruled not by a legitimate government but by the party. Correspondingly, the party does not govern China by law but, rather, by party policy and the will of its top leader(s). The personal will and decision of the leadership are above the law. The privilege of the ruling class is above the interests of the common people.

For more than 2,000 years, China had no practical legal tradition like that found in Western countries. Law existed in premodern China, but its main purpose was to shape the common people's behavior and impose imperial orders.[44] Law in imperial China was only applied to the common Chinese people. Under the Mao regime, the constitution and law together served as a rubber stamp. Law was replaced by party policy, and the policy was made by the top party leaders. Mao, as paramount leader and savior-prophet, was at the center of Chinese politics and served in an absolute dictator role. He exercised unfettered personal authority over the party, government, society, the military, the economy, and ideology. He promulgated his theory as ultimate truth and infallible dogma. China today can be characterized as an unlawful country, and the Chinese political system is actually personalism, nepotism, and dictatorship functioning together. Under the pressures of the reform movement, Deng began decentralizing personal power but still emphasized personal loyalty as the criterion for appointment. Chinese politics is essentially a personal politics by nature. The term *guanxi* represents a popular concept used to describe Chinese personal politics. *Guanxi,* which includes genetic and social *guanxi*s, refers to a system of connections. *Guanxi* is an important social resource of the Chinese people in politics and business because "it is not just that *guanxi* makes things easier; it is that *guanxi* makes things happen."[45] That is why in contemporary China nepotism is a very serious problem in both economic and political reform. At present, the richest people in China are those who hold power or have *guanxi*s to connect with power. It already has become a common phenomenon that many politicians convert their power to money, and that many rich men buy power by using money. Unlimited unchecked communist power and money work together to make Chinese politics dirtier.

The party/state controls over society are achieved by several basic means, mainly the *hukou* (registration system) and *danwei*, which tie "most Chinese to specific locales and work places."[46] *Danwei* as a basic organization implements the principles and tasks of the party and the government at local levels. A *danwei* controls its employees in everything from work performance to marriage and family planning. At this point, the *danwei* is very similar to the extended family or clan.[47] Broadly, there are two types of *danwei*—enterprise *danwei* and administrative *danwei*. A *danwei* controls employees basically through the *dangan* (personnel dossier) system. An employee cannot transfer to another *danwei* without his *dangan*. Economic reform, especially ownership reform, weakened the party's power over the state, and the state's power over *danwei*. Correspondingly, the *danwei*'s control function over employees has been loosened because private and foreign-funded enterprises are no longer required to receive the *dangan* when they hire employees. Citizens have more chances to change jobs and move from one place to another, but the *danwei* is still the center of an urban resident's life and dominates an employee's economic and political life.[48] Employees heavily rely upon *danwei* for their careers. In other words, employees' professional and political careers have been controlled by *danwei* or, more precisely, by the party/government, because enterprise and administrative *danwei* are directly controlled by the government.

The historical relationship between the party and legislatures in China shows that the party ignores and tramples on the law. Chinese legislatures were established for the first time in the last decade of the Qing dynasty. Legislatures in the period of the Nationalist government existed in name only. The National People's Congress (NPC), which was founded in 1954, never played an independent role in the Mao era but was only a tool of the party. The NPC was completely paralyzed during the ten years of the Cultural Revolution (1966–1976). In order to increase the new government's acceptance and heighten government efficiency, the post-Mao government began to restore the NPC's normal activities in 1978.[49] The reform engaged in legislative activity, supervision, representation, regime support, and improving relationships with the NPC and other organizations. The emphasis of the reform is to strengthen the role of the Standing Committee of the NPC, increase full-time professional legislators, and improve internal organizations, including establishing a chairmanship group and increasing the NPC's support staff. China's legal reform improved the accountability of the judicial and legal systems; expanded the education of lawyers, judges, and prosecutors; passed a number of statutes, including the Administrative Litigation Law, the Lawyers Law, the State Compensation Law, the Prison Law, the Criminal Law, and the Criminal Procedure Law;[50] heightened government efficiency; increased channels between the party and society; and caused the party to begin paying attention to social diversity. Some scholars have praised China for developing a sophisticated lawmaking system so that China's can no longer be regarded as a weak legislative system.[51] Undoubtedly, the NPC has become stronger, and Chinese legislatures have made considerable progress. Party policy completely replaced laws, and Chinese legislatures existed in name only before the reform movement began. The number of motions sharply increased in the reform period—by about twenty-seven times during the last two decades[52]—but that increase does not necessarily mean that the days of rule by law have already begun in China.

The reality is that power, party policy, and the top leader's decision usually supersede law in China. The Chinese legislative system has a long way to go to become an independent system and meet international norms. At present, the party still seriously interferes in NPC affairs "through its power of appointments."[53] The common people have no way to control deputies, and deputies have no requirement to speak for the people because the candidates for deputy are appointed by the party, not elected by the people. The party leaders have no need to listen to deputies because deputies have no essential legal rights to impeach party leaders. Structural reforms in the NPC, such as "free elections, campaigning, longer sessions and meaningful votes were rejected."[54] Other issues, such as legislative checks and balances, "were discussed but never adopted."[55] More importantly, the abnormal relations of the NCP and the party from the national to the local level have never been improved. The party is an unchecked power that easily leads to dictatorship. Generally speaking, Chinese citizens lack effective legal channels against arbitrary state action. A considerable number of the Chinese people are ignorant regarding legal affairs, and they do not know how to use the law to protect their rights; indeed, a large number of Chinese people respect the old Chinese tradition that a good man is never involved in litigation. Compared with the great volume of litigation cases, China is seriously short of professional lawyers and trained legal personnel.[56] Another serious legal problem in China is that law enforcement officials break the laws they are in charge of enforcing. For instance, arbitrary arrest and detention for political purposes remains a serious problem. Police continue to hold individuals without granting them access to their family or a lawyer, and trials continue to be conducted in secret.[57] All of these legal problems come from the party and serve to override juridical autonomy and interfere with the police, the courts, and legal proceedings.[58] According to party principle, law is the tool of the state and the ruling class. Therefore, "party interference and the destruction of the judicial system" are the main obstacles to Chinese legal reform.[59] Chinese legal experience has shown that it is impossible for China to step onto the democratic stage—that is, to become a country ruled by law—without ending one-party rule.

Law is legalized consensus, the formation of the public will. Civil society, or what Habermas calls the public sphere, is the warning system that adjusts the relationship between the state and society. Private and public autonomy are co-original and internally connected. A lawful country is based on a well-developed civil society because its legal system relies upon civil society as the source to improve the legal system and to make the state more legitimate. In turn, the civil society is the basic supporter of legitimate government. Therefore, a high degree of civil society is always associated with a democratic system. The degree of civil society is the criterion used to measure the degree of separation between the state and society.[60] Although the emergence of civil society is not a sufficient condition for democratization, it is a necessary precondition. Democratic institutions have little meaning without a well-developed civil society.[61]

However, there is little agreement on the definition of the term *civil society*.[62] From a Western viewpoint, at least, the term can be understood sociologically and politically. From a sociological perspective, civil society is the realm situated between the state and society and is made up of the basic building blocks of society. From a political perspective, civil society is a set of institutionalized relationships between the state and society based on democratic principles that are derived from the Anglo-American political tradition.[63] Basically, the term *civil society* can be considered as describing the realm of institutional social life, which is "self-generating, self-supporting, and autonomous from the state."[64] In China, *civil society* is a new phenomenon. In premodern China, there was neither a public realm between the state and society nor the separation of the state and society. Public service was merely an extension of the imperial office. The state control of society was based on "naked coercion or personal loyalty." In the republic era, the Nationalist Party tightly upheld a one-party system and made little progress toward a civil society. Ninety percent of the Chinese people lived in the countryside and received little education. According to a nationwide poll conducted in 1948, 73 percent of the Chinese population were illiterate. The old China was a sheet of loose sand, that is, it was in chaos, with no basic foundation for a civil society before 1949.[65]

In the Mao era, the government adopted the absolute totalitarian system, wherein the state itself shaped the society. Western scholars call this type of state a Leninist state. All Leninist states share some characteristics: they thoroughly penetrate society, control the economic system, supervise civil society and public opinion, and shape individuals' political conduct by means of secret police forces.[66] Mao also isolated China from the rest of the world; forbade the Chinese people to listen to shortwave radio under penalty of criminal law; cut off connections between the countryside and the city by the *hukou;* and prohibited peasants from moving from the countryside to the city, while urban residents were prohibited from moving from one place to another. Since the economic reform began in 1978, the market economy has weakened the vertical party/state control of society and created the basis for a civil society.[67] It is evident in the post-Mao era that professional organizations have developed rapidly, lawyers are moving out of government service to establish their own firms, private medicine and education are expanding fast, and the number of semiofficial newspapers and journals has increased over recent years.[68] However, among these associations, the mass organizations sponsored by the state are still the most influential and popular force. The most important positions in the mass organizations are appointed by the party; therefore, the organizations eventually become part of the government authority, and they are unwilling to break off formal relations with the party to seek autonomy from the party/state because they want to keep their own political and economic privileges.[69] Dissident activities are prohibited and are strictly suppressed. It is worth noting that the Tiananmen Square Incident actually interrupted the development of Chinese civil society, though some scholars argue that the failure of the democratic movement in 1989 was due to the first generation of powerful party leaders, not the weakness of civil society.[70] At present, the conflict between the state and society has not been resolved.[71] There is not enough evidence in China to indicate that it has emerged as a Western-style civil society that fully embodies the principles of self-regulation as well as separation of some institutions from the state.[72] Chinese political tradition and the party's coercive powers hinder the development of Chinese civil society.

THE STATUS OF THE INDIVIDUAL IN COMMUNIST CHINA

The role and status of the individual is the gauge used to evaluate the degree of social civilization. Traditional China was a family- and group-oriented country. The term government in Chinese *(gou jia)* refers to "nation-family." The family is the base of Chinese society and is a key to understanding the patriarchal system. In this context, Chinese society is an enlarged family. Historically, individuals, as family members, never truly stood independently. The state was above society, and society was above individuals. Individuals had the responsibility to obey their elders and government authorities but had no rights to fight for themselves.

In a global context, *The Universal Declaration of Human Rights,* promulgated by the United Nations (UN) after World War II in 1948, identified human rights as "a common standard of achievement for all peoples and all nations."[73] The declaration is a global legal document with comprehensive guiding principles to enlighten all people around the world to fight for their own human rights. Since it was issued, the Universal Declaration of Human Rights has assumed an incomparable significance in the moral, political, and legal spheres. In 1985, the UN recommended it as the authoritative definition of the standard of human rights.[74] Pope John Paul II highly praised the declaration as a "milestone on the long and difficult path of the human race."[75] Joseph Wronka has suggested that the "*Universal Declaration of Human Rights* should be the primary ethical and legal gauge of rights standards" in the twenty-first century.[76]

However, the Chinese government refused to have any dialogue with the outside world about human rights in the Mao era. Even though there was no official Chinese document or article in the Mao era that discussed human rights, the post-Mao government essentially abstained from talking about them both domestically and internationally. Three important Chinese official documents, the 1991 Human Rights White Paper, the 1995 White Paper, and the 1997 White Paper, detail the Chinese government's opinion on human rights.[77] The three documents share an emphasis on the differences between Western and Eastern cultures and define the term *human rights* as a Western product. The Universal Declaration of Human Rights, therefore, cannot be a universal truth. The documents assert that China made considerable progress to improve human rights in the Communist regime by demonstrating China's good human rights records.[78] They declare that China is a sovereign country and has its own right to decide how to practice human rights based on its circumstances. Therefore, Western countries should not impose westernized human rights on China. Chinese society would become disordered if the Chinese people practiced westernized human rights on Chinese soil. According to Chinese officials, the majority of Chinese people today prefer social and political stability as a means to improve their living standard. When Jiang Zemin visited the United States in 1997, he said that China's reform could not possibly succeed without social and political stability.[79] In addition, the Chinese government asserts that, of its population of almost 1.3 billion, 70 percent are low-educated peasants. It will take a long time for the Chinese people to learn democracy and fully implement the principles of human rights. According to Chinese official logic, it would destabilize society if China accepted the principle of human rights unconditionally.

However, the Chinese government's arguments that human rights are not universal rights are too weak to be convincing. First, human rights are not created by any single person or government. Human rights are the inalienable rights of humankind; as the American *Declaration of Independence* declares, "Life, Liberty, and the pursuit of Happiness" are self-evident truths. Second, human rights are not granted by any government or law but are based on individual dignity and worth. Governments only legalize and protect human rights. Every individual person has the same human rights before the law. Third, although every country has its own economic, political, and cultural traditions, human beings everywhere possess in essence the same human nature, dignity, and worth. Fourth, the Universal Declaration of Human Rights was approved by the UN General Assembly with forty-eight supporting votes, which represented an overwhelming majority of the membership at that time. This reflects the universal truth contained therein and a common understanding of human rights. *The Universal Declaration of Human Rights* declares that "Everyone is entitled to all the rights and freedoms set forth in this *Declaration*, without distinction of any kind, such as race, color, sex, language, religion, political or other opinion, national or social origin, property, birth or other status."[80]

Human rights come with the distinguishing characteristics of individuality, equality, and religion, but all of these characteristics conflict with the principles of the Chinese government/party. First, the individual is at the center of human rights and democratic societies. Louis Henkin has pointed out that "Individual liberty is one of the most cherished of American values."[81] In traditional China, not the individual, but the collective group, such as the family or organization, is at the center of society.[82] The party views individual persons as members of collectives, "views all rights as collectively based," and regards individualism as capitalism.[83] Socialist principles require that individuals take seriously their responsibilities to community and society.

Second, the principle of human rights in a democratic society is based on the principle that all men are created equal. Equality is one of the foundations of human rights. Equality means that all human beings possess a common nature that comes from the Creator of humankind,[84] and that human beings are capable of making moral choices and acting justly. Every person participates equally in social and political life. In the rigidly hierarchical historical China, people were not born equal. Some people were *jun-zi,* who were born to the ruling class, but some were "small men" born to the ruled class. According to Confucianism, individual rights were created by the government and granted only to the ruling class.[85] Mao asserted that human beings are divided into different classes, and that classes are unequal. The exploiting class in socialist society should be suppressed by the proletariat class according to Maoism. The abstract idea of equality is the capitalist utopia. The current economic reform movement promotes economic growth; meanwhile, the reform increases inequality, gives a green light to serious political and economic corruption, and widens the gap between rich and poor and between the ruling elite and the common people. Moreover, the party grants excessive political privilege to party members and officials. In turn, officials feed their personal desires and evil ambitions by using their political privilege. Thus inequality will become a serious social problem and contribute social turmoil if political reform does not coordinate with economic reform.

Third, in a democratic society religion shapes and is shaped by culture, politics, and human rights. Human rights, in the historical perspective, were derived from religious human rights. Human rights and religious rights work together under a democratic system. James E. Wood Jr. has stated it this way: "A foundation for religious human rights is to be found in the special relationship that religious rights have to all other human rights, both individual and social."[86] However, atheism is one of the principles of communism, and one of the ultimate tasks of the CPC is to abolish religion. Religion in China has been flourishing in the reform era, but only as the result of a compromised strategy of the party toward religion in the transition period. Religion is highly restricted by the government and the party. Religious activities are only allowed in temples and churches, not in public squares. In other words, religion was not permitted to shape culture and politics under communist rule. No religion is allowed to cross the line drawn by the party and government; to do so would subject it to harsh punishment. The party appears strong when it suppresses religions by force, but it is actually showing its weakness because a solid democratic society strengthens itself by supporting religious freedom.

In theory, under the Constitution of the People's Republic of China, the Chinese people fully enjoy all fundamental rights. There are four versions, the constitutions of 1954, 1975, 1978, and 1982. Although the most recent version, the Constitution of 1982, added the "Four Cardinal Principles" to strengthen the party powers, it clearly lists citizens' fundamental rights and duties from Article 22 through Article 56. According to the Constitution, all citizens of China are equal before the law and fully enjoy freedom of speech, press, assembly, association, procession, and demonstration. However, there is a wide gap between the law and the implementation of the law. In practice, China "emphasizes the social and economic aspects of human rights," and views "political rights and equality" as "bourgeois rights."[87] In contrast with the Mao regime, the post-Mao government gradually improved the human rights situation. In 1979, China began to attend meetings of the UN Human Rights Commission as an observer, and it became a member of the commission in 1982. In 1997, Beijing signed the UN Covenant on Economic, Social and Cultural Rights and hosted the UN Working Group on Arbitrary Detention.[88] Under international pressure, the government released some political prisoners and lifted some restrictions on the practice of human rights. According to the U.S. State Department's *2000 Country Reports on Human Rights Practices*,[89] there are still many serious human rights problems in

China, especially in political, religious, and ideological areas. In the fifty plus years under the Communist regime, there have been three massive persecutions: the Cultural Revolution in the Mao era, the Tiananmen Square Incident in the Deng era, and the anti–Falun Gong campaign in the Jiang regime. Some Westerners expect China to improve its stand on human rights continuously before the Beijing Olympic Games in 2008. However, so far there is no significant sign that China has changed its stand. All that has changed is its strategies toward human rights. The problem of human rights in China is a structural problem—the one-party system. China cannot fundamentally improve its human rights situation without eliminating the one-party system.

CONCLUSION

Since the early 1980s, China's economic growth has been the fastest in the world. In contrast, Chinese political reform is a very slow process. All measures of Chinese political reform are taken within the framework of the Communist Party of China. All achievements of political reform have not undermined the foundation of party power. Substantial political reform in China is needed to reform the party itself, that is, the one-party system. Jiang made it very clear that China did not need a multi-party system when he was interviewed by the Columbia Broadcasting System in September 2000.[90] The party will firmly uphold the one-party system as long as the party is in power. It is a naïve dream to fundamentally reform the Chinese political system under the leadership of the CPC. Thus two interrelated questions have been raised: Can China continue its economic reform and economic growth without political reform? And, will China move automatically toward democratization if it fulfills its economic goals and becomes a developed country? Obviously, the answer to both questions is no. Political reform in present-day China has become an urgent task, but it is a very difficult task, and it takes time. Since political reform is a more profound revolution than economic reform, it cannot be completed without social and political repercussions.

The goal of political reform in China should be to realize democratization. The fundamental obstacle to an acceptance of democratic principles in China is not, as Chinese officials have said, that China has a low level of economic development, that a large percentage of the Chinese people have a low level of education and do not know how to practice human rights, that China has no democratic tradition, or that the Chinese people today prefer political stability over improved living standards. Undoubtedly, all these problems, plus a low level of socioeconomic development, a weak civil society and legal tradition, the lack of independent opposition parties/groups, and the lack of a significant middle class and bourgeoisie, are obstacles to China's democratization. But what is the major obstacle to democratization in China? Twenty years of reform clearly show that the CPC is the ultimate obstacle to the process of democratization. It is very clear that the party not only remains in power but also resists accepting democratic principles. It would be too optimistic to believe that "if China continues its rapid pace of economic growth, the time will soon come when the role of the Communist Party will be over."[91] The concept that the party's era has ended is misleading. On the contrary, the party has never stopped political campaigns to resist democracy since the reform movement began. In the Deng era, the party launched the campaign pronouncing the Four Cardinal Principles in 1979, the campaign against bourgeois liberalization in 1981, and the campaign against spiritual pollution in 1983, and it suppressed the student movement in 1989. After Deng died, Jiang campaigned for a large-scale political movement against religious organizations, arrested many political dissidents, and banned democratic organizations from time to time. At present, no evidence indicates that the party will surrender its power or change its nature in the foreseeable future. Therefore, remaking China's public philosophy has become an urgent task in promoting the reform movement for democratization.

NOTES

1. James A. Dorn, ed., *China in the New Millennium* (Washington, D.C.: CATO Institute, 1998), p. 1.
2. Susan L. Shirk, "The Chinese Political System and the Political Strategy of Economic Reform," in *Bureaucracy, Politics and Decision Making in Post-Mao China,* eds. Kenneth G. Lieberthal and David M. Lampton (Berkeley: University of California Press, 1992), p. 59.
3. Dorn, *China in the New Millennium,* p. 5.
4. X. L. Ding, *The Decline of Communism in China: Legitimacy Crisis, 1977–1989* (New York: Cambridge University Press, 1994), p. 3.
5. Flemming Christiansen and Shirin M. Rai, *Chinese Politics and Society: An Introduction* (New York: Harvester Wheatsheaf, 1996), p. 315.
6. Bruce J. Dickson, "China's Democratization and the Taiwan Experience," *Asian Survey* 38 (April 1998), p. 350.
7. Lance L. P. Gore, "The Communist Legacy in Post-Mao Economic Growth," *China Journal* 41 (January 1999), p. 54.
8. Edward H. Crane, "Civil Society versus Political Society: China at a Crossroads," in *China in the New Millennium,* p. 237.
9. Zhong Yang, Jie Chen, and John Scheb, "Mass Political Culture in Beijing: Findings from Two Public Opinion Surveys," *Asian Survey* 38 (August 1998), p. 774.
10. Quoted in John Pomfret, "Corruption Charges Rock China's Leaders," *Washington Post,* January 10, 2002, p. A15.
11. Kenneth Lieberthal, *Governing China: From Revolution through Reform* (New York: W.W. Norton & Company, 1995), p. 181.

12. Shiping Zheng, *Party vs. State in Post-1949 China: The Institutional Dilemma* (New York: Cambridge University Press, 1998), p. 17.

13. Ibid., p. 9.

14. Christiansen and Rai, *Chinese Politics and Society,* p. 2.

15. Tai-Chun Kuo and Ramon H. Myers, *Understanding Communist China: Communist China Studies in the United States and the Republic of China, 1949–1978* (Stanford, Calif.: Hoover Institution Press, 1986), p. 17; Christiansen and Rai, *Chinese Politics and Society,* p. 2.

16. Zheng, *Party vs. State in Post-1949 China,* p. 17.

17. Ibid., p. 20.

18. Shirk, "The Chinese Political System and the Political Strategy of Economic Reform," p. 65.

19. Lieberthal, *Governing China,* pp. 192–208.

20. Bureau of Democracy, Human Rights, and Labor, U.S. Department of State, *1999 Country Reports on Human Rights Practices,* released 25 February 2000; available on-line at http//www.state.gov/www/global/human_rights/1999_hrp_report/china.html.

21. Zheng has said, "Once the paramount leader is gone, the revolutionary ideology becomes bankrupt, and the organizational discipline erodes, the party as we know it is over." See Zheng, *Party vs. State in Post-1949 China,* p. 263.

22. Ibid., p. 15.

23. Andrew J. Nathan, *Chinese Democracy* (New York: Knopf, 1985), p. 225.

24. Samuel P. Huntington, *The Third Wave: Democratization in the Late Twentieth Century.* (Norman: University of Oklahoma Press, 1991), p. 5.

25. Ibid.

26. Francis Fukuyama, *The End of History and the Last Man* (New York: Maxwell Macmillan International, 1992), p. 34.

27. Ibid.

28. Mingchien Joshua, *Modern Democracy in China* (Shanghai, China: Commercial Press, 1923), p. 1.

29. Ibid., pp. 7–12.

30. See Julia C. Strauss, *Strong Institutions in Weak Polities: State Building in Republican China* (Oxford, England: Clarendon Press, 1998).

31. Suzanne Ogden, *China's Unresolved Issues: Politics, Development, and Culture* (Englewood Cliffs, N.J.: Prentice Hall, 1995).

32. Shiping Hua, *Scientism and Humanism: Two Cultures in Post-Mao China* (Albany, N.Y.: State University of New York Press, 1995), p. 148.

33. Susan L. Shirk, *The Political Logic of Economic Reform in China* (Berkeley: University of California Press, 1993), p. 333.

34. Ibid., p. 334.

35. Yang, Chen, and Scheb, "Mass Political Culture in Beijing," p. 766.

36. See Christopher Marsh, *Making Russian Democracy Work: Social Capital, Economic Development, and Democratization* (Lewiston, N.Y.: Edwin Mellen Press, 2000), p. 14.

37. Tianjian Shi, *Political Participation in Beijing* (Cambridge, Mass.: Harvard University Press, 1997), pp. 8–22.

38. Bureau of Democracy, Human Rights, and Labor, U.S. Department of State, *1999 Country Reports on Human Rights Practices.*

39. Martin Fackler, "China Issues Internet Controls," *Washington Post*, January 18, 2002.

40. Christopher Marsh and Laura Whalen, "The Internet, E-social Capital, and Democratization in China," *American Journal of Chinese Studies* 8 (April 2000).

41. Shi, *Political Participation in Beijing*, pp. 8–27.

42. Nathan, *Chinese Democracy*, p. 227.

43. Shi, *Political Participation in Beijing*, p. 5.

44. Peter Ferdinand, "Social Change and the Chinese Communist Party: Domestic Problems of Rule," *Journal of International Affairs* 49 (Winter 1996), pp. 478–92.

45. Ju Yanan, *Understanding China: Center Stage of the Fourth Power* (Albany: State University of New York Press, 1996), p. 49.

46. Lieberthal, *Governing China*, p. 181.

47. Lowell Dittmer and Lu Xiaobo, "Personal Politics in the Chinese 'Danwei' under Reform," *Asian Survey* 36 (March 1996), pp. 246–67.

48. Shi, *Political Participation in Beijing*, pp. 1–4.

49. Kevin J. O'Brien, *Reform without Liberalization: China's National People's Congress and the Politics of Institutional Change* (New York: Cambridge University Press, 1990), p. 126.

50. Bureau of Democracy, Human Rights, and Labor, U.S. Department of State, *1999 Country Reports on Human Rights Practices.*

51. Murray Scot Tanner, *The Politics of Lawmaking in Post-Mao China: Institutions, Processes, and Democratic Prospects* (Oxford, England: Oxford University Press, 1998), p. 209.

52. Ibid., p. 79.

53. Ibid.

54. O'Brien, *Reform without Liberalization*, p. 177.

55. Ibid.

56. Suzanne Ogden, *China's Unresolved Issues: Politics, Development, and Culture* (Englewood Cliffs, N.J.: Prentice Hall, 1995), p. 202.

57. Bureau of Democracy, Human Rights, and Labor, U.S. Department of State, *1999 Country Reports on Human Rights Practices.*

58. Victor C. Falkenheim, ed., *Chinese Politics from Mao to Deng* (New York: Paragon House, 1989), p. 9; Ogden, *China's Unresolved Issues*, p. 194.

59. Ibid.

60. Stanley Lubman, "Introduction: The Future of Chinese Law," *China Quarterly* 138 (March 1995), p. 16.

61. Arthur Lewis Rosenbaum, *State and Society in China: The Consequences of Reform* (Boulder, Colo.: Westview Press, 1992), p. 9.

62. Heath B. Chamberlain, "Civil Society with Chinese Characteristics?" *China Journal* 39 (January 1998), p. 69.

63. Gordon White, Jude Howell, and Shang Xiaoyuan, *In Search of Civil Society: Market Reform and Social Change in Contemporary China* (Oxford, England: Clarendon Press, 1996), p. 4.

64. Edward X. Gu, "Cultural Intellectuals and the Politics of the Cultural Public Space in Communist China (1979–1989): A Case Study of Three Intellectual Groups," *Journal of Asian Studies* 58, no. 2 (May 1999), p. 392.

65. Alan P. L. Liu, *Mass Politics in the People's Republic: State and Society in Contemporary China* (Boulder, Colo.: Westview Press, 1996), p. 17.

66. Barrett L. McCormick, *Political Reform in Post-Mao China: Democracy and Bureaucracy in a Leninist State* (Berkeley: University of California Press, 1990), pp. 7–8.
67. White, Howell, and Shang, *In Search of Civil Society*, pp. 209–11.
68. Ibid., p. 214.
69. Ibid., p. 16.
70. See, for example, Rosenbaum, *State and Society in China*, p. 11.
71. McCormick, *Political Reform in Post-Mao China*, p. 201.
72. Chamberlain, "Civil Society with Chinese Characteristics?," p. 70.
73. Quoted in A. I. Melden, ed., *Human Rights* (Belmont, Calif.: Wadsworth Publishing Company, 1970), p. 145.
74. Joseph Wronka, *Human Rights and Social Policy in the 21st Century* (New York: University Press of America, 1992), p. xxi.
75. Quoted in ibid., p. xxii.
76. Ibid.
77. Ming Wang, "Chinese Opinion on Human Rights," *Orbis* 42 (Summer 1998), pp. 361–75.
78. Andrew J. Nathan and Robert S. Ross, *The Great Wall and the Empty Fortress: China's Search for Security* (New York: W.W. Norton & Company, 1998), p. 192.
79. Wang, "Chinese Opinion on Human Rights," pp. 361–75.
80. *The Universal Declaration of Human Rights*, article 3.
81. Garret Ward Sheldon, *The Political Philosophy of Thomas Jefferson* (Baltimore, Md.: Johns Hopkins University Press, 1991), p. 147.
82. R. Randle Edwards, Louis Henkin, and Andrew J. Nathan, "The Human Rights Idea in Contemporary China: A Comparative Perspective," in *Human Rights in Contemporary China*, ed. R. Randle Edwards (New York: Columbia University Press, 1986), p. 21.
83. Ann Kent, "Waiting for Rights: China's Human Rights and China's Constitutions, 1949–1989," *Human Rights Quarterly* 13 (1991), p. 174.
84. Ellis Sandoz, *A Government of Laws* (Baton Rouge: Louisiana State University Press, 1990), p. 13.
85. Andrew J. Nathan, "Sources of Chinese Rights Thinking," in *Human Rights in Contemporary China*, pp. 130–31.
86. James E. Wood Jr., *Church-State Relations in the Modern World* (Waco, Texas: J.M. Dawson Institute of Church-State Studies, 1998), p. 41.
87. Kent, "Waiting for Rights," p. 174.
88. Bureau of Democracy, Human Rights, and Labor, U.S. Department of State, *China: Country Report on Human Rights Practices for 1997*, released 30 January 1998.
89. Bureau of Democracy, Human Rights, and Labor, U.S. Department of State, *2000 Country Reports on Human Rights Practices*, released 23 February 2001; available on-line at http://www.state.gov/g/drl/rls.hrrpt/2000eap/index.cf?docid + 684.
90. *Dallas Chinese News*, September 15, 2000, p. E9.
91. C. H. Kwan, "The Role of the Chinese Communist Party Is Coming to an End," *Voice*, July 2000, p. 2.

CHAPTER 6

A Rapier: The Functions of Religion in China's Democratization

Political and religious institutions are the two main supporters of society. The relationship between religion and politics is the prism of social evolution. Jacques Gernet has referred to these two aspects as the "political sovereign" and the "doctrinal sovereign."[1] Both nation and religion are universal categories in Western modernity and in the development of Western expansion.[2] Therefore, religion and politics are inseparable and inevitably must work together. It is impossible to separate nation from religion when discussing modern democracy.[3] But can this principle be applied to China? There is no doubt that in democratic societies religion has played a key role in developing a market economy, advocating civil rights, maintaining social order, promoting public good, and defending the democratic system. Many religious activists, Chinese political dissidents, and Western scholars insist that Chinese religions can and should play a significant role in promoting China's democratization within the political system of the Communist Party of China (CPC). However, the party has not stopped persecuting Chinese religions since China began the reform movement in 1978. The party has mobilized its largest campaign against religious organizations, beginning in 1998. Although the conflict between some Chinese religious organizations and the government is growing in intensity, the government continues to persecute religious organizations. Therefore, some questions are raised here: Can Chinese religions play a key role without changes to the political system if religious organizations become involved in politics? Is it a good strategy for Chinese religious organizations to act alone to promote human rights and the democratic movement? How can Chinese religions play a significant role in the transition from the communist system to a democratic one? Can Chinese religion be used by the party? What are the historical tasks of Chinese religion in the twenty-first century?

THE CONNECTIONS BETWEEN RELIGION AND DEMOCRATIZATION

The connection between religion and democratization must be addressed before we can answer any of these questions. Religion at its inception had a political dimension and deeply influenced the evolution of society. Christianity at its beginning was regarded as an alien force, and Christians were persecuted by the Roman government. Even before the advent of Christianity, Rome realized that religion was inalienable from human life, which led the government to make political use of religion. After the Roman emperor Constantine I adopted the Christian faith and suspended the persecution of Christians in 313, he too made political use of religion. During the period from Saint Augustine to the Protestant Reformation, the belief was that "God is lord of the earthly city as well as the heavenly one."[4] Religion in most Western countries controlled the secular powers, and in social life theocratic ideas were popular and accepted as politically valid. The Middle Ages in Europe witnessed the unification of the realms of state and church, but the union was sometimes ugly in its results, leading, for example, to inquisitions, holy wars, witch hunts, and political and ecclesiastical corruption. One principle of the Reformation was that everyone has an equal right to pursue and find truth. When Martin Luther led a protest movement by posting ninety-five theses on a church door at Wittenberg on October 31, 1517, he opened a widespread attack on the doctrines and authority of the Roman Catholic Church. The Reformation resulted in the rise of individual rights and religious freedom and paved the way toward democracy.[5] In this way, as Jacques Gernet has noted, Christianity "has been associated with modernity."[6]

The Renaissance shifted the emphasis from divinity to humanity and upheld human dignity and worth. Reason became the fundamental criterion by which to judge everything in the Age of Reason. Thomas Hobbes and John Locke inherited the tradition of the Roman republic. Hobbes's social theory, however, left little room for God; and Locke's social contract theory was not based on divine justice, but on self-interest.[7] However, the people soon realized that human beings themselves were not capable of solving social problems, and that reason, science, and humanity were not the full preconditions for the establishment of a good social order. Whether these propositions are truth or myth is not the point; as the great theologian Thomas Aquinas pointed out, "If God did not exist, it would be necessary to create Him."[8]

The Pilgrims came to America seeking religious freedom. In this sense, the United States is the product of a search for religious freedom. Religious belief was the foundation of the new nation and the cornerstone of its social order. One reason the United States became such a peaceful and stable country is that it has learned to allow religion and democracy to work together. Ralph H. Gabriel has described this U.S. phenomenon in this way: American democratic principles include three democratic faiths. The primary doctrine of democratic faith is to affirm that a law exists that men did not make. The law includes the idea of natural rights and religious moral codes that are expressed in the Bible. The law forms the principle of individual life and establishes the foundation of the social order.[9] The second doctrine of democratic faith is "the free and responsible individual."[10] The individual is the center of society and is free to make decisions and choices; to express his or her thoughts; and to exercise freedom of action in the economic sphere,[11] including expressing individualism, owning private property, the "Law of Accumulation of Wealth," and the "Law of Competition."[12] The third doctrine of democratic faith is the mission of the United States. This doctrine asserts the conviction of the ultimate triumph of Christianity and democracy and provides for U.S. democracy the philosophy of unity.[13] Gabriel has highlighted the important role of religion, the inseparable relationship between religion and politics, and the great task of Christian mission. His revelations could be applied to the process of democratization in all countries around the world.

When religion is used for political purpose, it is called civil religion. Civil religion is one of the symbols of the fact that religion and democracy work together in the United States. The history of civil religion can be traced back as early as Niccolò Machiavelli (1469–1527), Hobbes (1588–1679), and Jean-Jacques Rousseau (1712–1778). American civil religion comes primarily from the Enlightenment and from Puritan thought. Civil religion has been part of American social and political life since the founding of the United States. Most U.S. presidents have made great efforts to promote civil religion. Usually, the inaugural address of U.S. presidents is an expression of the nation's civil religion. George Washington set the first example, so he is the founder of American civil religion as well as the founding father of the United States. After the United States Constitution was ratified in 1789, Thomas Jefferson was aware that it lacked any statement of divine meaning for the life of the American people. Therefore, Jefferson called for a second revolution that is "inward and spiritual."[14] Abraham Lincoln spoke of his own political religion to liberate Blacks from slavery. Dwight D. Eisenhower "consciously embarked on a crusade against 'atheistic communism' " and "summoned religious symbols to support his peacetime presidency." Richard M. Nixon used "civil religion and assigned to the people the attributes that once belonged to God, and he stood in the great tradition of civil religionists."[15] Ronald

Reagan "exalted civil religion to its highest point in American history."[16] George H. W. Bush used civil religion as a tool to defend the Persian Gulf War. Religion has had a pervasive influence on American society and has become the way of American life. When Alexis de Tocqueville traveled to the United States in the early nineteenth century, he observed that "the religious atmosphere of the country was the first thing that struck me on my arrival."[17] Derek H. Davis has put it this way: "Americans are a religious people."[18] Today, at the cultural level, civil religion as an American political ideology constitutes American political identity.[19] At the political level, religion as an institution engages in the political arena[20] and ensures freedom, liberty, and individual rights.[21]

According to Tocqueville, communist societies may govern without faith, but democratic societies cannot.[22] As a matter of fact, the Communist government in China also needs civil religion for political purposes. Maoism, to be sure, played the role of civil religion in China at least until Mao Zedong's death, and probably beyond it! Especially in the period of the Cultural Revolution, the former familial civil religion was replaced by Maoism, and the entire nation worshipped Mao—as a living god. Because of the role of religion in the political arena, the Chinese government tries to limit religious influence in Chinese society. In 1990, Cheng Linshu published an article in a Chinese official journal in which he publicly acknowledged that religion—as ideology, ethical code, religious faith, and cultural tradition—could be used to maintain and strengthen the socialist order and system.[23] In order to promote communist civil religion, on the one hand, the government suppressed Chinese religions. Even some Chinese official scholars have noted that it is unfortunate that socialist China has sought no use of religion in recent times.[24] On the other hand, in the post-Mao era, Deng Xiaoping and Jiang Zemin called for the Chinese people to read their books and unite all forces around the CPC they headed.

Religion is a rapier that can serve different political systems. The nature of religious functions is determined by the nature of the political system. Religious pluralism has served democratic principles in democratic societies. What is the role of religion in a democracy? First, the divine order tends to regulate the secular order. Democratic societies, generally, are based on the divine order. Nevertheless, religion and politics are two sides of the same coin. The nature of civil religion depends heavily upon the nature of the political system. As James David Fairbanks has noted, "Civil religion can serve as an important democratic constraint because of its emphasis on divinely bestowed rights and the nation's accountability to a higher power."[25] Civil religion can also threaten democratic values and serve as the tool of presidential tyranny in dictatorial countries. In world history, many military heroes became dictators and established dictatorships after they came to power, for example, Napoléon Bonaparte, Adolf Hitler, Joseph Stalin, Jiang Jieshi, and Mao. Washington was an exception, following what he saw as God's will in helping to create a democratic system. Civil religion under the two systems serves different functions. In China, the secular order is not regulated by the divine order. The Chinese communist government declares that Communist China is an atheist country that is a million times more democratic than capitalist societies.

Second, in democratic societies, the principle of the separation of church and state makes it possible for religion to become an independent force without government interference. The principle of freedom of religion ensures religious pluralism, which is a necessary precondition to guarantee individual rights and to strengthen a democratic system. As Davis notes, "From the time of the earliest European settlements in the sixteenth century, America's face has been one of religious diversity."[26] Four hundred years of American history have shown that religious pluralism does not threaten Christian America but, rather, expands the "possibilities of truth."[27] In the process of democratization, religion unites a nation (less formally than informally) under the divine order by helping the people to understand their own experience as it relates to a universal ultimate truth. Unlike the governments of democratic societies, the communist government in China is antireligious by nature. The Communists "think that every person is born with a bundle of anti-social attitudes within himself and seeks the redemption by themselves [the Communists] through violent revolution."[28] Under law, religion is an independent force separate from government, but in practice, the government controls religions tightly.

Finally, religion helps people to nurture their spiritual life. For many people, the purpose of human life is to "attain salvation by knowing God and obeying His will as revealed in Scripture."[29] The decline of a nation usually results from moral corruption along with economic crisis. In democratic societies, a common moral good must be based upon a common faith. Robert N. Bellah has pointed out that "Moral and religious understandings produce both a basic cultural legitimation and a standard of judgment for a society."[30] At this point, religion also helps the people reshape social structures at different levels. This function of civil religion was clearly seen in the civil rights movement of the 1960s in the United States and the reform movements of the 1980s and 1990s in Eastern European countries and the Soviet Union. However, religions in Communist China are required to serve the socialist construct and the central task of the party. Otherwise, religion is subject to persecution.

Western countries embrace many religions generally, but Christianity in particular. Although Christianity came to China only a century ago, the Chinese people have realized that Christianity is good for China's modernization. Some scholars have envisaged that Christianity as a system of faith, values, thinking, and culture has a manifold and pervasive influence in the process of world civilization and has significance for China's modernization in many aspects,[31] especially in remaking China's public philosophy. The Christian concept of sin helps Chinese self-understanding from a new perspective. The concepts of salvation and transcendence inspire the Chinese people more toward democracy. The Christian concept of ecumenism is important for the Chinese people as they seek to reconstruct the Chinese cultural system.[32] However, God reveals himself in different forms in different countries. China's modernization does not simply mean its Westernization or Christianization. Therefore, China should not move through the transition toward democracy by overthrowing everything associated with Chinese traditional culture.[33]

RELIGIOUS TRADITION IN CHINA

There has been a misunderstanding for a long time in Western societies, that China is not a religious country and that the Chinese people are not a religious people. Beginning about 2,500 years ago, Buddhism, Christianity, and Islam emerged, gradually becoming the three dominant world religions. The three religions dominate the three main cultural circles of the world. Christianity dominates the European cultural circle, which began with ancient Greece and Rome; Islam dominates the Arab cultural circle, which began with ancient Egypt and Babylon; and Buddhism dominates the Asian cultural circle, which began with India. Beginning with the Han dynasty, the three religions—one after the other—began their difficult journeys in China and were confronted with traditional Chinese culture. However, in the past 2,000 years, no one foreign religion has been able to conquer Chinese culture and become the dominant religion. Confucianism, as the mainstream of culture as well as religion, dominated China before 1919. The failure of the three world religions to dominate Chinese culture does not mean that there is no room for religion to develop on Chinese soil. Rather, different countries nurture different religions in a diverse world. The three major religions may someday assume a greater presence in China, but at present Chinese indigenous religions, as the dominant religions in China, continue to serve social and political functions.

China's religious heritage is made up of three religious traditions—Confucianism, Daoism, and Buddhism, the so-called *San Jiao*,[34] which together depict the religiousness of the Chinese people.[35] It is impossible to understand Chinese traditional culture and contemporary China without comprehending the three Chinese traditional religions. Li Shiqian, a famous Chinese scholar, described the three religions in this way 1,500 years ago: "Buddhism is the sun, Daoism the moon, and Confucianism the five planets."[36] However, some scholars do not see the three Chinese traditional religions as religions but as humanism and philosophy. Derk Bodde, for instance, states that it is better to understand *san jiao* as "three teachings" rather than "three religions." China is without any real linguistic equivalent for the word *religion*. According to Bodde, the Chinese word for religion is *jao,* which means "teaching," or "system of teaching." "Religion, in Western terms, means of course Christianity. When the Chinese use this term, they make no distinction between the theistic religions and purely moral teachings."[37] It is necessary to clarify some points in order to understand Chinese religion and its relationship to politics.

Etymologically, there are different meanings in Chinese for the terms *religion* and *teaching*. The word *religion* did not have an equivalent term in China until the late nineteenth century.[38] Based on the word's basic meaning in the West, the Chinese created the word *zong-jiao* for the term *religion*. *Zong* refers to clan, tribe, and ancestors; *jiao* refers to teaching. When the Chinese people put the words *zong* and *jiao* together for the equivalent of "religion," they were only reinforcing the Chinese understanding of the role of patriarchal religion. The term *teaching* for most Chinese means "to pass on knowledge," for example, of history, art, science, and technology. The term *religion* in any contemporary Chinese dictionary means "belief in god," "holy spirit," "retribution for sin," and "a hope of heaven." Obviously, the term *religion* has the same basic meaning in China as it does in Western countries. This explains why religion is only tolerated by the party/state, but teaching is encouraged.

Practically speaking, most of the Chinese people have practiced one of the religions of the *San Jiao*. According to official reports, there are more than 100 million religious believers in China, but "most profess Eastern faiths."[39] To ignore the three religions is to disregard the fact that the Chinese people have been religious practitioners. If the three religions are treated as the three teachings, it is exactly what the party and the Chinese government want.

Theoretically, the three Chinese religions have served religious aims. Some scholars deny that Confucianism is a religion, because Confucius did not perform miracles and refused to discuss death and the existence of gods. Confucianism does not have religious texts, systematic rituals, or formal organizations, but Confucius was very religious. When Confucius was a boy, he was fond of religious matters and performed religious ceremonies. The *Analects* records his prayers, fasting, and regular attendance at worship services. Confucius discussed God using the terms *shang-di* and *tian* (heaven). It is no wonder that Jingpan Chen affirms that Confucius was a "true heir of [the] best religious heritage." He concludes that Confucius was "not a teacher of religion, but a religious teacher."[40] According to Julia Ching, in China the term *state religion* always refers to Confucianism. Confucianism has served both secular and religious functions throughout history, but today it seems to be more a philosophy than a religion.[41]

In comparison with Confucianism, Daoism and Buddhism have served far greater religious functions in Chinese history. Daoism is a salvation religion that guides its believers beyond this transitory life to a happy eternity. It has a clearly enunciated belief in a hierarchy of gods, associates human weakness and sickness with sin, tries to heal such ills with the confession of sin and forgiveness, and bridges the gap between human beings and divine beings through the ritual practices of prayer and penance. Buddhism came to China and began its missionary venture in the first century A.D. Buddhism preaches karma, the Four Noble Truths, and the Eightfold Noble Paths and affirms a spiritual dimension through belief in meditation and transcendence that lie outside of time and history. Robert H. F. Thurman calls this process the "inner revolution" toward life, liberty, and the pursuit of real happiness.[42] Few scholars deny that Buddhism is "one of the world's three major universal religions, along with Christianity and Islam."[43] According to Chinese official reports, by 1997, there were 25,000 Daoist priests, 1,500 Daoist temples, 13,000 Buddhist temples, and 200,000 monks and nuns in China.[44] Among them are 120,000 lamas and nuns, more than 1,700 living Buddhas, 3,000 temples of Tibetan Buddhism, nearly 10,000 Bhiksu and senior monks, and more than 1,600 temples of Pali Buddhism.

Since the Han dynasty, the three Chinese traditional religions have assimilated aspects of one another and developed peacefully together. The development of the three religions constitutes the main picture of Chinese culture and contributes significantly to Chinese history. Some scholars point out that the three religions share one body and merge into one.[45] At the popular level, there are no divisions or mutually exclusive groups. Hence, it is best to treat Chinese religion as a unified system, because most believers do not sign an oath of affiliation with a particular religion. Many believers hold several religious faiths at the same time. But each of the three religions has its own fixed system of thought at the intellectual level, so their mutual exclusivity exists at this level. For more than 2,000 years, Buddhism has been an integral part of the Chinese culture. It is not so much that Buddhism conquered Chinese culture, but, rather, that Buddhism gradually was assimilated into Chinese culture.

CONFUCIANISM AS THE DOMINANT CHINESE RELIGION

In the development of the three traditional Chinese religions, although Daoism and Buddhism challenged Confucianism, Confucianism remained the main Chinese religious tradition from the Han dynasty through the period of premodern China. Confucianism not only occupied a dominant institutional and spiritual position in China but also established roots in Korea, Japan, and Vietnam as well as in other countries.[46] There is no doubt that Confucianism helped Chinese culture to survive and united the Chinese nation.[47] The effort to describe the religious dimension of Confucianism has been made by many scholars, including Hans Kung, Julia Ching, Chung-ying Cheng, William Theodore De Bary, Rodney L. Taylor, Tu Wei-ming, and Mary Evelyn Tucker. Kung, a Swiss theologian, speaks of world religions as three religious rivers. The first river is of Semitic origin with a prophetic character; the second river is of Indian origin with a mystical character; and the third river originated in China and bears a philosophical character. According to Kung and Ching, the central figure in Chinese traditional religion is "neither the prophet nor the mystic, but rather [the] sage: this is religion of wisdom."[48] Sagehood is the goal of Confucian religion. The central concept of the Confucian religion is "*tian*," or "heaven," in Western thought. *Tian* is at the center of the Confucian religious tradition and functions as an absolute. Taylor points out that the process of achieving sagehood is the movement of the individual toward *tian*—the absolute or ultimate.[49] Confucianism as a religion is a very broad system. In Western societies, the three models of cultural tradition—Graeco-Roman humanity, Christian theology, and natural science—constitute Western culture and dominate Western history. In contrast with Christianity, Confucianism has been more successful in combining the three aspects, that is, transcendence, humanity, and nature. Confucianism emphasizes humanity and spirituality without denigrating the aspect of transcendence.[50]

Tucker embraces the characteristics of Confucian religion by offering a new definition of religion and concludes that Confucianism provides a profound understanding of many religious questions to the Chinese people.[51] According to Tucker, religion occurs when human beings recognize "the limitations of phenomenal reality," and "undertake specific practices to effect self-transformation within a cosmological context."[52] Confucian tradition as religion is not separate from social, ethical, and political concerns. Confucianism is "concerned with encouraging moral and spiritual cultivation of the individual within a cosmological context."[53] Tu agrees that the religious dimension merged into Confucius's social and political concerns and was located in ultimate self-transformation, which involves identifying human beings within heaven, earth, and myriad things; realizing the limitation of the human being; recognizing self-transformation through practicing self-cultivation in moral behavior and spiritual life; and pursuing the union between heaven, earth, and all things.[54] Confucian religion pervades the whole of Chinese society. There is no clear distinction between Confucianism as a religion and Confucianism as a culture. The character of religious expression in China is, according to Laurence G. Thompson, "above all a manifestation of the Chinese culture." Therefore, Thompson uses the word *religion* in the singular to describe Chinese religion.[55]

The development of Confucianism went through three epochs. The period from the Han dynasty to the Tang dynasty could be considered the first epoch, characterized as traditional Confucianism. During this period, Confucianism became a dominant religion and began to expand its influence to neighboring countries. Beginning with the Song dynasty, Confucianism entered into the second epoch, characterized as neo-Confucianism (in Chinese, *lixue*). Neo-Confucianism assimilated Buddhist cosmology and Daoist ethical elements such as thrift, honesty, and effort. Confucianism became more vigorous in China and became an influential cultural phenomenon in some other Asian countries. However, Confucianism attracted little attention in Western countries during this period. After the people experienced Nazism in World War II, the inauguration of democratic systems spread over many countries, such as West Germany, Italy, Austria, Japan, and Korea.[56] However, since the 1960s, Western countries have experienced a "great disruption," including family breakdown, rising crime, and loss of trust.[57] Western liberalism, conservatism, and the third way tried to solve the crisis, but without success. With the development of Western material civilization, the conflicts between cultures have become increasingly intensive. Looking across the Pacific Ocean, Western countries found that Confucianism in some Asian countries had become a primary means to shape economic, political, and social structures. Those countries dominated by Confucianism appeared socially peaceful and harmonious. Western countries thus began to pay attention to the role of Confucianism, and Confucianism entered into its third epoch. Confucianism's influence now covers not only Asian countries but Western countries, too.

The trend of Confucianism in the third epoch reflects *zhong yong*—the "doctrine of the mean." According to Confucianism, *zhong yong* is a universal path that requires that people not go to extremes. The central way, or centrality, is the foundation of the world; harmony among human beings and nature and heaven is a universal path. It is, in theory and practice, different from liberal and biblical traditions as well as Hegelian contradiction theory. According to John N. Jonsson, professor of world religions at Baylor University, the doctrine of the mean is the resolution of social, cultural, and religious conflicts.[58] Western dialectical thinking views this resolution as the end product, but the doctrine of the mean views it as integral to the process itself. For example, the "One Country, Two Systems" policy relationship of Hong Kong and Beijing was a triumph of the doctrine of the mean. China's gradual approach, that is, following a central path for reform, also reflects the doctrine of the mean and enables China to receive a better result while avoiding the cost of a reform movement. Tu, in *Centrality and Commonality: An Essay on Confucian Religiousness*, recognizes the transcendental values of the doctrine of the mean and points out that the Confucian tradition has made profound contributions not only to China but also to world civilization in the twenty-first century. The doctrine of the mean is also a solution for Western countries seeking to adjust the relationship between the individual and the community and between the individual and the state. In this sense, the doctrine of the mean is the best teaching for the people in the practice of democracy, because democracy itself is a compromise between the state and the individual and between the state and civil society. At present, the doctrine of the mean can at least broaden the perspectives of decision makers and help them find alternative ways to fundamentally solve the contemporary conflicts between cultures. Like all other political systems, the democratic system is not perfect. The democratic system emphasizes rule by law; Confucianism emphasizes rule by virtue. It is better for domestic and international peace if modern democracy and Confucianism work together. However, Confucianism is a very complex system of thought. The use of Confucianism to promote democracy does not necessarily mean that Confucianism itself is a system of democratic thought. On the contrary, Confucianism makes little reference to the law or legal systems, including the judiciary. It makes no provision for a constitution and legislation; provides no room for civil society; has little interest in nationality; denies that everyone is born equal; and views the common people as important only for their labor, taxes, services, liturgy, and military service.[59] All these deficiencies in Confucianism must be reshaped in order for democratization to move forward in China.

CHINESE RELIGIONS AND CHRISTIANITY TOGETHER SERVE DEMOCRATIZATION

To serve democratization in China, different religions should coexist peacefully and coordinate harmoniously. Otherwise, the conflicts between religions would postpone the process of democratization, and even destroy democracy. Some Western scholars view Western Christendom as incompatible with the Confucian tradition, and some Chinese people treat Christianity as a foreign religion that does not fit Chinese traditional culture. There are profound historical roots for both viewpoints. Christian missionary activity in China began in the seventh century. The Nestorian Christian, Alopen, the first Christian missionary to China, arrived in Xian in 635. The Tang dynasty was the most glorious dynasty in Chinese history, and its emperors were relatively open-minded. So Alopen received an honor from the Chinese emperor Tang Tai Zong and was allowed to build Nestorian monasteries. The Nestorian monument was erected outside Xian in 781.[60] The second wave of the Christian mission was the Roman Catholic missionary movement. John Corvino, the first Catholic missionary and a zealous Franciscan monk, arrived in China in 1292 under the Yuan dynasty,[61] but the Catholic mission did not have much influence on China until Matteo Ricci arrived there in the sixteenth century.[62] Robert

Morrison, the first Protestant missionary, entered China in 1807. After the first Opium War, both Catholicism and Protestantism began to develop in China relatively fast. Under the Communist regime, Catholicism developed more slowly than Protestantism because "two unresolved issues—Vatican recognition of Taiwan and the consecration of bishops—continued to complicate the issues facing the church."[63] Sino-Vatican relations were broken off in 1957. By 1997, there were 4 million Catholics, 4,600 Catholic churches, 4,000 priests and missionary workers, 10 million Protestants, 12,000 Protestant churches, 25,000 meeting places, and 18,000 pastors and missionary workers throughout China.[64] Due to the fact that in 2001 Pope John Paul II publicly recognized the errors committed by the Catholic Church in China, it is expected that the relationship between the Vatican and China will improve in the future. The Vatican hopes to open some form of dialogue with China. China seems ready to talk, but, according to Chinese officials, with two conditions: first, the Vatican must cut its diplomatic relations with Taiwan, and, second, the Vatican cannot interfere in China's internal affairs on the pretext of religious issues. Therefore, both sides still have a long way to go to get along.

Although Christian missionaries worked in China for centuries, the Western missionaries were not very successful in converting the Chinese people, especially intellectuals. Ralph R. Covell has observed, "Whether Christian messengers attempted to present a Chinese gospel or one uncritically imported from a distant land, the results were virtually the same. The response to the Christian faith in China was always minimal, and the church never constituted more than a fraction of one percent of the national population. The Chinese masses never perceived that the biblical message addressed their deepest needs."[65] As "the Chinese have always been a religious people,"[66] why did the Christian mission experience so much difficulty in China? Theologically, the central Christian doctrines, such as creation, sin, and the Incarnation, contradict Confucianism and traditional Chinese culture. Gernet points out that "the concept of a God of truth, eternal and immutable, the dogma of the Incarnation—all this was more easily accessible to the inheritors of Greek thought than to the Chinese."[67] Politically, the contacts between China and Western Christianity before the nineteenth century were mutually beneficial, but the Christians were supported by gunships and protected by unequal treaties in the nineteenth century. Foreign churches and foreign missionaries enjoyed extraterritorial privileges in China. Some Western missionaries joined the Eight Power Allied Forces against China in 1900, as military officers who took part in the slaughter of Chinese civilians; some participated in the drafting of unequal treaties, including the Sino-British Treaty of Nanking in 1842, the Sino-American Treaty of Wanghea in 1844, and the Sino-American treaties of Tientsin in 1858; and some Western missionaries even called for restoring the Qing dynasty, an inhumane feudal society. Consequently, the Chinese people had little sympathy for Christianity.[68] Some Western missionaries had a tendency to criticize Chinese culture. Early Christian missionaries frequently rejected Chinese civilization and denounced the Chinese people. The first Protestant missionary, Robert Morrison, blamed the Chinese for being "selfish, deceitful and inhuman among themselves."[69] According to Jonsson, scientific dogma and dialectical materialism are also largely responsible for the failure of Western countries to appreciate Confucian thought.[70] Some Western missionaries even understood that destroying the traditional Chinese culture was the first task of the Christian mission in China. The Chinese people—especially the intellectuals—had theoretical difficulty accepting European-centered methodology. Christian ethics also contradict Confucian ethics. According to Confucianism, human beings are not born equal, and males and females should be treated differently.

Because of the influences of the Chinese cultural and religious tradition, foreign missionaries gradually recognized Chinese culture and tradition and founded the Chinese Union in the mid-nineteenth century.[71] At the end of the nineteenth century, the Chinese indigenous movement emerged, which attempted to restore traditional Chinese culture and attack Western culture and Christianity, but it made little progress. For both political and religious reasons, the Boxer Rebellion, an antiforeign uprising, broke out in 1900. The Boxers tried to drive all foreigners out of China by attacking Christian missions, slaughtering Western missionaries and Chinese converts, because they believed that the Westerners were destroying traditional Chinese culture. Seeking a workable solution, the National Conference of Missionaries was held in 1912 to develop indigenous Chinese churches. Influenced by the May Fourth Movement of 1919, the anti-Christian movement became stronger in the 1920s.[72] Under this high pressure, Christian missionaries formally stated in the 1920s that they did not intend to westernize China, and that the task of the missionary was to know the Chinese people and their culture. After the Nationalist government was officially established in Nanjing in 1927, Christianity gradually developed. It worked with Chinese traditional religions for more than twenty years, but this process was interrupted immediately after the Communist Party took power.

The most important reason for the Christian movement's slowdown in the second half of the twentieth century was that the Chinese Communist government suppressed Christians. Beginning in 1949, the party/state assumed a policy of "monitoring and regulating all religions," cutting Chinese religious organizations off from foreign influence. According to Chinese officials, the North American Associated Mission Boards did not "change their hostility toward China and would not give up their control of Chinese churches" after the founding of the People's Republic of China.[73] In *Religion under Socialism in China,* Zhufeng Luo explains that this is why the party decided to launch the Three-Self Movement[74]—for self-administration, self-support, and self-propagation—the most important tool of the Chinese government in the oppression of religions. Historically, the principles of the Three-Self Movement were proclaimed for the first time at the First Christian Conference in 1950,[75] which stressed that "the church must be organized by Chinese Christians themselves, not by foreigners or by the government,"[76] and that Christians must support the new China and cut off connections with imperialist powers. Soon a war developed between advocates of the independent Christian movement and the Three-Self Movement Committee. Wang Mindao, the pastor of the independent church with the largest congregation in Beijing,[77] strongly opposed the Three-Self Movement and believed that it had no biblical basis. He also saw the Three-Self Movement as not only un-Christian but also as plotting actively against the churches. Bishop K. H. Ting accused Wang of attempting to convince the Chinese people that the new government was oppressing Christianity and other religions. According to Ting, Wang was lacking in love toward the Chinese people and refused to talk about the imperialist aggression that had been committed against China.[78] Wang was jailed as a counterrevolutionary in 1955, but Ting's position rose rapidly, and he was selected to the committee of the Three-Self Movement.

In post-Mao China, the party/state continues to implement the Three-Self policy. An open letter of the Conference of the Standing Committee of the National Three-Self Movement, addressed to "brothers and sisters in Christ of all China," warned against those who were still hostile to China and attacked the Three-Self Movement. Meanwhile, some delegates raised the question, Why should a Chinese patriotic political organization control the ecclesiastic church?[79] In fact, the Chinese Christian Council (CCC) never separated from the Three-Self Movement, as Ting described before he retired in 1996: "In the past, one person had been both Chair of the Three-Self Movement and President of the CCC which meant the two were not split."[80] In the past, the Three-Self Movement and the CCC worked together to constitute the leadership of the official church, and many leading figures held positions in both organizations concurrently. Under this organizational structure, it was impossible for the CCC to solve the issue of church-state relations.

The 1980s was a good time to reassess the Three-Self Movement and to reorder church-state relations because the voices of political reform became a movement early in that decade. Bishop Ting showed his liberal position and set forth a proposal to the government in September 1988 in which he suggested that "the church should be in tune with socialism, but should not be a government department."[81] He tried to end political control over religion and predicted that the Three-Self Movement would be dissolved by 1991.[82] Ting's proposal was dropped because of the Tiananmen Square Incident of 1989. Afterward, he turned to support the Three-Self Movement again. At the opening of the Sixth National Chinese Christian Conference in 1996, Ting once more emphasized that the aim of the conference was very similar to that of conferences past: "First, to uphold the Three-Self."[83] The history of the development of the Three-Self Movement has clearly shown that the party/state tightly controls religion. The Three-Self Movement is the "instrument by which the churches were brought under the control of the state."[84] However, some scholars have praised the significant achievement of the Three-Self Movement in making fundamental changes to the status of religion, including changes in ideology among members of religious circles, changes in the souls and minds of religious figures who had been attached to imperialism and feudalism, changes in religious thinking, and changes in Christian theological thinking. All of these changes have enabled Chinese churches to work more harmoniously with the party/state.[85]

According to Document 19, issued by the Central Committee of the CPC in March 1982, the goal of the Three-Self Movement is to assist the party and government in implementing the party's policy toward religion. The Three-Self Movement must accept the leadership of the party; every church must register with the government according to the law; individual religious activities must be reported to the local committee of the Three-Self Movement; all places of religious activity must be reported to the provincial Bureau of Religious Affairs;[86] and all religious groups must submit a written report of their activities to the special committee of the government every six months. Based on the Three-Self Principles, no foreign religious organization is permitted to interfere in Chinese religious activities,[87] and no one church or religious organization was allowed to accept foreign funds until 1992. A new regulation that year changed this policy and permitted religious bodies and their affiliated organizations to accept foreign funds if they get a special permit from the government. At present, the Christian mission in China is still struggling. Christianity is a minority religion and face double challenges: traditional Chinese culture, and suppression by the Communist Party. The most difficult task for the Christian mission is dealing with the party. The most optimistic prediction says that the Christian population will not exceed 6 percent in the twenty-first century. Thus Chinese indigenous religions should help Christian missionary work in China in order to promote democratization.

THE PARTY, MARXISM, RELIGION, AND DEMOCRATIZATION

In the post-Mao era, both traditional Chinese religions and Western religions have developed faster and have begun establishing connections with world religious circles. In 1991, the China Christian Council officially joined the World Council of Churches, and the Chinese Catholic Church has sent representatives to some international religious conferences, such as the Fifth World Conference on Religion and Peace and World Catholic Youth Day. Religion has played only a marginal role in the process of democratization, however, because the Communist Party/government has limited religious gatherings to religious sites such as churches, temples, mosques, and other formal meeting places and has strictly prohibited religions from becoming involved in democratic political activities.

Legally speaking, Chinese citizens enjoy full freedom of religion under all versions of the Constitution of China. Article 88 of the Constitution of 1954 proclaims that "citizens of the People's Republic of China enjoy freedom of religious belief." According to Article 28 of the Constitution of 1975, Chinese citizens "have the freedom to practice a religion, the freedom to not practice a religion and to propagate atheism." And Article 36 of the Constitution of 1982 provides the following: "No state organ, public organization, or individual may compel citizens to believe in, or not to believe in, any religion; nor may they discriminate against citizens who believe in, or do not believe in, any religion. The state protects normal religious activities. No one may make use of religion to engage in activities that disrupt public order, impair the health of citizens, or interfere with the educational system of the state." [88] In the 1997 White Paper released by the State Council of China, the Chinese government recognized some basic international laws concerning human rights and religious rights, including the United Nations Charter; the Universal Declaration of Human Rights; the United Nations Declaration on the Elimination of All Forms of Intolerance and of Discrimination Based on Religion or Belief; the International Covenant on Economic, Social and Cultural Rights; and the International Covenant on Civil and Political Rights. Practically speaking, the Constitution encourages activities against religion. Based on the Constitution, the government pays equal attention to protecting the freedom not to believe in religion while stressing the protection of freedom of religious belief. Furthermore, China's Constitution basically protects only "normal religious activities," which are usually conducted by "a small number of people, as actuated by some abnormal purposes, conduct[ing] religious activities in an excessively frequent and long manner."[89] In order to eliminate "abnormal religious activities" and minimize religious influences on society, the Fifth National People's Congress adopted the Criminal Law of 1979 to restrict religious activities. Article 147 of that law reads, "A state functionary who unlawfully deprives others of their freedom of religious beliefs or violates the customs and habits of minority nationalities to a serious extent, will be sentenced to detention or imprisonment for not more than two years."[90] Article 99 states, "Those organizing and utilizing feudal superstitious beliefs and secret societies or sects to carry out counter-revolutionary activities will be sentenced to a fixed-term imprisonment of not less than five years."[91] The term *counterrevolutionary* is very ambiguous because there is no objective standard by which to evaluate it. Any activity in China can be defined as counterrevolutionary if the party/state sees it that way. Although the Ninth NPC passed a law in March 1999 to delete the term *counterrevolutionary* used in the previous criminal law, the party has applied this term in practice; for example, the party regards Falun Gong as counterrevolutionary. Since 1998, the campaign against Falun Gong has been intensified. According to China's *Human Rights Report 2000*, released by the Bureau of Democracy, approximately 100 or more Falun Gong adherents died in jail during the year.

In Communist China, most influential positions are held by party members. However, party members are actually forbidden to be faithful to God and to join others in worship. Freedom of religion does not mean that "the Communist Party members can freely believe in religion."[92] According to the party's constitution, party members, as disciples of Marxism, must believe in Marxist atheism. The party requires its 64 million members to "promote atheist thought in a positive way and persist in educating the masses of various ethnic groups with the Marxist perspective on religion."[93]

Marxism is the theoretical foundation of the CPC and the dominant ideology and guiding principle of socialist China. However, atheism is a central tenet of Marxism and the party. Marx clearly understood that religion was part of culture and was an ideology that supported capitalist society. When he was young, Marx was a member of the Hegel Youth Club, but there were disagreements concerning religion between Marx and Hegel. For Hegel, "God is the guarantee of the accidental world." Marx commented, "Obviously the reverse can also be said."[94] When Marx came to realize that it was necessary to eliminate religion to achieve political emancipation, he wrote that the criticism of religion is the premise of all criticism. According to Marx, God did not create man; man created God. Correspondingly, religion did not make man; man made religion in order to escape the misery of this world and to reach so-called supernatural beings in heaven. Religion was a negative feeling of the ruled class that was the reflection of their miserable life in capitalist society. Because the ruled class was unable to fulfill its hope in this world, that is, in the real world, the ruled class put their hope in heaven, in that other world. The ruling class used religion to anesthetize the people in order to maintain the capitalist system. At this point, religion is the opium of the people; the form of religion is identical with the form of society. Marx pointed out that "Religion is the general theory of that world. The struggle against religion is therefore indirectly the struggle against that world whose spiritual arena is religion."[95] Criticism of religion thus is transformed into criticism of earth, law, and politics.[96] The abolition of religion is the requirement for real happiness.[97] Logically, for Marxism, the abolition of religion and the abolition of the capitalist system are the same process—the communist movement toward the ultimate goal of the communistic society. Communism, in theory, has no room for religion.

When the Communist Party has put Marxism in practice, it has inevitably resulted in serious consequences. After the Russian Communist Party came to power in 1917, religious believers were immediately exiled or persecuted because Lenin viewed religion as "medieval mildew or one of the most odious things on earth."[98] The Soviet Union set an example for all other Communist countries. Cuba, North Korea, Vietnam, and China treated religion in the same way as the Soviet Union did. In China, the party believes that it is not religion but some ontological or philosophical belief system that "provides ultimate answers to ultimate questions on the meaning of human existence."[99] Ren Jiyu, an official theorist and the former director of the Institute of World Religions in the Chinese Social Science Academy, claims that "all religions are superstitions, but not all superstitions are religion." Religion generally is superior to pure superstition, but atheism is superior to all religion. Therefore, religion in China must be subordinate to Marxism and philosophy,[100] and religious organizations must accept party leadership. *Religion under Socialism in China*, one of twelve key projects in the Sixth Five-Year Plan for Economic and Social Development of China, was written by a group of scholars at the Institute for Research on Religion and represented official Chinese stances on religion. The book adopts Marxism as the guiding principle for research on religious issues; systematically explores the nature of religion in China, coordinating religion with socialist society and party policy toward religious belief;[101] and especially emphasizes the way to harmonize religion with socialist society, stressing that the leadership of the party and a commitment to socialism are the basic conditions for harmony to exist between religion and the socialist society.[102] Therefore, religious believers in China are required to support the party and the socialist system.[103] One of the goals of socialist society is to abolish religion, but the party does not believe that religion can be abolished through violent revolution because poverty, suffering, backwardness, and sickness are the main reasons for religion to continue in socialist society.[104] In addition, religion is a social phenomenon, and no one can expect to abolish it soon. In the primary stage of socialist society, the socialist system can use religion by using "democratic methods of discussion, of criticism, of persuasion and education."[105]

The nature of the party and Marxism determines the relationship between religion and the government. In Chinese history, there are four major historical sources the party can draw on in dealing with church-state relations in China: the ancient Chinese tradition that encouraged state control of religion; the New Cultural Movement of 1919 that promoted science and politics over religion; Marxism, which was introduced to China in 1921 as the theoretical foundation of an antireligious movement; and Mao, who set forth the united front policy to regulate church-state relations.[106] Mao's model, based on Marxism and under the leadership of the party, is still valid today. It is the typical model of party/state control of religion. Many scholars have observed that state control of religion is the distinguishing characteristic of church-state relations in China. The party/state control of religion in China has its own historical roots. After the Han dynasty (206 B.C.–A.D. 220) established Confucianism as the state religion, all dynasties that followed imposed state control of religion. Patriarchal religion and politics were the chief features of premodern China. For more than 2,000 years, the emperor's rule was the mandate of heaven; correspondingly, the imperial government held the sole right to perform the rituals in the worship of heaven. Under the Chinese patriarchal political system, the Board of Rites, one of the six Chinese imperial administrations, regulated religious affairs, including "the erection of temples, the ordination to the priesthood, and the conduct of the priests."[107] No one was permitted to build a monastery or temple without approval from the provincial governor. The churches had no right to ordain their own clergy; instead, the government did it for them. Priests' activities were monitored by government authority. No monastery or temple was allowed to accept any refugee for any reason. Any religious activity, belief, or speech had to be performed within the established religion and ideology, that is, Confucianism. Otherwise, it would be regarded as heterodoxy. Because the imperial government feared Western military power, Christianity was the only exception. Independent Christian organizations and activities were allowed and were free from government control.[108] It should be noted that state control of religion was not derived from Confucianism. On the contrary, for Confucianism, Nikolas K. Gvosdev argues, "the use of compulsion to regulate the beliefs and actions of others was a sign of weakness."[109]

The motivation for state control of religion in premodern China was that the Chinese government wanted to retain its power and maintain economic and political order. It clearly understood that religious forces might be used as a tool by other groups as "competitive centers of power."[110] Religious activities in the Republic of China still depended heavily on "prominent political figures." When the party and the patriarchal tradition work together under the Communist government, state control of religion becomes more severe. Under the rule of the party/state, the church-state relationship is essentially determined not by law but by party policy, which is above the national Constitution. The nature of party policy, based as it is on Marxism, is no doubt antireligious. Since the party came to power, the development of party policy on religion has gone through four general stages.[111] First, party policy treated religions as "imperialist religious forces" from 1949 to 1956. Second, the party launched a political campaign against capitalist ideology and religion from 1956 to 1965. Third, party policy went to extremes in regarding religion as enemy during the Cultural Revolution from 1966 to 1976. During the fourth stage, from 1978 to the present, the party has taken a moderate approach toward religion and "stresses that religion is a historical product that will disappear only when socioeconomic and cultural conditions have improved to the extent that people no longer require this 'opiate.' "[112] However, incidents of persecution of religious people in China have continued to occur from time to time. Davis observes that the persecution of religion "remains a serious problem in many parts of the world,"[113] and that in China many religious leaders have been detained for lengthy investigation and in some cases, beaten.[114]

Correspondingly, the development of church-state relations went through four periods in China. During the first stage, from 1949 to 1956, the government sought to establish the Three-Self Movement—to regulate Chinese churches in 1950, to control churches through the formation of the Chinese Protestant Anti-America and Aid Korea Movement between 1951 and 1954, and to control reformed churches through a political education campaign between 1954 and 1957. During the second stage, from 1957 to 1966, the state continued to control churches but softened its religious policy and sought the union of church and state by means of the socialist education movement to change believers' thinking. During the third stage, from 1966 to 1976, the government sought to destroy all churches. All religions were denounced and persecuted; all churches were closed; all religious activity was prohibited; and church properties were confiscated. During the last stage, from 1978 to the present, the state began to restore its soft-line religious policy, using religion for political purposes, but the government still consolidates its control of all churches.[115]

The pattern of church-state relations in Communist China is not one of mutual partnership. The party makes out guidelines to instruct the government, and the government as the agent of the party controls the churches. From the national level to the local level, both the party and the government set up corresponding departments to regulate religious associations. Religious policies are implemented by the Religious Affairs Bureau, which has a national office to direct the provincial and municipal bureaus, which in turn direct city- and county-level bureaus. Under the Religious Affairs Bureau, party policy is implemented by the major religious organizations, including the Buddhist Association of China, the China Taoist Association, the China Islamic Association, the Three-Self Patriotic Movement Committee of Protestant Churches of China, the China Christian Council, and the China Catholic Patriotic Association.[116] Interestingly, Confucianism has not been treated as a religion by the Chinese government. The Religious Affairs Bureau is directed by the United

Front Office, a party branch, and cooperates closely with the local Public Security Bureau, which is responsible for enforcing religious policies. If religious believers and organizations violate party policies, the Public Security Bureau punishes them according to criminal law. Registration is the government's key control mechanism. According to Regulation No. 145, on the Management of Places for Religious Activities, issued by Premier Li Peng in 1994, registration is based on the "three-fix" policy: patriotic association, a fixed meeting point, and activities confined to a specific geographic area. Although registered and unregistered churches are treated similarly in some areas because the party/government began losing its control over religion, local governments have carried out strict regulations, cracking down on unregistered churches and their members in most areas. Foreigners may conduct religious activities in Chinese territory but are only permitted to do so at sites approved by people's governments at or above the county level.

The current Chinese government also tightly controls the media, including television, newspapers, radio, public forums, and the Internet. The party censorship system makes it impossible for the Chinese people to organize private publishing houses or to publish articles that discuss religious human rights from a democratic perspective in official magazines. The government owns all land, and no one is permitted to build a church without a special government permit. Within this control system, one scholar asks, "How much freedom will these associations be given in the future to engage in religious activities?"[117] The relationship between church and state at present is very similar to the relation of father and son in ancient China. Churches must unconditionally obey the party/state. Religious bodies do not have the opportunity to negotiate a mutually beneficial relationship with the party/state.[118]

CONCLUSION

Religion has played an important role in the process of democratization worldwide. A democratic system cannot be sustained without religious support. In modern times, Christianity has been associated with democracy, but Christian missions in China have been confronted with a difficulty: Chinese traditional culture seeks to retain its traditional belief system, and the party essentially rejects Christianity and all other religions. This does not mean that the Chinese are a nonreligious people. China has many religions—not only the three traditional Chinese religions, but also other imported religions. Among these religions, Confucianism as religion and ideology remains dominant.

Religion has never been separated from the Chinese political system. Generally speaking, the nature and function of religion largely depend on the nature of the political system. The same religion can serve different types of political systems; Christianity, for example, served autocracy in the Middle Ages and democracy in modern times. This is why democratic countries in Asia have not found Confucianism to be an obstacle to democratization. Confucianism conditioned a highly centralized Chinese government in premodern China; some of Confucius's ideas, such as his doctrine of the mean (*zhong yong*) and his teaching principles, also can be used for democratization in modern China. However, Confucianism is a complicated system. To serve democratization, Confucianism must be reinterpreted and must work closely with Christianity.

Davis lists five aspects that threaten religious pluralism and religious liberty today worldwide. One of them is "the political power and influence of major religions,"[119] which can be applied in China today. The party/state control of religion has been a characteristic of Chinese politics in both ancient times and under the current communist regime. Based on the Constitution of the People's Republic of China, the Chinese people of all nationalities are under the leadership of the Communist Party of China and the guidance of Marxism-Leninism and Mao Zedong Thought. The essence of the relationship between religions and the Chinese government is the relationship between religions and the party. The essential characteristic of the relationship between religions and the party is that the party controls Chinese religions entirely. The party has persisted in persecuting religions since it came to power in 1949. The reform movement is opening a civil society and improving religious rights, but it has not changed the nature of the party. The party has changed only its strategy toward Chinese religion, not its standpoint on religion. Moreover, the party will further intensify its efforts to suppress religions by coercive force while the party is dying.

Although China's Constitution guarantees that "Citizens of the People's Republic of China enjoy freedom of religious belief," there is a gulf between the law and practice. In the framework of Chinese politics, the law is only an instrument of Communist politics. The party controls Chinese religion through various channels. First is its official ideology—Marxism-Maoism-Dengism. The ultimate goal of the party, based on Marxism, is to eliminate all forms of religion. Second is religious policy. Party policy and regulation are above the law in China. Third are semigovernment and government organizations. The associations of religions, as liaisons between religions and the government, put party policy into practice; the Religious Affairs Bureau, as an agency of the government, is the mediator between religious organizations and the party; the United Front Office represents the party in making religious policy; and the Public Security Bureau enforces the implementation of party policy and regulation among all religious groups and believers. Fourth are educational programs. All schools, colleges, and universities must follow party policy and educate students in Marxism, communism, and atheism.

Controlled by the party, Chinese religions at present play only a marginal role. Many Chinese people take a very pragmatic attitude toward religion because of persecution. Second, religious activities and influences are confined to specific meeting places in accordance with party policy. Third, religious groups are divided into two groups: registered religious organizations, and unregistered religious organizations (underground religious groups). By this registration, the party has minimized religious influences on Chinese society. Fourth, the Chinese official religion is becoming a civil religion. Civil religion in the communist system serves the goals of socialism and party politics. When civil religion serves communist politics, it becomes as dangerous as Christianity did serving Nazism in World War II. Fifth, the Three-Self Movement—self-administration, self-support, and self-propagation—is a typical model of the party's control of religion.

Three preconditions are essential for Chinese religion to play a key role in the process of democratization. First is the separation of the government from the party and of religion from the government/party. As long as the government/party interferes with religious affairs, Chinese religion cannot become an independent force to influence Chinese society and politics. Second, religious believers should have rights to take public office. However, all important posts in China are filled by the members of the Communist Party. According to the party's constitutions, all party members must be atheists; they are not allowed to believe in God. In other words, religious believers do not qualify for important positions in the public arena. Thus religions in China are unable to directly influence Chinese politics at the policy-making level. The third precondition is the establishment of a pluralistic culture. Chinese religious believers should be allowed to freely express their beliefs through public media, including TV, radio, art, literature, film, journalism, and other public forums.That these three preconditions have not yet been institutionalized can help explain why religion in China can play only a marginal role within the Communist system.

The party, as a system including theory, principles, regulations, policies, and organizations, is the fundamental cause that marginalizes the religious role in China's democratization, to block the revival of Chinese religions, and to change the nature of the function of Chinese religion. In order for Chinese religion to play a key role in China's democratization, the one-party system must be changed first. The future of Chinese religion in the twenty-first century essentially relies on Chinese political reform. At this point, China's religious movement must coordinate with the political reform movement. The call for religious human rights and freedom of religion in China would remain empty slogans without an end to the one-party system. Under the leadership of the CPC, religion is unable to act as an independent force to balance the social and political orders.

The party/state control of religion is the main obstacle to the implementation of freedom of religion. Therefore, it is urgent to call for the separation of church and state in China through legislation and educational programs and put it in practice as well. However, Democratization is not about how to Christianize China, but how to remake China's public philosophy, abandon Marxism, and change the party/state control system.

NOTES

1. See Jacques Gernet, *China and the Christian Impact: A Conflict of Cultures* (Cambridge, England: Cambridge University Press, 1985), p. 108.

2. Peter Van der Veer and Hartmut Lehmann, eds. *Nation and Religion: Perspectives on Europe and Asia* (Princeton, N.J.: Princeton University Press, 1999), p. 4.

3. Dipesh Chakrabarty, "Postcoloniality and the Artifice of History," *Representations* 37 (1992), pp. 1–26.

4. Robert N. Bellah, *The Broken Covenant: American Civil Religion in Time of Trial* (Chicago: University of Chicago Press, 1975), p. 26.

5. Crane Brinton, *The Shaping of Modern Thought* (Englewood Cliffs, N.J.: Prentice Hall, 1963), p. 24.

6. Gernet, *China and the Christian Impact,* p. 1.

7. Bellah, *The Broken Covenant,* p. 26.

8. John Markoff and Daniel Regan, "The Rise and Fall of Civil Religion: Comparative Perspectives," *Sociological Analysis* 42 (1982), p. 334.

9. Ralph H. Gabriel, *American Values: Continuity and Change* (Westport, Conn.: Greenwood Press, 1974), p. 106.

10. Ibid., p. 21.

11. Ibid., pp. 34, 167.

12. Ibid., p. 167.

13. Ibid., p. 25.

14. Quoted in Sanford Kessler, "Tocqueville on Civil Religion and Liberal Democracy," *Journal of Politics* 39 (1977), p. 35.

15. Richard V. Pierard and Robert D. Linder, *Civil Religion and the Presidency* (Grand Rapids, Mich.: Academic Press, 1988), p. viii.

16. Ibid., p. ix.

17. Quoted in Derek H. Davis, *Original Intent: Chief Justice Rehnquist and the Course of American Church-State Relations* (New York: Prometheus Books, 1991), p. 167.

18. Derek H. Davis, "Christian Faith and Political Involvement in Today's Culture War," *Journal of Church and State* 38 (Summer 1996), p. 477.

19. Rhys H. Williams and Susan M. Alexander, "Religious Rhetoric in American Populism: Civil Religion as Movement Ideology," *Journal for the Scientific Study of Religion* 33 (March 1994), p. 4.

20. Davis, "Christian Faith and Political Involvement in Today's Culture War," p. 477.

21. Quoted in Kessler, "Tocqueville on Civil Religion and Liberal Democracy," p. 123.

22. Kessler, "Tocqueville on Civil Religion and Liberal Democracy," p. 123.

23. Linshu Cheng, "The Basic Functions of Religion," *Studies on World Religions* 41, no. 3 (1990): pp. 84–93.

24. Chonqing Yu, "Discussion on Religions in the Socialist Period: Again on the Essence and Social Role of Religion," *Studies on World Religions* 30, no. 3 (1987), p. 126.

25. James David Fairbanks, "The Priestly Functions of the Presidency: A Discussion on the Literature on Civil Religion and Its Implications for the Study of Presidency Leadership," *Presidential Studies Quarterly* 11 (1981), p. 214.

26. Derek H. Davis, "Religious Pluralism and the Quest for Unity in American Life," *Journal of Church and State* 36 (Spring 1994), p. 245.

27. Ibid., p. 258.

28. Morris L. Ernst and David Loth, *Report on the American Communist* (New York: Capricorn Books, 1962), p. 189.

29. Kessler, "Tocqueville on Civil Religion and Liberal Democracy," p. 122.

30. Bellah, *The Broken Covenant*, p. xvi.

31. See, for example, Xinging Zhuo, "The Significance of Christianity for the Modernization of Chinese Society," *Crux* 33 (March 1997), p. 31.

32. Ibid., pp. 31–37.

33. Ibid., p. 31.

34. James E. Wood, Jr., "Religion and the State in China: Winter Is Past," *Journal of Church and State* 28 (Autumn 1986), p. 394.

35. See John N. Jonsson, "Introduction," in Kwong Chunwah, *Hong Kong's Religions in Transition* (Waco, Texas: Tao Foundation, 2000), p. ix.

36. Quoted in Stephen F. Teiser, "Introduction: The Spirits of Chinese Religion," in *Religions of China in Practice*, ed. Donald S. Lopez (Princeton, N.J.: Princeton University Press, 1996), p. 1.

37. Derk Bodde, *Chinese Thought, Society, and Science: The Intellectual and Social Background of Science and Teaching in Pre-modern China* (Honolulu: University of Hawaii Press, 1991), p. 148.

38. Julia Ching, *Chinese Religions* (Maryknoll, N.Y.: Orbis Books, 1993), p. 2.

39. Quoted in Bureau of Democracy, Human Rights, and Labor, U.S. Department of State, *1999 Country Reports on Human Rights Practices*, released 25 February 2000; available on-line at http//www.state.gov/www/global/human_rights/1999_hrp_report/china.html.

40. Jingpan Chen, *Confucius as a Teacher: Philosophy of Confucius with Special Reference to Its Educational Implications* (Beijing: Foreign Languages Press, 1990), p. 351.

41. Julia Ching, "Ethical Humanism as Religion?" in Hans Kung and Julia Ching, *Christianity and Chinese Religions* (New York: Doubleday, 1989), p. 87.

42. See Robert A. F. Thurman, *Inner Revolution: Life, Liberty, and the Pursuit of Real Happiness* (New York: Riverhead Books, 1998).

43. Christian Jochim, *Chinese Religions: A Cultural Perspective* (Englewood Cliffs, N.J.: Prentice-Hall, 1986), p. 10.

44. State Council of China, "1997 White Paper," *China's Religion* 12 (Spring 1998), p. 7.

45. Timothy Brook, "Rethinking Syncretism: The Unity of the Three Teachings

and Their Joint Worship in Late-Imperial China," *Journal of Chinese Religions* 21 (Fall 1993), pp. 13–14.

46. Mary Evelyn Tucker, "Religious Dimensions of Confucianism: Cosmology and Cultivation," *Philosophy East and West* 48 (January 1998), p. 10.

47. Daniel L. Overmyer, *Religions of China* (San Francisco: Harper & Row, 1986), p. 13.

48. Hans Kung and Julia Ching, *Christianity and Chinese Religions*, p. xiii.

49. Rodney L. Taylor, "The Religious Character of the Confucian Tradition," *Philosophy East and West* 48 (January 1998), p. 85.

50. Frank Whaling, "Christianity and Confucianism and Our Coming World Civilization: A European View," *Ching Feng* 38 (March 1995), p. 13.

51. Tucker, "Religious Dimensions of Confucianism," p. 11.

52. Ibid.

53. Ibid., p. 8.

54. Quoted in ibid., p. 12.

55. Laurence G. Thompson, *Chinese Religion: An Introduction*, 4th ed. (Belmont, Calif.: Wadsworth Publishing Company, 1989), p. 1.

56. Samuel P. Huntington, *The Third Wave: Democratization in the Late Twentieth Century* (Norman, Okla.: University of Oklahoma Press, 1991), p. 18.

57. See Francis Fukuyama, *The Great Disruption: Human Nature and the Reconstitution of Social Order* (New York: Free Press, 1999).

58. John N. Jonsson, conversation with author. Repeatedly expressed these viewpoints in numerous conversations with author in 2000.

59. Edward Shils, "Reflections on Civil Society and Civility in the Chinese Intellectual Tradition," in *Confucian Traditions in East Asian Modernity: Moral Education and Economic Culture in Japan and the Four Mini-Dragons*, ed. Wei-ming Tu (Cambridge, Mass.: Harvard University Press, 1996), pp. 52–71.

60. David B. Barrett, ed., *World Christian Encyclopedia* (New York: Oxford University Press, 1982), p. 232.

61. J. Theodore Mueller, *Great Missionaries to China* (Grand Rapids, Mich.: Zondervan Publishing House, 1947), p. 32.

62. Barrett, *World Christian Encyclopedia*, p. 232.

63. G. Thompson Brown, *Christianity in the People's Republic of China* (Atlanta, Ga.: John Knox Press, 1973), p. 196.

64. State Council of China, "1997 White Paper," p. 7.

65. Ralph R. Covell, *Confucius, the Buddha, and Christ: A History of the Gospel in Chinese* (New York: Orbis Books, 1986), p. 4.

66. Ibid.

67. Gernet, *China and the Christian Impact*, p. 3.

68. Kan Baoping, "The Christian Church in Its Chinese Context," in *Contemporary Religious Trends within the Socio-Political Climate of East Asia*, ed. John N. Jonsson (Waco, Texas: Baylor University, 1996, mimeographed), pp. 10–20.

69. Quoted in Xiaoqun Xu, "The Dilemma of Accommodation: Reconciling Christianity and Chinese Culture in the 1920s," *Historian* 60 (Fall 1997), p. 22.

70. Jonsson, conversation with the author.

71. Jessie G. Lutz and R. Ray Lutz, "Karl Gutzlaff's Approach to Indigenization: The Chinese Union," in *Christianity in China: From the Eighteenth Century to the Present*, ed. Daniel Bays (Stanford, Calif.: Stanford University Press, 1996), p. 269.

72. Cyriac K. Pullapilly, ed., *Chinese Politics and Christian Missions: The Anti-Christian Movements of 1920–28* (Notre Dame, Ind.: Cross Cultural Publications, 1988), pp. 1–3.

73. Zhufeng Luo, ed., *Religion under Socialism in China* (Armonk, N.Y.: M.E. Sharpe, 1991), p. 11.

74. Ibid., pp. 55–56.

75. See George Petterson, *Christianity in Communist China* (Waco, Texas: Word Books Publisher, 1969), p. 168.

76. Raymond L. Whitehead, ed., *No Longer Strangers: Selected Writings of K. H. Ting* (New York: Orbis Books, 1989), p. 146.

77. Francis P. Jones, ed., *Documents of the Three-Self Movement: Source Materials for the Study of the Protestant Church in Communist China* (New York: National Council of the Churches of Christ in the U.S.A., 1963), p. xv.

78. Whitehead, *No Longer Strangers*, 141–43.

79. Weifan Wang, "A Church Leader of Vision," *Chinese Theological Review* 10 (1994), p. 89.

80. K. H. Ting, "Greetings to the Sixth National Chinese Christian Conference," *Chinese Theological Review* 12 (1996), p. 23.

81. Quoted in Alan Hanter and Kim-Kwong Chan, *Protestantism in Contemporary China* (Cambridge, England: Cambridge University Press, 1993), p. 62.

82. Ibid., p. 94.

83. Ting, "Greetings to the Sixth National Chinese Christian Conference," p. 122.

84. Wood, "Religion and the State in China: Winter Is Past," p. 401.

85. Luo, *Religion under Socialism in China*, p. 72–92.

86. See James E. Wood Jr., *Church-State Relations in the Modern World* (Waco, Texas: J.M. Dawson Institute of Church-State Studies, 1998), pp. 197–201.

87. Ibid., p. 199.

88. Barrett, *World Christian Encyclopedia*, p. 234.

89. Eric Kolodner, "Religious Rights in China: A Comparison of International Human Rights Law and Chinese Domestic Legislation," *Human Rights Quarterly* 16 (1994), p. 470.

90. Ibid.

91. Quoted in Bob Whyte, "The Future of Religion in China," *Religion in the Communist Lands* 8 (1980), p. 7.

92. Kolodner, "Religious Rights in China," p. 467.

93. *People's Daily*, 11 March 1999.

94. Quoted in Saul K. Padover, *On Religion: Karl Marx* (Sydney: McGraw-Hill, 1974), p. xv.

95. Ibid.

96. Ibid. p. 36.

97. Ibid.

98. David McLellan, *Marxism and Religion: A Description and Assessment of the Marxist Critique of Christianity* (New York: Harper & Row, 1987), p. 4.

99. Johan D. van der Vyver and John Witte Jr., eds., *Religious Human Rights in Global Perspective: Legal Perspectives* (Boston: Martinus Nijhoff Publishers, 1997), p. 146.

100. Quoted in Julia Ching, *Probing China's Soul: Religion, Politics, and Protest in the People's Republic of China* (San Francisco: Harper & Row, 1990), p. 135.

101. Luo, *Religion under Socialism in China,* p. xv.
102. Ibid., p. 115.
103. Ibid., p. 141.
104. Ibid., p. 4.
105. Quoted in Kevin Boyle and Juliet Sheen, *Freedom of Religion and Belief* (New York: Routledge, 1997), p. 183.
106. See Richard Van Housten, ed., *Wise as Serpents, Harmless as Doves* (Pasadena, Calif.: William Carey Library, 1988), p. x-xii.
107. C. K. Yang, *Religion in Chinese Society: A Study of Contemporary Social Functions of Religion and Some of Their Historical Factors* (Berkeley: University of California Press, 1961), p. 187.
108. Ibid., p. 191.
109. Nikolas K. Gvosdev, "Finding the Roots of Religious Liberty in the 'Asian Tradition' " (Waco, Texas, Baylor University, 2000, mimeographed), p. 4.
110. Yang, *Religion in Chinese Society,* p. 180.
111. Boyle and Sheen, *Freedom of Religion and Belief,* p. 180.
112. Kolodner, "Religious Rights in China," p. 466.
113. Derek H. Davis, "Thoughts on Religious Persecution around the Globe: Problems and Solutions," *Journal of Church and State* 40 (Spring 1998), p. 279.
114. Ibid., p. 283.
115. See Housten, *Wise as Serpents, Harmless as Doves,* pp. xiv-xxiv.
116. Ibid., p. ix.
117. Whyte, "The Future of Religion in China," p. 8.
118. Ibid., p. xxiv.
119. Davis, "Thoughts on Religious Persecution around the Globe," p. 279.

CHAPTER 7

The Double Missions of Chinese Education

Economic prosperity and democratization rely largely on education because education is the ultimate source to empower human beings and mold the new generation.[1] *Education* in the modern sense is a broader term. Any process that involves teaching or training the mind and character to impart knowledge and develop skills can be called education. Both formal school education and self-education are important. We all need to update our knowledge through education from time to time. It is clear that education is the most powerful force shaping the evolution of a society and that it has become one of the foundations of world civilization, social order, and democratization.[2] Economically, education is a decisive factor in the transformation of a society from the agricultural sector to industrialization and services; ideologically, education helps to propagandize modern ideology and make people democratic-minded; sociologically, education helps to prevent the emergence of a hereditary aristocracy;[3] and politically, education serves the needs of governance by nurturing government officials and officials-to-be.

Why has China achieved such rapid economic growth in the last two decades? One explanation is that the rapid expansion of education promoted productive forces, in the sciences and technologies in particular. To maintain the communist system and ideology, the Communist Party has put considerable emphasis on political education. Chinese education doubtless serves the general task of the CPC. As Suzanne Ogden has noted, "The educational system has served as one of the primary vehicles for conveying the values of Chinese culture, development, and socialist political culture."[4] Therefore, China's educational system may be understood as a subsystem of the political system and the primary instrument to sustain a social order and modern society.[5]

The most serious problems in premodern China over several centuries were backwardness and autocracy, because China lacked education in the modern sense. The May Fourth Movement of 1919 for the first time set forth the slogan Science and Democracy, to directly target backwardness and autocracy. However, these two serious problems remain years after the May Fourth Movement. Blame for this must be placed in part on Chinese education. Although China had the earliest and largest educational system in the world and placed an extraordinarily high value on education before the sixteenth century,[6] it lagged behind the developed countries after that time. At present, China is still at least twenty years behind the developed countries, even though China's educational system rapidly expanded in the post-Mao Zedong era. There are 1.2 million scientists and technologists in the United States and 900,000 in the former Soviet Union, but China has only 200,000.[7] Lynn Paine has noted, "Education must play a central role if China's modernization is to progress."[8] The question raised here is how education can fulfill its double mission of promoting both economic prosperity and the democratic spirit of the Chinese people within the Communist political system. Remaking China's public philosophy must involve reforming China's educational system.

THE SHADOW OF CHINESE TRADITIONAL EDUCATION

The contemporary Chinese educational system is deeply influenced by two traditions: traditional Chinese educational thought and Marxism-Maoism. In order to understand the communist educational system, it is necessary to examine Chinese traditional educational thought and systems first. China's educational history can be traced back 4,000 years. During the Western Zhou dynasty, the Chinese educational system became more sophisticated.[9] Ancient Chinese education reached the "most glorious stage" in the Sui dynasty and the Tang dynasty.[10] Confucianism was at the center of education in premodern China. Confucius's greatest contribution to education was that he persistently practiced his motto *you jiao wu lei*—"education for all." This motto suggested that there should be no class distinction in education and that all people essentially possess four qualities: benevolence, righteousness, propriety, and wisdom.[11] According to Confucianism, "By nature, men are nearly alike; by practice, they get to be wide apart."[12] Education leads to differences in morality and knowledge, but all can improve themselves through education. Based on this educational philosophy, Confucius tried to teach anyone who came to him for learning, even those who could not afford to pay for the instruction.[13] Yet education for all could not become popular practice in premodern

China, even in the republic era. Education was a privilege of wealthy families before the Communist regime. Generally, only those who were members of nobility and destined to become *jun zi*, or government officials, had opportunities to receive formal education. Due to the fact that women had the lowest social status in Chinese society, they never had the right to a formal education. Some upper-class women received education, but it was limited to learning women's virtues and domestic skills, such as housekeeping, cooking, sewing, and knitting.

The educational goal for Confucius was twofold: to cultivate individuals and to serve politics. As Sally Borthwick has noted, "the transformation of the masses *(jiao hua)* and the cultivation of talent for office *(yu cai)*" were the major functions of ancient Chinese education.[14] The two tasks were interrelated, but cultivating individuals was the precondition to nurturing talented people for public office and shaping a good social order. Unlike Daoism, Confucianism never taught the people pessimistically to flee from the real world and become political nihilists. To the contrary, Confucius taught the people to devote themselves to society.[15] According to Confucianism, schools and teachers should pass on knowledge, which is the basis of education. The Four Books and the Five Classics were the main textbooks. The six arts—rites, music, archery, chariot-riding, history, and mathematics—were the main categories of education.[16] The ultimate purpose of education was to serve society, government, and emperor. To be a *jun zi*, one had to receive education as well as serve the country. Hence political education is one of the characteristics of Confucian educational thought. Confucian political teaching strongly emphasizes loyalty—to parents at home and to rulers in public. Loyalty was the first and most important criterion for the Chinese governments in recruiting and training Chinese officials. Influenced by this educational view, Chinese intellectuals and officials placed great emphasis on self-training in loyalty in order to take public office. This may partly explain why the highly centralized Chinese government lasted more than 2,000 years.

The Chinese rulers realized long ago that punishment and teaching should work together to maintain a good social order. According to Confucianism, if a society is governed only by law and regulation, its members will have no shame if they violate it. If the rulers teach the common people virtue, however, the people will voluntarily walk in the right track; disobedience to the law will be accompanied by shame. Therefore, teaching people virtue was one of the basic characteristics of Chinese traditional education. *Jen* (love) and *li* (proper conduct) are the two key concepts of Confucian moral teachings and contain three aspects: first, ethical value, including love, proper conduct, filial piety, and the doctrine of the mean; second, intellectual value, including the arts, loyalty, and faithfulness; and third, religious teaching, including the doctrine of heaven, the doctrine of humankind, and communication between heaven and humankind. Of course, Confucius emphasized the significance of knowledge for the cultivation of self as well: "Though dull, he will surely become intelligent; though weak, he will surely become strong."

Chinese traditional education served Chinese patriarchal politics. The unique characteristic of Chinese education in the world is the civil service examination system, which was designed primarily for the selection of officials rather than for the education of the elite. The imperial government understood that the administrative system had a limited function over the entire country given China's size and population, but that education was a necessary tool for the rulers to control the minds of the Chinese people. The examination system became a symbol of centralized power in China, directly serving ideological control efforts and the development of a highly centralized political system. When the embryonic form of the civil service examination came into existence in the Han dynasty, it was called "district recommendation upon village selection."[17] This system required the local administrative unit, or village, to recommend men who were determined to devote themselves to public service.[18] The examination system gradually shifted the emphasis from the recommendation alone to "a composite of four processes: education, administrative experience, recommendation, and examination."[19] In order to coordinate the process of the examination, the government established the Imperial Academy. Later, enrollment in the Imperial Academy became the path to becoming a government official. Although the examination system was open only to a small number of people with political connections, it was significant and started the Chinese scholarly tradition; that is, Chinese scholars and officials merged into one organic whole. This Chinese educational tradition was neither an aristocracy nor a bourgeois plutocracy, but it has been called "governance by scholars."[20]

The civil service examination system was officially established in the Sui dynasty and was perfected in the Tang dynasty. The Tang dynasty emphasized the competitive side of the examination and made it possible in theory for anyone to take the examination, but the government still did not allow merchants and artisans to take the examination.[21] They were excluded because they made profits for themselves and could be considered as selfish men. According to Confucianism, only filial sons could become honest officials. To strengthen the examination system, two departments—the Ministry of Rites and the Ministry of Personnel—coordinated the examination during the Tang dynasty. The Ministry of Rites examined a student's literary skills; the Ministry of Personnel examined a student's administrative abilities. Candidates were allowed to send writing samples to leading scholar-officials before taking their examinations, however, in order to receive good recommendations. Under this policy, it was difficult for the examiners to fairly judge performance on the examination. The Song dynasty basically followed the examination pattern of the Tang dynasty but required that candidates' names be withheld from the exam to assure anonymity and to prevent favoritism.[22] The Ming dynasty made extensive changes to the examination system. Before the Ming dynasty, those recommended for the examination were required to take it only once. Everyone who passed the examination and began work as a minor official hoped one day to achieve a high official office. The examination in the Ming dynasty was divided into three levels: the Prefectural County Examination for the Cultivated Talent, the Provincial Examination for the Recommended Man, and the Metropolitan Examination for the Doctor of Letters. The Cultivated Talent and the Recommended Man were not qualified to be high officials. The new Doctor of Letters was required to continue studying for another examination for three years. If he passed the second examination, he would become a high official even without having the experiences of a minor official.[23]

As a consequence, the quality of the officials coming out of this examination system became worse and worse. First, the high-level officials lacked administrative ability and talent; a lot of them actually were bookish. Second, the "eight-part essay"—a stereotyped writing and literary composition in rigid form and with poor ideas—became a fixed format for all candidates to follow, destroyed human talent, and suppressed the Chinese elites. The original purpose of the examination system was to recruit the best-qualified people as officials, but it went in the opposite direction after the Ming dynasty. In the Qing dynasty, many rich families hired talented scholars to prepare about ten eight-part essays for their children to memorize, and the children simply wrote down what they remembered. The examination system in the Qing dynasty became completely "a policy of fooling the people."[24] Third, Confucian scholars normally spent fifteen to twenty years in preparation for taking the examinations at the local, provincial, and imperial levels before they finally were qualified to be scholar-officials in the imperial bureaucracy. Consequently, the gulf between pure knowledge and practice expanded.[25] Because experimentation and technology were looked down on, few Chinese people were truly devoted to these areas. Thus the ruling class lost its vitality and the Chinese dynasties were in decline from the time of the Qing dynasty.

It is undeniable that there was a positive side to the civil service examination system. It nurtured the most perfect civilian governmental system in the world and played a significant role in uniting the Chinese nation through its centralized control, thus providing the empire with a well-educated bureaucracy,[26] expanding the resources to recruit elites, bringing Chinese literature into a glorious period during the Tang and Song dynasties, and giving intellectuals an impetus for hard study. Sun Yat-sen, the founding father of the Republic of China, highly praised the examination system as "the oldest and best of its kind in the world"[27] and proposed the examination bureaucracy as one branch at the same level as the executive, legislative, judicial, and control powers within the Five-Power Constitution.[28] The Nationalist government passed the examination law in 1933; it applied to those who were seeking government posts.[29] After the Nationalist government settled in Taiwan, all schools there continued to adopt Confucian moral teachings as educational mottoes to serve the government, including *li, yi, lian,* and *chi* (propriety, righteousness, uncorrupt ability, and self-respect). Article 158 of the Constitution of the Republic of China affirmed traditional morality as the aim of education.[30] However, the examination system led intellectuals to pursue wealth and high official positions, corrupting their souls in some respects; it narrowed the function of Chinese education; it became an obstacle to the development of the economy and technology; and it supported the highly centralized government and helped the dictatorial system block the democratic process. Consequently, the Chinese feudal society was stagnant for a long time.

In the middle of the nineteenth century, Chinese reformers launched education reform and brought Chinese education into the modern era. Modern Chinese education went through three stages before the Communist Party came to power. The first stage began in the middle of the nineteenth century. Their defeat in the first Opium War shocked the Chinese people and triggered the Self-Strengthening Movement. Some Chinese elites saw the disadvantages of the examination system and placed blame on the Chinese education system. They suggested that self-strength is born of power; power is born of knowledge; and knowledge is born of both Chinese and Western learning.[31] The results would be too slow if people studied only in Chinese schools.[32] They also advocated learning from Western culture and reforming the educational system. As for the relation of Chinese learning and Western learning, Zhang Zhitong has pointed out that "Chinese learning was inner learning; Western learning was outer learning. Chinese learning was for regulating the body and mind; Western learning was for managing the affairs of the world."[33] The slogan of education reform at the first stage was "Chinese learning was for basis and Western learning for use." The reformers made great efforts to train talented people who had both Chinese and Western knowledge; they also began promoting the establishment of modern schools and sending students to foreign schools. The first foreign language institute in China was founded in 1862; the first technical school was established in 1866; and the first naval academy came into existence in 1881. During this stage, education reform basically focused on the content of education but did not touch the educational institutions. Therefore, this stage could be considered the transitional period from ancient education to modern education.

The failure of the second Opium War indicated that the slogan "Chinese learning was for basis and Western learning for use" could not solve China's problems. The reformers realized that the fundamental causes of China's slow development were not an inadequate Chinese education but, rather, the weak Chinese political system. Then some reformers began to make efforts to change the educational institutions. Two reform programs were the decisive factors in bringing China's educational system into the modern period. First, China reorganized the old-style academies and established a new, national school system. In 1904, the courts issued edicts establishing a national system, including normal schools, primary schools, civil middle schools, military middle schools, civil high schools, military high schools, language schools, industrial schools, schools of diligent accomplishment, and the institute of officials.[34] Second, China abolished the civil service examination system in 1905. During the second stage, Chinese educational growth was spectacular. The number of schools increased seventy-three-fold from 1903 to 1909.[35]

In the third stage of modern education, from 1912 to 1949, Chinese education was focused on "popular education" to enlighten the Chinese people. The revolution of 1911 overthrew the last Chinese emperor, but Yuan Shikai restored the imperial system for a short period of time (100 days). This restoration made Chinese elites rethink the disadvantages of Chinese traditional culture and education. They realized that China could not achieve modernization without changing the minds and souls of the Chinese people through education. The May Fourth Movement was modern China's Renaissance; it fiercely attacked the feudal educational system and enlightened the Chinese people. Unfortunately, it also paved the way for Marxism and the Communist Party to develop in China.

EDUCATION UNDER THE CHINESE COMMUNIST GOVERNMENT

After the founding of the People's Republic of China, the Communist Party and the government put education high on their list of priorities and made significant progress in the area. All Chinese people, according to the Constitution of the People's Republic of China, have equal opportunities to receive an education. The dream of universal education began to be realized for the first time in Chinese history. Chinese education expanded rapidly from the 1950s through the first half of the 1960s. The number of university and college graduates increased nearly 9 times, from 21,000 in 1949 to 186,000 in 1965; the number of secondary school graduates increased 6.6 times, from 352,000 in 1949 to 2,325,000 in 1960; and the number of primary school graduates increased more than 10 times, from 646,000 in 1949 to 66,676,000 in 1965.[36]

Like education in premodern China, education in the Mao era emphasized politics. This characteristic was reflected in every period of the development of Chinese education under the Communist regime. First, the initial period from 1949 to 1956 allowed China to explore contemporary educational theory and practice. Meanwhile, the Chinese government called on the people to understand and implement Mao's thought and the party's educational policy, systematically criticize old educational thoughts, and learn from the Soviet educational model. After China finished the transformation from private ownership to public ownership in 1957, Chinese education entered into the second period (1957–1965). Inspired by Mao's 1956 speech, "Let a hundred flowers bloom, let a hundred schools of thought contend," the Chinese people enjoyed a short period of improved education, but Mao soon campaigned the Great Leap Forward and the Anti-Rightist Movement. These political movements negatively impacted Chinese education's recovery. Due to the failure of the Great Leap Forward, educational standards were reasserted and readjusted. The party reaffirmed that the schools must be designated "as conduits for bright students to become future leaders, scientists, and professionals."[37] In the third period, from 1966 to 1976, China's educational system slipped into complete chaos. During the Cultural Revolution, knowledge was regarded as counterrevolutionary, and intellectuals were viewed as a force alien to socialist government. Most schools were closed; the university entrance examination was abolished; and all intellectuals were forcibly reeducated through physical work. Students were urged to criticize teachers, administrators, experts, and other capitalist leaders;[38] most teachers in urban areas were sent to the countryside to be reeducated; and some of them were tortured, even killed. In this period, political education was the only topic in Chinese education. This is one of the reasons why the Chinese economy collapsed during the Cultural Revolution.

The communist educational system in the Mao era was guided by the principles of Marxism-Maoism. Several viewpoints of Marx that directly affected Maoist educational thought and systems deserve mention. First, nature and society together is the basis of education; human beings are part of nature and society. Based on this theory, the natural and social environments make human beings; educational thought and systems are determined by the nature of society. Logically, communist educational thought and systems are determined by the communist political system. Second, knowledge is derived from human practice, which is the starting point of education, the purpose of education, the development of cognition, and the sole criterion to test the truth. This theory discouraged students from studying basic scientific knowledge. Third, the greatest practice is political activity. All practice that strays from communist practice is viewed as revisionism. Therefore, according to Marxism, education is a part of politics and must serve proletariat politics. Marx especially stressed the political role in changing the political superstructure of the capitalist society and establishing the communist society.

In upholding Marxism, Mao's educational philosophy can be characterized as three principles: political education (education serves proletariat politics); mass education (professional educators must be reeducated; the masses can be educated by themselves through political campaigns); and education through practice (it is required that students come out into society to learn from workers and peasants; this is called socialist education). The educational model in the Mao era was an antiexpert or revolution-centered model. According to Mao, there were only two kinds of knowledge since class society came into being: the knowledge of the struggle for production, and the knowledge of the class struggle. Mao described the relation of the two in this way: "Natural science and social science are the crystallization of these two kinds of knowledge, and philosophy is the generalization and summation of the knowledge of nature and the knowledge of society."[39] According to Mao, "All work in schools is for the purpose of transforming the students ideologically. Political education is a link of the center, and it is undesirable to teach too many subjects. Class education, Party education and work must be strengthened."[40] Curriculum should be meaningful to the class struggle; textbooks should be political. Mao viewed intellectuals as part of the bourgeoisie and sent students to the countryside for ideological reeducation. "The class struggle [was] a principal subject" for students," Mao said; if students "[knew] nothing about the class struggle," they could not be "considered as university graduates."[41] The school was the battlefield between proletariats and capitalists. Schools must guide students and teachers to criticize non-Marxist pedagogy and the bourgeoisie. The aim of education was to "serve proletarian politics and be integrated with productive labor."[42] Mao believed that knowledge was less important than productive labor because the socialist-motivated people could produce the miracles of a socialist economy. Productive labor was the basis of learning, teaching, and education. Furthermore, the more knowledge the people possess, the more dangerous the people are to the socialist system. Schools at all levels under Mao's regime were required to list productive labor as a part of regular academic plans. Therefore, political education and productive labor constituted the major features of the curriculum in the Mao era.[43] Such education policy, Maoists argued, "produces perpetual revolutionaries" to defend the communist political system.[44]

After Deng Xiaoping regained power in 1977, he altered the emphasis of education from politics to sciences and technology and used education as a vehicle to promote his reform program. Deng regarded education as the key to the Four Modernizations and made educational reform his first priority. He believed that "the key to achieving China's modernization is the development of science and technology, and unless we pay special attention to education, it will be impossible to develop science and technology."[45] The guiding principle of education before 1978 was to coordinate education with the political ideology of the party. The Third Plenum of the party in 1978 recognized that the revolution-centered model was incorrect. Deng emphasized education in training students to contribute to the process of the Four Modernizations. In order to accelerate the development of education, he suggested the following priorities for the new era: (1) improving the quality of education and raising the level of teaching; (2) strengthening order and discipline in the schools; (3) making certain that education kept pace with the needs of China's economic development; and (4) respecting the work of teachers and raising their professional level.[46]

The Chinese educational model in the reform era might be considered as an economy-centered model. The Chinese government made nine years of education compulsory for all children; ensured financial sources of funding for education; promoted vocational and technical education; and reformed enrollment planning for higher education and the system of job assignment after graduation.[47] Chinese education developed rapidly in the 1980s, including preschool education, primary education, secondary education, and higher education. According to official sources, 20 million children were registered to attend nurseries and kindergartens by 1982,[48] and there were 146,269,600 pupils in primary schools in 1980.[49] According to the Chinese government, science and technology were the keys, education is the foundation, and primary education is the foundation for the foundation.[50] The Seventh Five-Year Plan (1986–1990) further affirmed that universal elementary education was "a major foundation for and a mark of modern civilization."[51] It was reported that in 1980 there were 55,080,800 students in ordinary secondary schools, 453,600 in agricultural and vocational middle schools, and 1,243,400 in specialized secondary schools.[52] The task of secondary education is twofold: preparing students for higher education, and training labor forces for the national economy. In the Mao era, university students were required to spend the majority of their time going out into society to learn from the workers, peasants, and soldiers, to take part in the class struggles, and to criticize the bourgeoisie.[53] After Mao died, the State Council restored the enrollment examination system for higher education, reformed the centralized educational system, and made efforts to promote the different types of universities, including regular colleges and universities, the Central Television University, and short-term vocational colleges. The government also encouraged the Chinese people to take the self-study examination. The State Council in 1983 approved the establishment of a National Examination Guidance Committee to formulate a unified standard for the examination of self-study. The number of higher education institutions dramatically increased, from 675 in 1980 to 1,016 in 1985,[54] with 1,143,700 undergraduate students enrolled in colleges and universities and 17,700 postgraduate students.[55]

China's educational system has continued to develop from the 1990s to the present. First, Chinese educational law and regulation have been improved. The Chinese government has promulgated many laws to guarantee the educational rights of Chinese people, including the Law of Compulsory Education of the People's Republic of China, the Law of Teachers of the People's Republic of China, the Law of Protection over Juveniles of the People's Republic of China, and the Education Law of the People's Republic of China. The Ministry of Education has issued more than 200 sets of administrative rules and regulations to promote the development of Chinese education. Second, Chinese educational facilities and enrollment have been dramatically expanding. According to the Xinhua News Agency, by the end of 1999, there were 582,322 primary schools countrywide with an enrollment of 135,549,600; and there were 64,400 common junior middle schools and 38,600 senior high schools nationwide with an enrollment of 58,116,500. Now, more than 95 percent of the Chinese population has access to the nine-year compulsory education system. It is predicted that about 95 percent of illiterate young people will learn to read and write by 2010.[56] The Chinese government has made efforts to develop special education. More than 1,520 special schools have been opened for disabled students, with a total enrollment of 371,600. The government has paid special attention to higher education. In 2002, there were 1,396 common colleges and universities nationwide offering 3,205,000 seats in bachelor's programs, 390,000 seats in master's programs, and 100,000 seats in doctoral programs. Meanwhile, China continues to expand higher education in various ways, such as self-study and adult education programs. More than 800 colleges and universities provide adult education programs, offering 5,591,600 seats for bachelor and associate bachelor's programs. By 2002, more than 1,295,000 people had obtained associate bachelor's degrees through self-study programs.[57] International exchange programs have been expanding as well. From 1978 to 1998, more than 320,000 Chinese students went to 103 countries to study; 50,000 of them were sent by the state, 100,000 by the government units that employ them, and 170,000 went at their own expense.[58] Since 1979, China has hosted 340,000 foreign students from more than 160 countries. About 110,000 students have returned to China after graduation, and they have made great contributions to China's economic and social development. According to the *People's Daily*, China has begun setting up a standard for eligibility of students studying abroad. By 1999, the number of foreign students studying in Chinese universities had increased at an annual rate of 20 percent, to reach 50,000 studying at some 300 institutions of higher learning.[59] All these statistics show that education in China has arrived at a new stage.

UNRESOLVED EDUCATIONAL PROBLEMS

China has achieved magnificent progress in the educational arena since it launched the economic reform program, but fundamental structural problems have not yet been resolved. In premodern China, education overemphasized politics and ethics and was divorced from science and technology. Then, education actually became part of the government recruitment system and lost its essential educational functions. In the Mao era, education went to an extreme revolutionary model. Communist political education replaced all other basic educational functions, bringing the Chinese economy to the verge of collapse. In the post-Mao era, communist politics still pervade education, and democracy is rejected. Therefore, China's educational system faces great challenges. First, access to information has become increasingly important. Education in this new century should train the people to utilize information, develop new ways of thinking, and operate a variety of research facilities with suitable methods. Second, globalization is a modern phenomenon. Any major achievement depends upon international cooperation. Economics, politics, ideology, religion, science and technology, and information are transnational. In order to conform to the process of globalization, education should take responsibility for training people to understand a foreign country's history, economy, politics, ideology, religion, language, and traditions. Third, the term *education* today describes a very broad category that includes preinfant education (for unborn children), infant education, elementary education, secondary education, higher education, professional education, adult education, and continuing education. Correspondingly, the content of education should include scientific education, art education, moral education, professional education, information and computer education, liberal education, classical education, secular education, religious education, and democratic education. Facing the new century and new situation, China should reform its educational system, structure, mechanism, curricula, and overarching concept to support economic development and democracy.

Reforming the Centralized Control System

The highly centralized control system over education must be reformed. The Chinese educational system is a weak bureaucratic actor because the party tightly controls Chinese education,[60] the so-called socialist education model with Chinese characteristics. Paul Mort has observed that it takes about thirty years for a new educational idea to be translated into action in the United States, but it takes only a very short period of time in Communist China. Two reasons can explain this. First, the party has the power to do whatever it wants. There is no other branch to check its power. Second, state decisions are identical with party decisions. The Chinese educational system is constructed within the party system.[61] The highest level of educational organization in China from 1949 to 1985 was the Ministry of Education, which reported directly to the State Council.[62] In turn, the State Council was controlled by the Political Bureau of the CPC. During the Cultural Revolution, Mao attacked the Ministry of Education and destroyed the educational system. When educational reforms began in 1978, the Ministry of Education had returned to its former position. In order to firmly control education, the party decided that the State Council would replace the Ministry of Education with the State Education Commission, which is one level above all the other ministries and thus able to legislate policy for all schools and universities.[63] The State Education Commission is responsible for determining broad policies and selecting textbooks, providing curricula outlines, and running higher education through the university entrance-examination system. The branches of the State Education Commission at provincial, city, and county levels must implement the policies and regulations that are made by higher-level offices. Provincial authorities run the secondary educational system through their control of the secondary school entrance exams. The local governments provide the majority of funds for local elementary and secondary schools.[64] Although the educational authorities have been decentralized, the State Education Commission retains the key decision-making power over education.[65] With the economic reform expanding, economic power has been shifting from the central government to local governments. In other words, local governments have taken more responsibilities for developing their own economies, educational systems, and other civil services.

At this point, the central government has no reason to hold the right to control local education affairs. To maintain its centralized system and ideological control, the government placed restrictions on private schools and completely monopolized the Chinese education system before 1984.[66] After that time, China began to allow the establishment of private schools in large cities, but there were only 45,000 non-government-run schools in China in 1999, accounting for 5.2 percent of all the country's schools, and 1,240 non-government universities. Most non-government schools and universities are located in economically advanced areas.[67] The government has not granted the right for private schools to compete fairly with public schools; for example, the private schools have no rights to confer diplomas, and students in private colleges are not eligible to apply for study-aid loan from banks. Therefore, privatization is part of educational reform.

Removing Communist Education from the System

Communist education must be removed from Chinese education. In premodern China, the education system was treated as the tool of politics, and education as a whole was designed to recruit imperial officials. Under the Nationalist government, schools became increasingly politicized and served as propaganda centers for the doctrine of the Guomindang. Students in both elementary and middle schools were required to study the Three People's Principles, listen to the "Last Will and Testament of Sun Yat-sen" every Monday morning, and sing the new national anthem.[68] After the Communist Party came to power, Mao "adopted the position of an emperor figure," passing on his own words and thoughts through education.[69] The objectives of communist education were to contribute to the ideological conversion of the Chinese people and intensify party control.[70] Under the Maoist regime, ideological training was the key to education. Lu Dingyi, the head of the Central Propaganda Department of the CPC, speaking at the People's Congress in April 1960, put the developing Chinese defiance of Western established educational principles into bold and explicit words: "We hold the view that education should serve the politics of the proletariat; the bourgeois class is of the opinion that 'education is for education's sake': this means that education should serve the politics of the bourgeois class. We hold the view that education should be combined with productive labor; the bourgeois class thinks that education and productive labor should be separated. We hold the view that education should be directed by the party, on the line of the masses; the bourgeois class thinks that only expert staff can direct education."[71] The Chinese government put politics at the center of the curriculum in different ways; for instance, textbooks utilized symbols to achieve certain behavioral patterns and to provide a political context for the learning process. Politics also became a "distinct subject of study."[72] During the Cultural Revolution, students were required to read aloud from *Mao Zhu Xi Yu Lu (Mao's Quotations)* in every class session and to follow his superior instruction.

According to Chinese officials, the purpose of primary education is to cultivate the pupil's moral character of loving the motherland and supporting the Communist Party;[73] the purpose of middle schools is to train socialist workers and qualified students for higher education;[74] the purpose of high schools is to train specialized professionals with political awareness and communist morality;[75] and the purpose of higher education is to produce students who are socialist-minded with knowledge and skills in their own fields.[76] Although the post-Mao government has been departing from the old educational model, it has never given up communist education. The party/government continues to stifle intellectual activities by promoting political campaigns—such as anti–cultural contamination, anti–spiritual pollution, and anti–bourgeois liberalization—to prevent intellectuals from borrowing Western ideas. After China restored the university entrance examination system, candidates were required to take an examination on communist politics. Some new examination formats have been implemented, such as "3 + 2" (Chinese, mathematics, and foreign language plus history and geography), 3 + comprehensive art examination, and 3 + comprehensive science examination. Those students destined for science study are no longer required to take the political subject exam, but all students are still required to take political courses after they enroll in the university. At present, three standard political courses remain in the curriculum of higher education: History of the Chinese Communist Party, Marxist Economics, and Marxist Philosophy.[77] Although the titles of the standard political courses have changed from time to time, the nature of ideological control over students and intellectuals has never changed. Recently, a new required course entitled Communist Ideals and Professional Morality was added to the curriculum.[78] Students are not qualified to graduate without passing the communist political courses. This political education costs students time, constrains students' initiative, and results in lower academic competitiveness of Chinese students in the global society. Therefore, educational reform in China necessarily involves a curriculum reform.

Introducing Democratic Education

Democratic education should be introduced into the Chinese education system. The school is a microsociety and a miniature political system. Students should be encouraged to practice democratic principles because students are the future of a society.[79] Teachers should be committed to teaching democratic principles and discussing public policy because teachers are the communicators of democratic values in the classroom.[80]

Although Western-style schools were established in China 150 years ago, their purpose was to "train people to know how to operate foreign machines, produce modern guns, weapons, warships, commercial ships, and train a group of scholars qualified to be interpreters of foreign languages."[81] Influenced by the New Cultural Movement of 1919 and Western scholars such as John Dewey, Bertrand Russell, Paul Monroe, G. R. Twiss, W. A. McCall, and Helen Parkhurst, the Nationalist government pushed education in the "direction of democratic education."[82] The modern university in China came into existence in the second half of the nineteenth century. The main concern of the Nationalist government was to expand enrollments in the sciences in order to develop the national economy. Major subjects in the nationalist period were arts, sciences, law, commerce, medicine, agriculture, and engineering. In the 1930s, the Chinese government adopted several measures in the field of higher education, including the geographic and financial rationalization of higher institutions, the establishment of academic chairs in place of college and departmental organization, a clear national procedure for monitoring all academic appointments, a final examination and a thesis for all graduating students to ensure strong initiation in a discipline, and the introduction of province- or citywide academic examinations at the end of secondary school as a unified means of selection for university entrance.[83] By 1947, university departments of political science and law flourished, constituting 24 percent of the total enrollment.[84] The Mao regime regarded Western democracy as subversive to the socialist system and discontinued the process of democratic education. In 1965, about 65.5 percent of all students were enrolled in applied science majors; only 0.6 percent studied political science and law. The rest of the students were enrolled in other departments, such as applied arts, pure theoretical sciences, humanities, and finance and economics.[85] Enrollments in political science and law dropped from 37,682 in 1947 to 7,338 in 1949, 4,144 in 1965, and to only 410 by 1976.[86] The post-Mao government basically has focused on economic growth and has remained ambivalent about its political implications.[87] The Four Modernizations formula clearly shows that the party neglects questions of political democratization.[88]

Correspondingly, the Chinese government does not allow Chinese scholars and teachers autonomy and academic freedom. Academic freedom is the precondition for scholars to explore science and technology. Modern universities in France and Germany enjoy great autonomy in relation to the state; and the modern British university system is largely free from state controls although it retains connections to the church. The United States inherited the British legacy. U.S. colleges and universities from the seventeenth to the early nineteenth centuries were mainly "dominated by churchmen, whose governmental style they reflected and whose members dominated their boards."[89] Civil liberties and democratic principles were introduced into U.S. universities a long time ago, but there was neither autonomy nor academic freedom in premodern China.[90] The civil service examination system dominated Chinese education for 1,400 years and "controlled canonical knowledge within the Hanlin Academy."[91] (The Hanlin Academy, *Hanlin yuan*, was a very important institution in the central administration of the Chinese empire.) At present, professors in China are not allowed to conduct any independent research project that departs from the Four Cardinal Principles, and all professors must teach what the party tells them to; otherwise they are subject to various punishments.

Religious education is part of a democratic education. Religious studies are regular course offerings in democratic societies and help the people to understand the importance of religious liberty.[92] Western missionaries mostly came to China in the nineteenth century and started teaching a modern, secular curriculum. While Chinese reformers of the Self-Strengthening Movement found that power was born both of Chinese and Western knowledge, nineteenth-century Western missionaries argued that "knowledge was power, and what we wanted in China was power consecrated to the service of Christ."[93] Christian education in China was started by Protestant missionaries along the east coast in the mid-nineteenth century. The early missionary goal focused on evangelism through conversion that provided members and leaders for the Christian Church.[94] According to a report of the Chinese Ministry of Education, approximately 4 million students out of the school-age population of 100 million enrolled in missionary schools during the period of the Republic of China. The number of students in the missionary schools was comparatively small, but the influence of these schools was great.[95] However, by fall 1952, all foreign-related colleges had ceased to exist in recognizable form. A seventy-year history of Christian education had been ended by the Communist Party.[96] The characteristics of communist education are secular and antireligious. In the Mao era, education emphasized materialism and Darwinism to answer the basic questions of human existence. Religious education was completely prohibited. In post-Mao China, schools and universities have offered some courses on religious history within the Marxist framework, but they have not been permitted to provide courses on Christian faith and other religious values. The funny thing is that the Chinese government has also required seminaries to teach religion by using Marxist principles. By 1997, there were only seventy-three seminaries for 1.3 billion Chinese people, according to the white paper released by the State Council. Thus China has a great shortage of professional religious scholars.

At present, the Internet is one of the most effective channels for receiving and disseminating democratic ideas and practices. Therefore, the Internet should be opened up for democratic education. China started online educational services in 1998. According to the Xinhua News Agency, Chinese universities enrolled more than 200,000 students via the Internet in 2000.[97] More than 1.5 million people in China are now receiving college-level instruction via the Internet, television, and radio.[98] However, Wei Yu, the deputy minister of education, points out that online educational information is "a part of the socialist education system"; therefore, only the State Education Mission has the right to manage the service.[99] The development of Internet education in China is slow because the party/state put many restrictions on Internet service. Therefore, it is still questionable whether the Internet will become a tool for democratization in China's foreseeable future.

Reforming the Educational Mechanism

The educational mechanism must be further reformed. Sufficient educational funding is a precondition for the educational system to function effectively. Education expenses before 1992 stayed below 4 percent of GNP, at only about 32 yuan per person (about U.S.$3.8).[100] Actually, educational investment has continued to decrease because of inflation. In

1998, the Chinese government invested 294 billion yuan in education, 150 billion yuan of it on compulsory education, an eighteenfold increase compared with 1986.[101] China will spend some 250 billion yuan (U.S.$28.7 billion) annually on higher education in the first decade of the twenty-first century.[102] The government also set up an annual foundation to sponsor 600,000 school dropouts from poor families to take up their schooling again.[103] Meanwhile, the government receives educational funds from foreign countries and international organizations. The first donation, of U.S.$18,266,000, by the World Bank has been allocated to twenty counties for building more than 2 million square miles of schools and buying more books for reading rooms and desks and chairs for students. The World Bank's second donation, of U.S.$13 million, was given to eleven cities, eighteen poor counties, and eleven normal schools to carry out the nine-year compulsory education programs and to improve the quality of teaching.[104] Obviously, the Chinese government has gradually invested more and more capital in education. However, China's economy has not received the same percentage returns from education. According to research on the contribution of higher education to economic growth in China, the share of expenditures on education is 8.84 percent in an annual GDP increase of 9.58 percent, but only 0.48 percent of economic growth is due to higher education.[105] Another report, on worldwide competitiveness, shows that in 2000 China's scientific competitiveness rank dropped by three places. These statistics indicate that the allocation of education funds in China is not appropriate. They raise a serious question, of how the Chinese government can most wisely invest educational funds to support economic development. According to a report in *China Education Daily*, of all monies spent on compulsory education, only 2 percent is from the state treasury, 70 percent comes from townships, and the rest comes from provincial governments.[106] The central government must do more for basic education.

Because of the lack of education funds, nine-year compulsory education has not achieved an ideal result. Consequently, the illiteracy rate remains an impediment to modernization. In China, an "illiterate" is defined as anyone twelve years of age or older who could read no more than 500 Chinese characters, and a "semi-illiterate" as anyone with knowledge of no more than 1,500 Chinese characters.[107] Before 1949, approximately 80 percent of the 400 million-plus population was illiterate.[108] Without a doubt, the Chinese Communist government has made great efforts to eliminate illiteracy. More than 90 percent of school-age children were enrolled in school by 1980, and more than 95 percent by 1999. The Constitution of China ratified in 1982 made it clear for the first time that primary education would be compulsory for all children. Article 19 of the Constitution states, "The state runs schools of various type, makes primary education compulsory and universal, develops secondary, vocational, and higher education and promotes preschool education." By 1982, the illiterate or semiliterate population dropped to 23.5 percent of the total population. By 1999, China had eliminated illiteracy among 2,990,000 people nationwide.[109] The Chinese government claimed in 2000 that China had accomplished the goals of nine-year compulsory education as a whole and had eliminated youth illiteracy as a whole. About 240 million young people and children were receiving education in the schools nationwide.[110] However, "nine-year compulsory education as a whole" only refers to the target of 85 percent of the Chinese population. The remaining 15 percent of the population lives mainly in the countryside, especially in poor regions in western China. The reform movement created large numbers of rich people, but at the same time it widened the gulf between rich and poor and between rural areas and urban areas. In some remote areas of the western part of China, many children are not willing to accept education because they view it as useless and cannot afford the expense. It should be noted that although it is so-called compulsory education, only small portions of tuition payments are exempted. In addition, textbooks are increasingly expensive—more than 100 yuan per semester for primary school students and 200 yuan per term for middle school students. Students in some rural areas are unable to afford tuition and textbook expenses and donations based on their parent's incomes. In urban areas, tuition is more expensive. According to a survey, in Shanghai tuition is 14,000 yuan for three years of kindergarten, 16,500 yuan for five years of primary school, 30,000 yuan for seven years of secondary school, and 46,000 yuan for four years of college.[111] Altogether, a family needs to pay tuition fees of 106,5000 yuan for a student's education from kindergarten through undergraduate college. The tuition fee is too high for many Chinese families in both rural and urban areas. Since China carried out the family responsibility system, more and more students have left school to help their families with farmwork.[112] Some local governments have adopted regulations to require compliance with the Constitution's requirements for education. According to the regulations, people who have not completed their elementary education cannot be appointed as cadres, cannot be hired by enterprises, and are not permitted to join the army. However, a very difficult task still remains for China to further reduce the illiteracy rate. The basic capability of reading and writing is a precondition for learning and practicing democracy. Obviously, since the reform movement, the growing illiteracy rate is an obstacle to democratization. A serious question today is how the government can support basic education and reinforce compulsory education nationwide.

To establish an effective educational mechanism, China needs more qualified teachers. Teachers are the core of education. China has a long tradition of honoring and respecting teachers, but during the Cultural Revolution teachers were labeled as the "stinking ninth category." In the post-Mao era, the Chinese government has reaffirmed that teachers are the key to schools' success in meeting the needs of Chinese modernization. Deng called public attention to the importance of creating an atmosphere of respect for knowledge and for intellectuals. In order to promote teachers' initiative, the government raised teachers' salaries, improved their housing conditions, expanded preservice teacher-training programs, and the National People's Congress designated September 10 as National Teacher's Day at its January 1985 meeting. However, teachers have ranked among the lowest-paid professionals and have had few benefits during the post-Mao era, such as housing, salary, and health insurance, although the party has made efforts to improve the situation. One hundred thousand secondary school teachers left their jobs between 1985 and 1988.[113] Many young university professors have left their teaching positions for business (*xia hai*) and foreign countries (*tao jin*). The average age of China's professors in 1983 was 65, that of associate professors was 53.5, and the average age of lecturers was 45.[114] Most self-sponsored students who left China to study abroad have stayed in foreign countries after they graduated. After the September 11 terrorist attacks, most Chinese students still consider returning to China their last choice. Consequently, the number of students per teacher in Chinese classrooms has grown larger, and educational quality in China has decreased.

CONCLUSION

Ideology, economy, religion, politics, and education are part of an integrated system and work together in the same cultural system. It is impossible for a country to achieve democratization without an advanced educational system. To remake China's public philosophy, it is necessary to reform the Chinese educational system and bring Chinese education to a higher level. China had the earliest and largest educational system in the world, but premodern China became a backward country with a low educational level. Approximately 80 percent of the Chinese population was illiterate before 1949. This is one important explanation for how China maintained its absolute monarchical political system for more than 2,000 years. After the founding of the People's Republic of China, the Chinese government made magnificent progress in educational areas. Education has become an important source in contributing to the Four Modernizations since Deng's reform movement began. However, educational problems in China remain, such as the highly centralized educational system, communist political education, lack of democratic education, inefficient educational mechanisms, and so forth. At present, the Communist government not only retains tight control over the educational system, but it also applies the Communist ideology to the educational curriculum at every level. This seriously affects students in their ways of thinking and in their attitudes toward Chinese society. All these problems derive from the Chinese political system. China's educational problem is a structural problem. The Chinese political system must be reformed when reforming China's educational system, conception, structure, and mechanism.

NOTES

1. Stewart E. Fraser, *Education and Communism in China: An Anthology of Commentary and Documents* (Hong Kong: International Studies Group, 1969), p. 1.

2. Alexander Woodside and Benjamin A. Elman, "Introduction," in *Education and Society in Late Imperial China, 1600–1900,* eds. Benjamin A. Elman and Alexander Woodside (Berkeley: University of California Press, 1994), p. 1.

3. Chang-tu Hu, *Chinese Education under Communism* (New York: Bureau of Publication, 1962), pp. 16–17.

4. Suzanne Ogden, *China's Unresolved Issues: Politics, Development, and Culture* (Englewood Cliffs, N.J.: Prentice-Hall, 1995), p. 317.

5. Harmon Zeigler, *The Political World of the High School Teacher* (Corvalis, Oreg.: University of Oregon, 1966), p. xi.

6. Woodside and Elman, "Introduction," p. 1.

7. Suzanne Pepper, *China's Education Reform in the 1980s: Policies, Issues, and Historical Perspectives* (Berkeley, Calif.: Center for Chinese Studies, 1990), p. 2.

8. Lynn Paine, "The Educational Policy Process: A Case Study of Bureaucratic Action in China," in *Bureaucracy, Politics, and Decision Making in Post-Mao China,* eds. Kenneth G. Lieberthal and David M. Lampton (Berkeley: University of California Press, 1992), p. 182.

9. John F. Cleverley, *The Schooling of China: Tradition and Modernity in Chinese Education* (Boston: G. Allen & Unwin, 1985), p. 1.

10. Editorial Committee, *Education and Science* (Beijing: Foreign Languages Press, 1983), p. 2.

11. John N. Hawkins, *Mao Tse-Tung and Education: His Thoughts and Teachings* (Hamden, Conn.: Linnet Books, 1974), pp. 26–27.

12. Quoted in Jingpan Chen, *Confucius as a Teacher: Philosophy of Confucius with Special Reference to Its Educational Implications* (Beijing: Foreign Languages Press, 1990), p. 455.

13. Chen, *Confucius as a Teacher,* p. 175.

14. Sally Borthwick, *Education and Social Change in China: The Beginnings of the Modern Era* (Stanford, Calif.: Hoover Institution Press, 1983), p. 4.

15. Chen, *Confucius as a Teacher,* p. 175.

16. Cleverley, *The Schooling of China,* p. 2.

17. Mu Chien, *Traditional Government in Imperial China: A Critical Analysis* (New York: St. Martin's Press, 1982), p. 17.

18. Ibid., p. 51.

19. Ibid., p. 17.

20. Ibid.

21. Ibid., p. 51

22. Ibid., p. 79.

23. Ibid., p. 112.

24. Ibid., p. 134.
25. Ruth Hayhoe, *China's Universities and the Open Door* (Armonk, N.Y.: M.E. Sharpe, 1989), p. 13.
26. Chien, *Traditional Government in Imperial China*, p. 52.
27. Quoted in Cleverley, *The Schooling of China*, p. 21.
28. Chien, *Traditional Government in Imperial China*, p. 50.
29. Cleverley, *The Schooling of China*, pp. 21–22.
30. Ibid., p. 3.
31. William Ayers, *Chang Chih-tung and Educational Reform in China* (Cambridge, Mass.: Harvard University Press, 1971), p. 153.
32. Ibid., p. 134.
33. Quoted in Ibid., p. 160.
34. Marianne Bastid, *Educational Reform in Early Twentieth-Century China* (Ann Arbor: Center for Chinese Studies, University of Michigan, 1988), p. ix.
35. Ibid., p. 89.
36. Shuang Guang, "Education and Economic Development: Evidence from China," *Comparative Economic Studies* 39 (Fall/Winter 1997), p. 69.
37. Franklin Parker and Betty June Parker, *Education in the People's Republic of China, Past and Present: An Annotated Bibliography* (New York: Garland Publishing, 1986), p. xxxiv.
38. Ibid., p. xxxv.
39. Mao Zedong, "Rectify the Party's Style of Work" (February 1942), in *Selected Works of Mao Zedong*, vol. 2 (Beijing: Foreign Languages Press, 1965), p. 39.
40. Mao Zedong, "Instruction on the Question of Consolidating the Anti-Japanese Military and Political College" (6 October 1966), *Current Background* 897 (10 December 1969), p. 10.
41. Mao Zedong, "Summary of Talk with Mao Yan-hsing" (5 July 1964), *Current Background* 888 (August 1969), p. 14.
42. Mao Zedong, "A Talk Delivered in 1958," *Current Background* 888 (August 1969), p. 7.
43. K. E. Priestley, *Education in China* (Hong Kong: Green Pagoda Press, 1961), pp. 14–15.
44. Parker and Parker, *Education in the People's Republic of China, Past and Present*, p. xxxii.
45. Deng Xiaoping, "Speech at the National Conference on Education (April 22, 1978)," *Selected Works of Deng Xiaoping: 1975–1982* (Beijing: Foreign Languages Press, 1984), p. 53.
46. Ibid., pp. 6–12.
47. Keith Lewin, Su Hui, Angela Little, and Zheng Jiwei, *Educational Innovation in China* (Burnt Mill, Harlow, England: Longman House, 1994), pp. 20–21.
48. Shi Ming Hu and Eli Seifman, eds., *Education and Socialist Modernization: A Documentary History of Education in the People's Republic of China, 1977–1986*. (New York: AMS, 1987), p. 12.
49. China Handbook Editorial Committee, *Education and Science*, p. 10.
50. *People's Daily*, 12 August 1979, p. 1.
51. "Proposal of the Central Committee of the Chinese Communist Party for the Seventh Five-Year Plan for National Economic and Social Development (September 23, 1985)," *Beijing Review* 40 (October 1985), p. 15.

52. China Handbook Editorial Committee, *Education and Science,* p. 10.
53. Hu and Seifman, *Education and Socialist Modernization,* p. 31.
54. Hayhoe, *China's Universities and the Open Door,* p. 42.
55. China Handbook Editorial Committee, *Education and Science,* p. 10.
56. Xinhua News Agency, 28 October 2000, 12 May 2000.
57. China Education and Research Network, available at http://www.edu.cn/HomePage/english/index.shtml.
58. Xinhau News Agency, 16 December 1999.
59. Xinhau News Agency, 9 March 2000.
60. Paine, "The Educational Policy Process," p. 181.
61. See Thomas C. Schmidt, "Organization and Structure," in *China's Schools in Flux,* eds. Ronald N. Montaperto and Jaya Henderson (White Plains, N.Y.: M.E. Sharpe, 1979), p. 40.
62. Ibid., pp. 42–45.
63. Ogden, *China's Unresolved Issues,* p. 319.
64. Paine, "The Educational Policy Process," p. 186.
65. Hayhoe, *China's Universities and the Open Door,* p. 43.
66. Chin-Tsao Chen, "The Necessities, Possibilities, and Difficulties of Establishing a Wholly Foreign-Owned Private School in the People's Republic of China" (Ph.D. diss., Wilmington College, 1997); available on-line at http://wwwlib.umi.com/dissertations/fullcit/9729130.
67. Xinhua News Agency, 22 May 2000.
68. Cleverley, *The Schooling of China,* p. 60.
69. Ruth Hayhoe, *China's Universities 1895–1995: A Century of Cultural Conflict* (New York: Garland Publishing, 1996), p. 23.
70. Priestley, *Education in China,* p. 8.
71. Quoted in Ibid., p. 2.
72. Gregory R. Anrig, "Curriculum," in *China's Schools in Flux,* eds. Ronald N. Montaperto and Jaya Henderson (Armonk, N.Y.: M.E. Sharpe, 1979), p. 88.
73. China Handbook Editorial Committee, *Education and Science,* p. 35.
74. Ibid., p. 37.
75. Ibid., pp. 42–43.
76. Ibid., p. 47.
77. Quoted in Hayhoe, *China's Universities and the Open Door,* p. 33.
78. Hayhoe, *China's Universities and the Open Door,* p. 52.
79. Mary A. Hepburn, ed., *Democratic Education in Schools and Classrooms* (Washington, D.C.: National Council for the Social Studies, 1983), p. 1.
80. Zeigler, *The Political World of the High School Teacher,* p. 151.
81. Lu-Dzai Djung, *A History of Democratic Education in Modern China* (Shanghai, China: Commercial Press, 1933), p. 2.
82. Ibid., pp. 7–10.
83. Hayhoe, *China's Universities and the Open Door,* p. 17.
84. Editorial Committee, *Achievement of Education in China: Statistics 1949–1983* (Beijing: People's Education Press, 1984), p. 62.
85. Hayhoe, *China's Universities and the Open Door,* p. 30.
86. Editorial Committee, *Achievement of Education in China,* p. 54.
87. Hayhoe, *China's Universities and the Open Door,* p. 29.
88. Ibid., p. 28.

89. Hayhoe, *China's Universities 1895–1995*, p. 8.
90. Ibid., p. 10.
91. Ibid., p. 13.
92. Derek H. Davis and Robert H. Haener III, "An Examination of Church-State Curriculum in American Higher Education," *Journal of Church and State* 38 (Winter 1996), p. 169.
93. Quoted in Cleverley, *The Schooling of China*, p. 32.
94. William Purviance Fenn, *Christian Higher Education in Changing China: 1880–1950* (Grand Rapids, Mich.: William B. Eerdmans Publishing Company, 1976), pp. 24–25.
95. James B. Webster, *Christian Education and the National Consciousness in China* (New York: E.P. Duttton & Company, 1923), p. 27.
96. Fenn, *Christian Higher Education in Changing China*, p. 225.
97. Xinhua News Agency, 26 June 2000.
98. Ibid., 3 April 2000.
99. Ibid., 5 April 2000.
100. Paine, "The Educational Policy Process," p. 182.
101. Xinhua News Agency, 27 December 1999.
102. Ibid., 11 October 1999.
103. Ibid., 24 May 1999.
104. Ibid., 14 April 2000.
105. Yuwen Cui, "Quality Education and International competition," *Journal of Beijing Normal University*, no. 1, 2000, p. 59.
106. *China Education Daily*, 27 October 2000.
107. *China Daily*, 4 August 1983, p. 4.
108. Xinhua News Agency, 2 March 2000.
109. Ibid., 28 February 2000.
110. Ibid., 2 March 2000.
111. *People's Daily*, 13 July 13, 2001.
112. Hu and Seifman, *Education and Socialist Modernization*, p. 18.
113. Paine, "The Educational Policy Process," p. 202.
114. Gaojiao Zhang, "Higher Education Front," *China Report* 24 (13 March 1985), pp. 37–40.

CHAPTER 8

Remaking China's Public Philosophy and China's Future

The process of remaking China's public philosophy is a profound revolution that will have a great impact on China's future. The term *China* generally refers to the mainland, Taiwan, Hong Kong, and Macao, but particularly to the mainland. Taiwan, Hong Kong, and Macao have adopted different economic and political systems from the mainland, as the second system of the so-called one country, two systems. With the spread of globalization, greater China—cultural China—becomes a fascinating phenomenon. Since Hong Kong and Macao have returned to the People's Republic of China, the two special regions have established close relations with mainland China under the guidance of the central government. Nowadays, Hong Kong, Macao, and the mainland are becoming more and more similar, although Hong Kong and Macao Chinese have had quite different experiences. Some Western scholars have begun to question whether the policy of one country, two systems is still functioning.

The peoples of Hong Kong and Macao have openly criticized the central government. There is little doubt that citizens residing in Hong Kong and Macao are eager to remake China's public philosophy in order to retain their established lifestyles and living standards. As for relations between Taiwan and mainland China, it is quite evident that the unification of the mainland with Taiwan is the common will of the Chinese government and the majority of the Chinese people. The government clearly sees Taiwan's strategic position in the world and wants to unite Taiwan with the mainland as soon as possible. Mainland China will never relinquish this mission under any circumstance. The common desire for unification is due not only to patriotic nationalism but also arises from traditional Chinese culture—the idea of a great union. Western countries must understand this point in order to make their own China policies. However, there is a gulf between Taiwan and the mainland in terms of both political and economic systems and cultural traditions. The election of Chen Shuibian as president of Taiwan in 2000 strongly indicated that the Taiwanese were trying to drift away from the mainland. Although Chen is not a strong president, he represents the will of the majority of the Taiwanese people. The more serious signal sent to the Beijing government is the result of the Taiwan's parliamentary elections in November 2001. The Nationalist Party lost its dominant position for the first time since the Nationalist government fled the mainland in 1949. In the 225-seat Legislative Yuan, the Democratic Progressive Party improved its position, from 66 seats to 87, as the Nationalists dropped from 123 to 68 seats. The election results imply that the Taiwanese dislike the current political system of mainland China and that the Democratic Progressive Party and Taiwan might move toward independence while getting support from the Taiwanese people and establishing a higher international profile for Taiwan. Taiwan is unlikely to be convinced that unification with the mainland can be accomplished peacefully absent a complete reconstruction of China's public philosophy. In the first official reaction to the parliamentary election, spokesman Zhang Mingqing of China's Taiwan Affairs Office on December 5, 2001 warned Taiwan that China would pay a lot of attention to the direction of Taiwan's polices toward the mainland in the wake of the election and that any attempt to wage pro-independence policies would fail to get public support. Some analysts believe that China lacks the military capability to take over Taiwan at present. Nobody knows for sure when China will possess such a capability. Probably, China will never have the chance to unify Taiwan with the mainland because China is unable to develop sophisticated weapons and military forces.

Will China give up its quest for unification with Taiwan if China continues to lack the military capability? It is clear that the Chinese government will definitely not let Taiwan go if it declares independence. Without a doubt, Taiwan is an important strategic partner to the United States. The George W. Bush administration promised many times after September 11 that the United States would take responsibility for defending Taiwan,[1] because it would be a great threat to U.S. interests if the People's Republic of China attacked Taiwan. If China attempted to unite Taiwan and the mainland by military force, it could trigger a massive war worldwide. The best solution for China is a peaceful unification with Taiwan, achieved through remaking China's public philosophy. Therefore, remaking China's public philosophy is not only a sacred mission for all the Chinese people, including mainland Chinese, Taiwan Chinese, Hong Kong Chinese, Macao Chinese, overseas Chinese, and ethnic Chinese, but it also has regional and global significance. All Chinese people and peacemakers worldwide should promote this great mission.

THE CAPITALIST SYSTEM AND CHINA'S DEMOCRATIZATION

The purpose of remaking China's public philosophy is to peacefully make China a democratic society and a true member of the global village. How can this be initiated? Modern democratic societies are based on capitalism. China had the most advanced civilization in the world before the fourteenth century. Unfortunately, its glorious past did not lead China to become a capitalist society. Was this a mistake of Chinese history? No. Capitalism in China was developing naturally during the Ming dynasty, but this natural process was interrupted by foreign invasions in premodern China, by civil wars and the Guomindang's corruption in the republic era, and by the communist political system of the People's Republic of China. Immanuel Wallerstein has conjectured that the rise of capitalism was caused by four collapses: "The collapse of the seigniors, the collapse of the states, the collapse of the Church, and the collapse of the Mongols."[2] Several reasons for these collapses can be identified. First, capitalism is always closely tied with a particular political system. A market economy is not a pure economic system, but rather "the market becomes itself an important political mechanism."[3] Second, the emergence of capitalism in Europe was inspired by intellectual movements such as the Protestant Reformation, the Renaissance, and Baconian-Newtonian science. Third, private property rights and a sovereign state allowed capitalism to develop.[4] The legalization of private ownership is fundamental to the development of a market economy, and "commodification is a second," because private property rights act "as an incentive for entrepreneurial risk."[5]

In comparison with Europe, Western-style intellectual enlightenment, private property legislation, and a modern nation-state never emerged in China before the Revolution of 1911. Moreover, the Chinese government took a negative attitude toward Western societies and carried out a strict closed-door policy when the capitalist system first emerged in the West. China lost its first opportunity to reform its economic and political structure in the first wave of democratization (1828–1926). As the second wave of democratization spread to many countries from the West to the East after World War II, China did not even consider reconstructing its political system because the Nationalist government and the CPC were involved in the Third Civil War from 1945 to 1949. In the Mao era, the party sharply denounced capitalism and concentrated on the class struggle from 1950 to 1976. China thereby lost a second opportunity to align itself with emerging democratic thought. The world began to experience a third wave of democracy in 1974 that is still continuing;[6] however, during this period,

China was bogged down in domestic chaos—the Cultural Revolution. Although the Chinese government has emphasized economic development since 1978, the Chinese historical lesson suggests that China will not achieve the "fifth modernization"—democratization—even if it succeeds economically, as long as the Chinese government continues to resist the capitalist system as a whole.

In the Mao era, the party propagandized its view that the socialist society is the paradise of human beings and the capitalist society is the hell of human beings. Educated in the communist ideology, most Chinese people at that time viewed capitalist society as a symbol of inequality, corruption, murder, drugs, prostitution, and smuggling. Having seen the reality of capitalist societies after China opened its doors to the rest of the world, however, the Chinese people felt that they were being cheated. They gradually realized the connection between the capitalist system and modernity and democracy,[7] but official Chinese ideology in the post-Mao era still rejects the capitalist system overall. The Chinese government insists that the socialist society is superior to the capitalist society; the capitalist society is only a necessary stage toward the establishment of the socialist society. While the Chinese government adopted some capitalist measures for its economic reforms, Chinese official documents have never affirmed the validity of the capitalist system as a whole. However, to get maximum support from the people of all ranks of Chinese society, the owners of private companies have been allowed to become members of the CPC; in fact, private owners now make up 20 percent of the total party membership. Thus, some analysts declare that the party has entered into a new stage: postcommunism. Unfortunately, these private owners are merging with followers of the party leadership. They are not gravediggers for the socialist society. On the contrary, they open a way for Chinese officials and businessmen to work together, thereby opening the way to serious political and economic corruption. This corruption is leading the Chinese people to turn against the party and is speeding up its collapse.

The Chinese government unarguably has made good efforts at moving toward modernization. Internationally, it has signed various legal documents to conform to global norms. Domestically, the political environment appears more flexible than ever before, but the party has not been willing to alter its old public philosophy even after winning the right to host the Olympic Games of 2008 in Beijing. Although the last Chinese emperor was overthrown ninety years ago, neither the Nationalist government nor the Communist government has truly reformed the old Chinese public philosophy. The patriarchal Chinese culture, tradition, politics, and religion are still deeply embedded there. In contrast with other nations, no country in the world has been more overshadowed by the influence of its historical cultural burden than China.[8] Is China's traditional culture still meaningful to contemporary China, in the call for a new public philosophy? Making China a capitalist society does not mean abolishing Chinese traditional culture completely. Edward Friedman has suggested that the Chinese traditional culture caused China's democratic failure,[9] but there are more people, Wang Gungwu observes, "outside mainland China who are appreciative of traditional culture than there are within."[10] The relationship between Chinese traditional culture and democracy has been and will continue to be debatable. Two points need to be clarified. First, remaking China's public philosophy is not the same as remaking Chinese culture. History is a river of continuation and discontinuation; the Chinese traditional culture as the base of the Chinese nation will never lose its validity. In the process of remaking China's public philosophy, only those elements of Chinese culture that no longer fit democratic principles will be discarded. Second, every nation has its own cultural tradition. The way of Chinese life has basically followed its own cultural tradition. Capitalist China, too, can accommodate traditional Chinese culture. Westernization cannot solve China's problems. In fact, China will lose its cultural roots if it denies everything in its past at the cultural level. Chinese traditional culture as a whole is not compatible with democratic principles at the political level, but remaking public philosophy does not contradict the use of positive elements of Chinese traditional culture in the process of democratization. Confucianism as religion and culture has a global significance in contemporary time. The third epoch of Confucianism is still vigorously ongoing and contributes to Western culture, but it is worth noting that the government's rehabilitation of Confucianism in recent years, including aspects such as filial piety, loyalty, and nepotism, is intended to serve the government's political purpose.[11]

Economy has its relatively independent characteristic, though the five aspects of society—ideology, economy, politics, religion, and education—are interrelated and support a society. Otherwise, we could not explain why the Chinese economy has developed rapidly while political reform has made little progress in the past years. China's economy is now one of the nine largest in the world, and China has become a regional power. China's economy has continuously developed and, fortunately, it stepped out from under the shadow of the Asian financial crisis of 2000. If China retains its current economic growth rate, its economy may become the world's largest within fifty years. Even if it slows down, China's economy could possibly become the second largest in the world by 2020.[12] China's magnificent economic achievement has caught the world's attention as one of the most important phenomena of the global economy in recent decades.[13] However, the high growth rate of the Chinese economy does not mean that China has become a capitalist society. There are various reactions to China's economic development in Western societies. Some people are shocked by the rise of the Eastern giant and consider China to be a major threat to the West.[14] Some view China as a potential threat to

Western societies based on its size and location.[15] Some see that China's economic growth does not threaten other countries but challenges other developed countries as a new competitor.[16] Some ignore the magnificent changes that occurred in China in the past and believe that "China is a small market that matters relatively little to the world."[17] Some think that China and America were strategic partners in the mid-1980s but became strong rivals beginning in the 1990s.[18] Some welcome China's transition and regard its economic growth and political stability as a positive contribution to the global order.[19] The focus of their concerns is whether or not Chinese economic development is good for the global village. The answer is evident: China's role in international society is determined not by the power of its economy but by the nature of the nation—by capitalism/democracy versus socialism/dictatorship. It is a typical example that China was not invited to join the G8 Summit held in June 2003 in France, although China's GDP has surpassed that of Russia, Canada, and Italy.

It is true that the boundaries of previous international alliances have been blurred since September 11. Possibly, international camps will be realigned. China's role in the global village is becoming ambiguous, but this situation will not last too long. The foundation for forming alliances is either through democratic principles or through nondemocratic principles. In the long term, whether or not China threatens the global order depends not on China's economic power and geographic location but on the nature of the Chinese political system. If China's public philosophy is gradually remade, if China smoothly transfers to a democratic system, it will be a peacemaker in the global village no matter how strong China is. If democracy prevails, the more powerful China is, the better it is for the global order.

HAS CHINA CHANGED ITS SOCIALIST IDENTITY?

A nation's identity is determined by the nature of the state. China is a socialist/communist country, as determined by the nature of the state/party. Quite a few scholars have indicated that its economic reform is changing China's identity. The Chinese people, indeed, have suffered from poverty, but an improvement in living standards is not the sole purpose for the Chinese people to devote themselves to the economic reform movement. When their living standard reaches a certain level, they demand political participation and democracy. This political enthusiasm essentially contradicts the party's will because the motivation for the party to promote reform programs is to strengthen its power. According to official Chinese documents, the reform movement is the second socialist revolution. The purpose of the first socialist revolution in 1949 was to transform political power and ownership, yet the purpose of the second socialist revolution is to realize a socialist modernization and develop a socialist economy with Chinese characteristics. Hence the market economy in China is called the "socialist market economy." When the CPC defines the Chinese market economy by socialism, it does not necessarily mean that the party understands the term *market economy* incorrectly. On the contrary, the party clearly understands that there is a fundamental conflict between a free market economy and the socialist system. In order to save the socialist system, the party pursues the pragmatic formula of stimulating economic reform by adopting both socialist principles and capitalist means. Therefore, what changed for the party in the post-Mao era was not the political system but only economic measures. Deng's philosophy of the reform movement may look like a new idea, but obviously it is a refurbished version of the slogan "Chinese learning is for basis, Western learning is for use," adopted by the Self-Strengthening Movement in the nineteenth century.

It was inevitable that China's rapid economic growth would also generate other changes in all social aspects. Hence, some scholars have suggested that China has been departing from communism and state socialism.[20] Ideologically, Marxism and Maoism have been reassessed. The ideological emphasis has shifted from class struggle to economic development. The slogan Four Modernizations inspires the enthusiasm of the Chinese people to devote themselves to the socialist reconstruction. The ideological alteration opened the way for the party and the government to focus on the economy. Economically, China is moving from an agricultural country to an industrial country. Science and technology have developed rapidly; the living standard of the Chinese people has dramatically increased. The traditional planned economy is moving into the socialist market economy, and sole public ownership has been replaced by six types of ownership. The rapid economic growth has also created a large middle class and a large number of internal migrants, expanded urbanization, and led to the accumulation of a great amount of capital. China's recent accession to the WTO will further expand economic growth and economic reform. Politically, since the death of Deng Xiaoping, a single charismatic leader no longer holds all power and controls the entire country. China is moving from an absolute monarchical system to an authoritarian system, as intellectuals and technocrats gradually take key positions in the party and the government. Spiritually, freedom of religion has been officially recognized. All citizens are legally permitted to practice their personal religious faith as long as they do not organize independent religious groups that threaten the state. At present, at least five types of culture—Chinese traditional culture, Marxism-Maoism-Dengism, Western culture, religious culture, and nationalism—are coexisting and developing. The cultural development of recent years could be described as the decline of Marxism and the official culture; the renaissance of Western political science, philosophy, and other non-Marxist thought; and the renaissance of Chinese traditional thought.[21] Educationally, China's nine-year compulsory education system has been strictly enforced. The illiteracy rate has been dramatically reduced, and all types of educational facilities have rapidly expanded, including preschools, elementary schools, secondary schools, high schools, vocational schools, higher education, adult education, self-study programs, TV and radio universities, and Internet universities. The development of education greatly contributes to economic growth and paves the way for civil society and democracy.

China's transitions appear imbalanced, however, between the north and the south, between the west and the east, between the city and the countryside, and among economic, political, and cultural spheres. When some foreigners travel from the northern part of China to the southern part, they think that China's south seems to be a different country.[22] Some scholars have even noted that China really consists of many different Chinas, linguistically and ethnically.[23] Generally, China's south and east are more advanced in economy and finance; China's north is more political; and China's west and its rural areas are relatively backward. Edward Friedman has observed that the true Chinese culture is in the southern part of China.[24] The central government is losing control at the local level because of decentralization, but government authority at the provincial level is gaining power. The Chinese people in advanced areas are more concerned about ideological culture and politics. Young people are inclined to reject Chinese traditional culture and the "new Confucian nationalism,"[25] and they are thirsty for Western thought. All these imbalances do not mean that China is divided. China remains a unified country of fifty-six nationalities. The Chinese people fear disunity and chaos, and no Chinese person speaks out in favor of separatism, or splitism.[26] Essentially, the imbalances indicate that China is moving toward becoming a diverse society, but there has been no solid public philosophy to guide the Chinese people. It is time to promote a new public philosophy—one that will enable China to transform itself into a democracy.

Has China's recent progress changed its identity? For people who experience daily life in China over only a short period of time, it is difficult to identify the nature of mainland China. The lifestyle of the Chinese people, including their dress, food, housing, transportation, street life, nightlife, means of entertainment, and use of modern communication equipment, is not significantly different from lifestyles in capitalist societies. One scholar has further observed that "America is everywhere in China. It is not only a matter of Coca-Cola, McDonald's, Boeing, pop music, and basketball; it is also evident in mind-sets and behaviors."[27] When official foreign delegations visit China, they see and hear good things because their activities are arranged by Chinese officials. It is no wonder that they are surprised by China's impressive changes and conclude that China is becoming a capitalist society, that China is no longer a meaningful communist country, and that what communism is left in China is only the Communist Party itself. Moreover, some scholars believe that the party is dead. They think that as China becomes more and more like Western societies, it is on the verge of becoming a democratic system.

However, lifestyles and living standards cannot represent the nature of a nation. China will not necessarily carry out a democratic system even if it becomes a global economic power. A careful observation of the Chinese way of life—including religious freedoms, human rights, censorship, and the election and legislative systems—will show that the majority of the Chinese people still do not live like Western people. At present, China "remains unchanged in its political nature."[28] Although official Chinese documents do not clarify where China is going and what China's identity will be in the future, it is very clear that the Constitution of the People's Republic of China, the Constitution of the Chinese Communist Party, the constitutions of all mass organizations, and all official documents insist that the Four Cardinal Principles—Marxism-Leninism and Mao Zedong thought, the leadership of the party, the proletariat dictatorship, and the socialist road—are the theoretical foundation of China. When the Four Cardinal Principles are implemented in Chinese ideology, economy, politics, religion, and education, Chinese ideology becomes Marxist ideology with Deng's and Jiang Zemin's characteristics; Chinese economics is called the socialist market economy; Chinese politics remains a highly centralized political system; religions are tightly controlled by the party/state; and education has no choice but to serve the goals of the party. The combination of the Four Cardinal Principles and the five aspects of society in the post-Mao era indicates that the socialist system is still present.[29]

According to J. Howard W. Rhys, "national identity does not depend on racial heritage" but on cultural factors and political systems.[30] Therefore, China's transitions from state socialism, including the political system, economic development, and ideological censorship, "are far from complete,"[31] even though China has begun its transition from a communist to a postcommunist authoritarian regime and has achieved significant progress in many areas.[32] The state/party dictatorship remains stable,[33] but China is no longer the typical totalitarian dictatorship. The fact that China failed to control SARS in 2003, for example, reflects the nature of the CPC. One journalist has tried to distinguish totalitarianism and authoritarianism in this way: "A totalitarian government arrests, tortures and murders," but an authoritarian government "leaves many of these functions to the private sector." Therefore, "we should oppose the establishment of totalitarian regimes, we should encourage the evolution of authoritarian regimes toward a more humane society."[34] From this point of view, China is neither a capitalist society nor a typical Leninist state but a hybrid socialist society.

GLOBALIZATION AND CHALLENGES

Globalization is the integration of the world's economies. In the process of globalization, developments in science and technology have made today's global village smaller and smaller. The process of economic development in every single country is essentially a part of the process of globalization. If all countries coordinate their development well, globalization will proceed faster. The process of remaking China's public philosophy involves globalization. China, with the world's third-largest territory and largest population, can possibly achieve the world's largest GNP. There cannot be integrated globalization without China's full participation. Conversely, China's economic development also relies heavily on foreign investment, trade, access to science and technology, and cultural exchanges. China cannot realize the four modernizations without international assistance. From this perspective, international pressures can be considered an important factor in pushing the Chinese government to move gradually toward modern democracy. In other words, an open-door policy should include both economics and politics. The Chinese government should abide by international law and allow the Chinese people communication with Western countries via various means.

Development and peace are the two key global issues.[35] In the world conference of "The Twenty-first Century Forum" held in Beijing in June 2000, 500 well-known politicians, scholars, and entrepreneurs from different countries discussed the characteristics of economic globalization and agreed that economic globalization points toward the emergence of seven tendencies in the twenty-first century.[36] First, information is becoming the greatest driving force to promote economic growth. Second, technology is acting as an independent commodity. In turn, this commodity enables technology to develop further. Third, private capital is becoming the mainstream of international capital. Fourth, the international economic system has been reorganized in order to fit the new characteristics of globalization. Fifth, globalization has increased the demand for technocrats, scientists, and intellectuals in both developed and developing countries. Therefore, high-quality elites are moving from one country to another without boundaries. Sixth, globalization is intensifying the connections and cooperation among countries. Seventh, reform and an open-door policy together are becoming the rule in developing countries. All these tendencies require China to do more in order to be compatible with international economic norms and implement WTO regulations.

The CPC was mysterious to Western countries before 1949. Communist China was far from the inner circle of international society before it regained a seat in the United Nations in 1972. A conventional opinion is that China was isolated, but few people know that the Communist government tried to develop a normal relationship with the United States and was rebuffed by Washington at the time of the founding of the People's Republic of China. Both sides were responsible for the fact of China's isolation. Under Mao's self-sufficiency policy, China went to an extreme and conformed to no one in the world but to itself. When the U.S. government realized that a stronger relationship would be good for both countries, President John F. Kennedy made efforts to improve the Sino-American relationship.[37] In 1963, Roger Hilsman, an assistant secretary of state, claimed that the United States was in favor of keeping the "door open" to China if China gave up its "venomous hatred" of the United States.[38] However, for various reasons, such as Kennedy's assassination, the Vietnam War, and the Cultural Revolution, the process of the normalization of Sino-American relations was interrupted. After Richard Nixon became president in 1969, he immediately declared, "The policy of this country at this time will be to continue to oppose Communist China's admission to the United Nations,"[39] but he soon changed his attitude toward China after secret negotiations between two countries. Nixon was the first U.S. president to visit Communist China and signed the *Shanghai Communiqué,* which marked a new chapter in Sino-American relations. The Jimmy Carter administration accepted the Communists' three "nonnegotiable conditions" of normalization: "Termination of the United States–Republic of China defense treaty, establishment of diplomatic relations with the government in Beijing instead of with Taipei, and withdrawal of the United States military forces from Taiwan."[40] Since then, the relationship between China and the United States has been officially normalized. The two events—the normalization of Sino-American relations and the restoration of China's seat in the United Nations—opened the way for China to play an active role in international society.

Since 1978, China's international position has become more and more important. Deng carried out the open-door policy and gradually established extensive economic relationships with foreign countries. After the U.S. Congress approved China's most-favored-nation (MFN) trade status in 2001, China became more closely linked to the world economy.[41] China's accession to the WTO means that China will further open its market, eliminate restrictions on imports, accept international norms, and deepen the reform of state-owned enterprises. This implies that China will become a substantial part of the global economy. The direct consequences of China's accession to the WTO are in the economic area. There is no doubt, however, that WTO membership will impact China's political reform in the long term, but it will be a slow process. In this sense, China is still outside international society at present. Unless the current economic reform brings not only economic prosperity but also social stability and democracy, China will not become a real insider in the international community.[42]

Capitalist economy is the driving force of globalization. State ownership in China as the cornerstone of the socialist society has been shaken, but China's economy has not been totally privatized.[43] About 70 percent of gross assets were still owned by the state in 1997, yet state-owned enterprises generated only 34 percent of China's total industrial output.[44] Ownership reform has met with strong resistance from the highest circles of the Communist Party. The party is reluctant to give up state ownership as the dominant ownership in the Chinese economy because the party fears losing its power base. The party believes that the Four Cardinal Principles, not privatization, are the key to the development of the Chinese economy. Thomas G. Rawski argues that "privatization is no magic potion for prosperity."[45] In fact, capitalist markets and privatization are two sides of the same coin. The market economy requires private ownership to coordinate with the modern enterprise system. Certainly, modern enterprise models include private property rights and the right to make investment decisions.[46] In the second half of the 1980s, some former socialist countries engaged in reform and "harmonized their economies with those of the capitalist West."[47] That is why those countries have transformed from socialist systems to a democratic system. However, the party/state in China upholds the socialist market economy and runs the market economy by socialist principles rather than allowing the market to run itself. At this point, the socialist market economy can only be called a semi–market economy. China's economic reform is an unfinished economic revolution. The party/state must withdraw from the socialist market economy and further develop private ownership to escape the cycle of stop-and-go growth.[48] Otherwise, China's economic growth rate could fall to as low as 5 percent by 2020.[49]

In addition, China is confronted with many serious challenges in its economic development toward globalization. First, China's population is growing even though the government tightly controls the birthrate. It has been estimated that there will be 1.6 billion Chinese people by 2035. The Chinese population is five times as large as the U.S. population, but China's arable land is only 60 percent of that in the United States. China has about 7 percent of the earth's total agricultural land, but it must feed 22 percent of the world's population. In addition, China's agricultural land will be further reduced as urbanization increases. Therefore, China will face a great shortage of food and must take a variety of measures to reduce its population growth rate. Second, due to ownership reform and optimization of the labor force, the unemployment rate has increased. In 1993, 4.2 million people were *xia gang* (laid off); this figure reached 5.7 million in 1997. Zeng Peiyan, the director of the State Planning Commission, reported in early March 2002 to a National People's Congress meeting that the total number of unemployed and stepped-down workers from state-owned enterprises was around 12 million. However, according to China's White Paper, issued by the News Bureau of the State Council on April 19, 2002, from 1998 to 2001 the aggregate number of stepped-down workers from state-owned enterprises in China totaled 25.5 million.[50] Third, the gulf between rich and poor has widened. The widening income gap is not only "between developed and underdeveloped regions," but also "between rich and poor people of the same region or city."[51] Moreover, unfair income allocation has been a serious political issue since 1980 and has resulted in critical social problems. More than twenty bombs set off in 2001 indicated that the conflict between rich and poor is intensifying. A so-called stable era in China has ended. Fourth, "inflation has remained at a high level" because of rampant foreign investment and excessive growth in currency circulation.[52] Fifth, environmental problems have seriously affected the ecosystems of China and neighboring countries. China will become the largest producer of carbon dioxide in the world within ten to twenty years. It will cost at least U.S.$2 billion to solve these environmental problems. Sixth, China lacks natural resources and relies heavily on Middle Eastern countries for petroleum imports. The demand for petroleum in China is increasing as the economy is growing. Chinese domestic energy needs already exceed the output of energy. China will need to import more petroleum in the future if it does not make a breakthrough (i.e., discover new oil resources within China and/or shift to another energy source). While China has one-fifth of the world's population, it "has only 7 percent of its fresh water and cropland, 3 percent of its forests, and 2 percent of its oil."[53] Seventh, it is urgent for China to establish a social welfare system. Otherwise, 320 million people over sixty years old will be a great burden to Chinese enterprises in 2040. Eighth, other problems also need to be taken into consideration, such as an underdeveloped transportation system, monetary instability, bottlenecks in energy and raw material supplies, and legal issues. All of these have resulted from economic development. Conversely, these problems restrict Chinese economic reform and lead to social problems such as inequality, bribery, corruption, the crisis of faith, and moral collapse.

Another global issue is peace. Today's world is filled with conflicts and wars, between the south and the north, between the West and the East, between civilization and barbarism, between religious moderation and religious extremism, and even between higher- and lower-level cultures. The international and domestic threat of terrorism has become critical worldwide since September 11. Other forms of violence occur frequently, such as physical abuse, murder, shooting, robbery, and torture. Before China broke off its formal relationship with the Soviet Union, Chinese officials propagandized that imperialism was the sole source of these conflicts because imperialist countries wanted to expand their capital and exploited their colonial assets. After that time, the Chinese government declared that the two superpowers—the Soviet Union and the United States—were the most dangerous enemy to the world because they scrambled for spheres of influence and wanted more territory and natural resources. Since China has carried out an open-door policy, the Chinese government has viewed three forces—nationalism, terrorism, and extremism—as the greatest enemy to international peace and domestic stability.

Since September 11, many Western scholars have become aware that the Chinese government is intentionally tightening its internal control in the name of antiterrorism. The government decided to crack down on international and domestic antagonistic forces, separatists, perpetrators of domestic violence, and religious extremists before the Sixteenth National Congress of the Communist Party of China. While visiting China in February 2002, President Bush expressed his concerns on human rights and religious freedom. Nevertheless, no evidence has shown that the Chinese government has stopped persecuting political dissidents and religious persons. Social stability should be built on a base of social and cultural norms. It is impossible to maintain social stability forever by delivering harsh punishment or banning civil society. Only democracy can make a peaceful world and fundamentally guarantee individual rights for the long term. China will face great instability if it attempts to maintain its social stability only by coercive power and fails to promote political reform. By this token, internationally, prosecution of an unjust war hardly ends war permanently; the world cannot establish permanent peace by means of peacekeeping troops. Generally speaking, "the more democratic countries become, the less likely they are to fight wars against each other. The more dictatorial they are, the more war prone they become."[54]

The issue of Chinese development specifically refers to economic growth, but in a broader sense, the concept of development includes political, cultural, and social progress, too. The issue of democracy is part of the issue of development and is the central issue of globalization. There will be no integrated globalization without democratization. By this premise, the process of remaking China's public philosophy is the same as the process of globalization. It can be argued that democratic systems in different countries share basic similarities, though they also have their own special characteristics. Some Asian countries and regions, such as Japan, South Korea, and Taiwan, have long sought an Asian-style democracy. Their democratic systems embrace both basic Western democratic principles and strong Asian traditions. However, this does not imply that China is an Asian-style democratic country. On the contrary, civil society in China is very weak because the state has failed to create the political and legal structure to protect most forms of social self-organization.[55] The Chinese people do not have the right to request a change of government. Within the current Chinese political framework, all power is held by the

Communist Party. One top leader—the general secretary of the party—practically owns the party's power and has the right to appoint his successor. No other social organization can check the party's power. The party exercises its absolute power and control over 31 provinces and more than 2,000 counties. This unitary political system, on the one hand, needs to centralize its power in order to control the entire country. On the other hand, it produces a conflict between the central government and local governments. Local governments seek autonomy, but they do not use legal measures, instead finding loopholes in the system. Chen Yun, the former vice president of China, describes this phenomenon as the "traffic-light philosophy," meaning that the localities treat the central policies strategically: "When the red light is on, they make a detour and proceed as they were going; when the yellow light is on, they ignore it and keep going at the same speed; and when the green light is on, they rush ahead at full throttle."[56] Under this political system, official corruption has, surprisingly, increased since the reform movement began. In 1998, for example, twelve Chinese officials at the provincial rank were involved in criminal economic activities, seventeen were involved in such activities in 1999, and twenty-two in 2000. Apparently, the one-party system fundamentally contradicts the current economic reform and triggers voices of social discontent. Only political reform can soften and solve the conflict and guarantee that economic reform will go forward. Therefore, democracy is the convergent point of these two global issues.

THE FUTURE OF CHINA

Many scholars have tried to predict China's future, but their predictions are quite varied because it is not easy to foresee China's future in the coming century; not even in the next fifty years. Jack A. Goldstone expects a terminal crisis in China within the next ten to twenty years,[57] while the others predict that China will become an economic and political power soon. Following our examination in previous chapters of China's transitions in the five aspects of Chinese society, it is believable that China might dramatically change its model in market economy and mechanisms. Within fifty years, the gap between China and developed countries in terms of GDP will be getting narrower, but the gap in terms of per capita income could widen. It is possible that China will catch up with Japan and become the second world power in fifty years. China's urbanization will definitely increase; as many as 70 percent of the Chinese population may reside in urban areas by 2050. However, it is difficult to precisely predict China's future in other aspects. Any glowing prediction of China's future easily becomes a form of utopianism because economic growth could come from both economic mechanisms and political institutions. The fact that China's economic growth is declining indicates that political reform has become a focal point to further develop the economy. China's economy reached its height in 1992, with a GNP growth rate of about 14 percent, but after that, China's economic growth began declining, dropping to 10.5 percent in 1995, 9.6 percent in 1996, 8.8 percent in 1998, and about 7.5 percent in 2001. According to Dai Xianlong, president of the Bank of China, the goal for 2002 was 7 percent. Based on World Bank reports, between 2000 and 2025, China's GNP can only reach 6.6 percent.

The future of China's economic growth, on the one hand, depends on further economic reform in industrial structure, fiscal policy, state ownership of enterprises, the financial system, the social security system, and market mechanisms. On the other hand, it really depends on China's full reform movement and fostering a democratic system, and ultimately, on China's willingness to remake its public philosophy. Democracy would not appear remote if China would remake its public philosophy. However, there is no pure evidence that China will become a democratic society in the near future. Richard Bernstein and Ross H. Munro offer three reasons to justify this argument. First, the Chinese political culture restricts the development of democracy and for 3,000 years "has developed no concept of limited government, or protections of individual rights, or independence of the judiciary and the media."[58] Second, the CPC gives no sign of surrendering its powers at present. Third, if China were to carry out a democratic system, it would have to give up the right to control Taiwan: "Democracy in China would force China's leaders to acknowledge the rights of the people of Taiwan."[59] However, according to Jiang's speech at the meeting celebrating the eightieth anniversary of the founding of the CPC, the party will strengthen its power further in the future, uphold its ideological line, consolidate its class foundation, adhere to democratic centralism, and handle party affairs and the policy of strict party discipline. It is obvious that China is changing, but the party as the last fortress of antidemocracy is trying to resist the changes.

Shaohua Hu in his recent book expresses a different opinion. He predicts that China "will become democratic by 2011," and that the one-party system will be history by that time.[60] From a historical perspective, the more specific the prediction, the less realistic it is. Hu's overly optimistic telescoping is probably a utopian dream and is misleading to both the Chinese people and readers in Western countries. China studies are the base for Western countries to make foreign policy regarding China. The U.S. government has admitted that "America has not had a unified and coherent China policy."[61] To avoid this mistake, Western countries should thoroughly study China in terms of foreign policy making.

To remake China's public philosophy, it is necessary to clarify some misconceptions that are scattered in official Chinese reports. The first misconception is that the Chinese people are only concerned with material life, not with political and spiritual life. Chinese officials often say that democracy is not urgent for most Chinese people. Some Western scholars echo this view and point out that the majority of Chinese peasants do not have political interests at all. It is true that many Chinese people have viewed the improvement of living standards as the top priority, but this does not mean that the Chinese people have completely lost interest in politics. With the development of economic reform, more and more of the common people demand individual rights and political freedom, but the party is unwilling to share power with the Chinese people. The failures of democratic initiatives were not because China lacked a democratic culture and self-consciousness,[62] but because the democratic movement was confronted with strong resistance, especially from the party system.

The second misconception is the notion that China is a sovereign country, and that Western countries are not supposed to impose Western-style democracy on China. Basic democratic principles are universal and can be applied not only to Western societies but also to Eastern societies, for example, Japan and South Korea. Obviously, the Chinese government has used a double standard to practice politics. While it rejects Western democracy by asserting diversity, it does not allow opposition groups/parties to exist at home. China as a member of the global village should abide by international law and conform its politics to global norms. The idea of the sovereign country is not an excuse to reject the practice of universal principles. Current international policies will "affect the relationship between the individual and the state over the coming years."[63] The Chinese government has always propagandized that the capitalist system is hypocritical democracy, and that socialist China will create a higher-level democratic system. This misconception allows China to create its own democratic model with Chinese socialist characteristics without changing the current political system. In fact, the socialist system fundamentally contradicts modern democracy. The socialist experiences in the past eighty years have proven that the Leninist state is a monstrous dictatorship. The common people in China have indeed suffered under the so-called socialist democracy.

The third misconception is that political reform will result in social instability. No one can deny the fact that a dynamic social structure is the main driving force of social development, even if China's high economic growth rate in the past came from its social stability. Democracy creates dynamic social stability, which provides the best configuration for a society to develop. The real motivation for the party to resist democracy is not that it fears social instability, but that it fears losing its absolute power. That is why the Chinese government views political dissidents, intellectual organizations, independent religious bodies, and internal migrants as unstable elements. It is worth noting that internal and external migrants are not the source of social instability. The increase in migration is both the cause and the result of the reform movement, reflecting the expansion of a market economy and the erosion of state authority. Migrants come from different places with their own cultural traditions, and they exchange ideas and learn about one another in a variety of ways when they join social groups, work units, and communities. Because migrants have different cultural backgrounds, there are many conflicts among them. In order to preserve their own identities and live together peacefully, they have little choice but to open their minds and listen to the views of others. No doubt, this is a necessary process in learning democracy. Therefore, the law should permit individuals to move from one place to another freely and protect their rights.

The one-party system is the ultimate obstacle blocking the process of democratization in China. As long as the Communist Party is in power, it essentially resists democracy. What are the basic strategies the party uses to resist democracy? First, it challenges basic democratic principles. Individual freedom is the core of democracy. Martin Luther King Jr. declared, "There is nothing in all the world greater than freedom. It is worth paying for; it is worth losing a job for; it is worth going to jail for. I would rather be a free pauper than a rich slave. I would rather die in abject poverty with my convictions than live in inordinate riches with the lack of self-respect."[64] In traditional China, the state stood alone; individuals were "inexorably bound to a collectivity—the family, clan or village—which simplified the state's tasks of maintaining order."[65] Traditional Chinese culture is "group-orientated and essentially hostile to individualism,"[66] though some scholars argue that the Confucian self-cultivation tradition in the nineteenth-century neo-Confucian stage reflected modern liberalism.[67] Democratic culture is individual-centered, nurtured by religious faith, empowered by science and technology, and regulated by laws. However, the CPC views individualism as a capitalist idea and a threat to the party's authority. According to official Chinese ideology, the masses are the fundamental driving force for the development of history; every single person is only a member of collectives; and individualism is the theory of the abstract equality of capitalism. Therefore, individuals must dedicate their hearts and souls to the party and the course of communist movement. The party/state controls individuals basically in two ways. First, it controls them through a system, such as the party system, mass organization, *hukou* (registration), and *dangan* (personnel dossiers). Second, the party/state manipulates individuals through ideological control, such as education, censoring public speech and publishing, and monitoring religion and civil society. A democratic system is based on human beings' having equality and dignity and on fully protecting individual rights, including civil rights, political rights, and religious rights. It is recognized that the observance and protection of human rights in China have improved since the reform movement began in 1978, but what the state/party has changed in this regard is not its stance but only its strategies.

In addition to the fact that the party resists the democratic system, some scholars argue that China is not ready for democracy. Democracy is based on the free expression of human will, and the Chinese people as a whole are unable to practice democracy because of China's population, economy, and education. Therefore, China's future is uncertain. There are at least three possibilities for China's future: quasi democracy, civil war, and vast upheaval.[68] Although this statement is overly pessimistic, it implies that it will take time for the Chinese people to prepare for democracy. In order to nurture their self-consciousness, it is very important to promote popular and quality education. China's educational system is far behind the level of developed countries' systems. Government spending for education is currently only 4 percent of GNP, while the world average totaled 5.1 percent of GNP in the early 1990s.[69] Each person share is only 32 yuan (about U.S.$4) per year for education, based on the total educational investment. It is urgent for China to reevaluate its educational purpose, reform the educational system, adjust the educational curriculum, and introduce some new educational content to the classroom.

Another means to nurture individual consciousness is through the protection of personal religious faith. Notably, religion as an important cultural phenomenon and political force has been acknowledged as an agent of globalization that serves democratization. Throughout the world's history, religion has served a vital role through the influence of missionaries, conquerors, and other migrants.[70] People in ancient times did not think of religion as a choice, but the Protestant Reformation made it possible for religion to be viewed as the individual's communication with God. In modern societies, the people are able to make religion a choice because they are offered "a variety of possibilities, including religious possibilities."[71] Although China historically has had a variety of religious experiences, state control of religion has been the basic characteristic from ancient times to the present. The party/state in China today has clearly understood that religion can be an alien force acting against the state, but also that it can be used for the state.[72] Thus the party/state has never loosened its control of religion. It is a very difficult task to fight for religious freedom in the communist system. The European people fought for religious liberty for several hundred years. The American people took more than 100 years to fight for the principle of separation of church and state, from the time of the first colony to the ratifications of the United States Constitution and the first ten amendments. It will take time, too, for the Chinese people to fully enjoy individual freedom of religion.

The second basic strategy the party uses to resist democracy is its insistence that Marxism/Maoism is the sole theory and principle to guide the Chinese people through the current transitions. According to the Constitution of the People's Republic of China, Marxism is the guiding principle of the Chinese people and the theoretical foundation of the party. In reality, as it did in other former socialist countries, Marxism failed in both theory and practice in the Mao era.[73] According to a survey conducted in the 1980s, more than 60 percent of the college students from forty-seven Chinese universities did not believe that communism is the future of China.[74] The majority of a provincial city's people's deputies did not believe that Marxism is the only ideology that can lead the Chinese people to happiness. Especially after the Tiananmen Square Incident in 1989, the Chinese people have discovered that Marxism is in "tension with both Chinese traditional culture and the values of modernization."[75] According to a recent survey, the majority of potential governors after the Sixteenth National Conference of the CPC will be those people called *lao san jie* in Chinese—people who were born between 1947 and 1952 and who were sent to the countryside for reeducation. These new communist leaders cannot possibly become true Marxist followers. Obviously, although Marxist ideology is no longer a restraint on current transitions,[76] the party still uses Marxism as a whip to beat the common people. To remake China's public philosophy, the Chinese people must remove Marxism-Maoism-Dengism-Jiangism as the official ideology of China; abandon the fantasy that these "isms" are the guiding principles in economics, politics, the military, science, culture, ethics, religion, and daily life; and drop Marxism as a required course in universities, high schools, and secondary schools. To abolish the fantasy that Marxism is the sole universal truth, it is necessary to promote pluralism. A democratic society should represent different political theories and different interest groups. Pluralism fundamentally guarantees a diverse society, and "it might be the precondition for democracy,"[77] although pluralism does not necessarily lead to democracy. The Chinese government must safeguard a sphere in which individuals and groups can hold different values and can act without the interference of the party/state. Some concepts are especially important to pluralism, such as freedom of expression, moral pluralism, political pluralism,[78] ideological diversity, and capitalist economic organization.[79] The state should not seek to resolve conflicts among values when they arise.[80]

Third, the most important strategy the party uses to resist democracy is its insistence that democracy be practiced under the party's leadership. Some analysts point out that only the CPC can govern China—at least for now—because any other parties in China are the tools of the Communist Party. The ultimate goal of the party and the principles of democracy are completely contradictory. Clearly enough, the defeats of democracy in the Communist era were caused by the party. If the top party leader had compromised with the democratic movement in 1989, China would have democratized peacefully.[81] In Western countries, political parties have helped democracy and have checked governmental authority with accountability and freedom. Maurice Duverger, a leading European scholar of political parties, asserted long ago that "liberty and the party system coincide."[82] Political parties provide channels for citizens to affect decision making, give political leaders reliable bases, keep the balance between the state and civil society and individuals, protect their own rights and dissents, expose corruption, and create new ideas to stimulate social development.[83] The reason the party stands opposed to democracy in China is evident. In Western democratic societies, the term *party* is also used in its plural form, *parties,* but the term *party* in the communist political context is used only in the single, capitalized form *PARTY*. China does not have any legitimate opposition party at present. Any unchecked power will ultimately become tyrannical. The democratic system should be based on the theory and practice of the separation of powers among executive, legislative, and judicial branches. The democratic system must be based on the principle of multiparty competition as well as the presence of pressure groups and a free press. A democratic system involves majority rule. The minority should accept the majority's victory in an election. The ruling majority in a representative democratic government should respect minorities and protect minority rights. The one-party system in China inevitably results in small-group rule—party rule. Therefore, the central purpose of remaking China's public philosophy is to put an end to the one-party system.

No political system is perfect. The democratic system is no exception. A democratic country is not a paradise and must be continually perfected. The power of the modern democratic system is based not on its ability to eliminate every single social problem but on its ability to resolve the problems within its system. Without a doubt, there are still many social problems in democratic societies, such as violence, drugs, sexual abuse, discrimination, and so forth. Like the relation of a virus to a physical body, the existence of social problems in democratic societies does not reflect defects in their social structure. The central problem of a democratic society does not spring from democracy but is part of democracy itself.[84] After September 11, many people began rethinking democracy. Due to the fact that the democratic system is an open system, some people take advantage of democratic society. That is why democratic society seems so vulnerable. Therefore, the positive attitude toward problems in a democracy is to adjust the relationship between individual liberty and social responsibility. There is no reason to blame the democratic system itself. Modern democracy is the best political system devised so far by humanity. At least for now, no other new political assumptions can prevail over and replace the modern democratic system. The democratic system may possibly constitute the "end point of mankind's ideological evolution" and the "final form of human government,"[85] even though it will continuously meet confrontations from all directions. Remaking China's public philosophy is part of this process. Therefore, it is not only important and urgent, but the process should courageously face all challenges to come!

NOTES

1. *The Washington Post*, April 26, 2001, p. A1.

2. Immanuel Wallerstein, "The West, Capitalism, and the Modern World-system," in *China and Historical Capitalism: Genealogies of Sinological Knowledge*, ed. Timothy Brook and Gregory Blue (Cambridge, England: Cambridge University Press, 1999), p. 43.

3. Ibid., p. 19.

4. Ibid., p. 15.

5. Ibid., pp. 19–22.

6. Samuel P. Huntington, *The Third Wave: Democratization in the Late Twentieth Century* (Norman: University of Oklahoma Press, 1991), p. 21.

7. Timothy Brook, "Capitalism and the Writing of Modern History in China," in *China and Historical Capitalism: Genealogies of Sinological Knowledge*, ed. Timothy Brook and Gregory Blue (Cambridge, England: Cambridge University Press, 1999), p. 112.

8. Chen Jain, "The China Challenge in the Twenty-first Century," *Peaceworks* 21 (1998), p. 4.

9. Edward Friedman, *National Identity and Democratic Prospects in Socialist China* (Armonk, N.Y.: M.E. Sharpe, 1999), p. 339.

10. Gungwu Wang, *The Chinese Way: China's Position in International Relations* (Stockholm: Scandinavian University Press, 1995), pp. 59–64.

11. Werner Meissner, "New Intellectual Currents in the People's Republic of China," in *China in Transition: Issues and Policies*, ed. David C. B. Teather and Herbert S. Yee (New York: St. Martin's Press, 1999), 3–24. According to Meissner, "the rehabilitation of Confucianism in recent years has served a dual purpose: (1) Confucianism means order and obedience to one's superior, devotion to the State, and puts the interests of the group above the interests of the individual and thus helps to promote the desperately needed social order and stability; and (2) Confucianism as an ideology could provide the Chinese people with some sort of national identity. In short, National-Confucianism could serve as a bulwark against the ideological incursions from the West" (p. 9).

12. Nicholas R. Lardy, *China's Unfinished Economic Revolution* (Washington, D.C.: Brookings Institution Press, 1998), p. 215.

13. Chen, "The China Challenge in the Twenty-first Century," p. 1.

14. Cheng Li, *Rediscovering China: Dynamics and Dilemmas of Reform* (New York: Rowman & Littlefield Publishers, 1997), p. 312.

15. Wang, *The Chinese Way*, p. 69.

16. Chen, "The China Challenge in the Twenty-first Century," p. 3.

17. Gerald Segal, "Does China Matter?" *Foreign Affairs* (September/October 1999), pp. 24–36.

18. Richard Bernstein and Ross H. Munro, *The Coming Conflict with China* (New York: Alfred A. Knopf, 1997), p. 1.

19. Li, *Rediscovering China*, pp. 312–15.

20. This viewpoint forms the central argument of the following two books: Edwin A. Winckler, ed., *Transition from Communism in China* (Boulder, Colo.: Lynne Rienner Publishers, 1999); and Yanqi Tong, *Transitions from State in Hungary and China* (New York: Rowman & Littlefield Publishers, 1997).

21. Werner Meissner, "Western Political Science in China," in *Chinese Thought in a Global Context*, ed. Karl-Heinz Pohl (Boston: Brill, 1999), p. 359.
22. Friedman, *National Identity and Democratic Prospects in Socialist China*, p. 3.
23. Robert W. McGee and Danny Kin-Kong Lam, "Hong Kong's Option to Secede," *Harvard International Law Journal* 33, no. 2 (Spring 1992), p. 438.
24. Friedman, *National Identity and Democratic Prospects in Socialist China*, p. 341.
25. Ibid., p. 14.
26. Ibid., p. 341.
27. Philippe Massonnet, *The New China: Money, Sex, and Power* (Boston: Tuttle Publishing, 2000), p. 188.
28. Bernstein and Munro, *The Coming Conflict with China*, p. 15.
29. Tong, *Transitions from State in Hungary and China*, p. 1.
30. J. Howard W. Rhys, "Religion and National Identity," *Faculty of Religious Studies* 19 (Spring 1991), p. 47.
31. Tong, *Transitions from State in Hungary and China*, p. 234.
32. Minxin Pei, *From Reform to Revolution: The Demise of Communism in China and the Soviet Union* (Cambridge, Mass.: Harvard University Press, 1994), p. 7.
33. Friedman, *National Identity and Democratic Prospects in Socialist China*, p. 319.
34. *New York Times*, 21 April 1981, p. 6.
35. Jingping Ding, *China's Domestic Economy in Regional Context* (Washington, D.C.: Center for Strategic & International Studies, 1995), p. 55.
36. *Sino-Us Evening News* 106 (June 20, 2000), p. 1.
37. Shia-ling Liu, *U.S. Foreign Policy toward Communist China in the 1970's: The Misadventures of Presidents Nixon, Ford, and Carter* (Taibei: Kuang Lu Publishing Company, 1988), p. 3.
38. Quoted in Kwan Ha Yim, ed., *China and the U.S., 1964–72* (New York: Facts on File, 1975), p. 3.
39. Ibid., p. 181.
40. Liu, *U.S. Foreign Policy toward Communist China in the 1970's*, pp. 31–32.
41. Ding, *China's Domestic Economy in Regional Context*, p. 2.
42. Chen, "The China Challenge in the Twenty-first Century," p. vi.
43. Lance L. P. Gore, "The Communist Legacy in Post-Mao Economic Growth," *The China Journal* 41 (January 1999), p. 26.
44. Ibid., pp. 26–27.
45. Thomas G. Rawski, "Reforming China's Economy: What Have We Learned," *The China Journal* 41 (January 1999), p. 155.
46. Ding, *China's Domestic Economy in Regional Context*, p. 64.
47. Wang, *The Chinese Way*. p. 26.
48. Ding, *China's Domestic Economy in Regional Context*, p. 68.
49. Nicholas R. Lardy, *China's Unfinished Economic Revolution* (Washington, D.C.: Brookings Institution Press, 1998), pp. 214–15.
50. Zhang Kai, "Unemployment Growing in China," *Hong Kong Fourth Internationalist Journal, October Review* 29, no. 2 (30 June 2002).
51. Massonnet, *The New China*, p. 4.
52. Ding, *China's Domestic Economy in Regional Context*, pp. 17–18.
53. K. K. Wong, "The Challenge of Sustainable Development," in *China in Transition: Issues and Policies*, ed. David C. B. Teather and Herbert S. Yee (New York: St. Martin's Press, 1999), p. 175.

54. Bernstein and Munro, *The Coming Conflict with China*, p. 18.

55. Friedman, *National Identity and Democratic Prospects in Socialist China*, p. 321.

56. Quoted in Lucian W. Pye, "The State and the Individual: An Overview Interpretation," in *The Individual and the State in China*, ed. Brain Hook (Oxford, England: Clarendon Press, 1996), p. 32.

57. Jack A. Goldstone, "The Coming Chinese Collapse," *Foreign Policy* 99 (Summer 1995), p. 43.

58. Bernstein and Munro, *The Coming Conflict with China*, pp. 15–17.

59. Ibid.

60. Shaohua Hu, *Explaining Chinese Democratization* (Westport, Conn.: Praeger Publishers, 2000), p. 160.

61. U.S. Congress, House Committee on Foreign Affairs, *The Future of United States–China Policy: Joint Hearings before the Subcommittees on Economic Policy, Trade, and Environment; International Security, International Organizations, and Human Rights; and Asia and the Pacific, of the Committee on Foreign Affairs, House of Representatives*, 103d Cong., 1st sess., 20 May 1993.

62. Friedman, *National Identity and Democratic Prospects in Socialist China*, p. 339.

63. Hook, *The Individual and the State in China*, p. 6.

64. Martin Luther King Jr., *I Have a Dream*, ed. Lotte Hoskins (New York: Grosset & Dunlap, 1968), p. 45.

65. Hook, *The Individual and the State in China*, p. 27.

66. Pye, "The State and the Individual," p. 17.

67. According to William Theodore De Bary, "The thought of Chu Hsi [Zhu Xi] begins and ends with the aim of 'learning for the sake of one's self' a phrase which recalls Confucius's dictum in the *Analects* that learning should be for the sake of oneself and not for the pleasing of others. . . . When Western notions of liberalism and individualism reached East Asia in the 19th century, [they] emphasized the discrete or isolated individual. This contrasts with the Confucian personalism [that] conceived of the person as a member of the large human body, never abstracted from society, but always living in a dynamic relation to others, to a biological and historical continuum, and to the organic process of the Way. In fact the importance of individual autonomy or being able to follow one's own inclination was not foreign to traditional ways of thinking, but there may indeed be a certain Neo-Confucian predilection expressed in the choice of these terms to represent the nineteenth-century." See De Bary, *The Liberal Tradition in China* (New York: Columbia University Press, 1983), pp. 21, 43.

68. See Ju Yanan, *Understanding China: Center Stage of the Fourth Power* (Albany: State University of New York Press, 1996).

69. Stanley Rosen, "Education and Economic Reform," in *The China Handbook*, ed. Christopher Hudson (Chicago: Fitzroy Dearborn Publishers, 1997), p. 250.

70. Madeleine Cousineau, ed. *Religion in a Changing World* (Westport, Conn.: Praeger, 1998), p. xiii.

71. Ibid., p. 1.

72. Graeme Lang, "Religions and Regimes in China," in *Religion in a Changing World*, ed. Madeleine Cousineau (Westport, Conn.: Praeger, 1998), p. 149.

73. A. James Gregor, *Marxism, China, and Development: Reflections on Theory and Reality* (New Brunswick, N.J.: Transaction Publishers, 1995), p. 56.

74. Xiangyan Liu, "Wenping Re," in *Five Waves* (Beijing: People's University Press, 1989), p. 132.

75. Suzanne Ogden, *China's Unresolved Issues: Politics, Development, and Culture* (Englewood Cliffs, N.J.: Prentice Hall, 1995), p. 312.

76. Tong, *Transitions from State in Hungary and China*, p. 235.

77. Merle Goldman, "Politically Engaged Intellectuals in the Deng-Jiang Era: A Changing Relationship with the Party-State," *China Quarterly* 138 (June 1994), p. 48.

78. See William A. Galston, "Expressive Liberty, Moral Pluralism, Political Pluralism: Three Sources of Liberal Theory," *William and Mary Law Review* 40 (March 1999), p. 869.

79. Ramon H. Myers, ed., *Two Societies in Opposition: The Republic of China and the People's Republic of China after Forty Years* (Stanford, Calif.: Hoover Institution Press, 1991), p. xlv.

80. See Albert W. Dzur, "Value Pluralism versus Political Liberalism?" *Social Theory and Practice* 24 (Fall 1998), p. 375.

81. Friedman, *National Identity and Democratic Prospects in Socialist China*, p. 339.

82. Quoted in A. James Reichley, *The Life of the Parties: A History of American Political Parties* (New York: Free Press, 1992), p. 3.

83. Ibid., pp. 414–15.

84. James Coleman and Donald Cressey, *Social Problems* (New York: Harper & Row, 1984), p. 66.

85. Francis Fukuyama, *The End of History and the Last Man* (New York: Maxwell Macmillan International, 1992), p. xi.

Bibliography

BOOKS

Anrig, Gregory R. "Curriculum." In *China's Schools in Flux,* eds. Ronald N. Montaperto and Jaya Henderson. Armonk, N.Y.: M.E. Sharpe, 1979.

Ayers, William. *Chang Chih-tung and Educational Reform in China.* Cambridge, Mass.: Harvard University Press, 1971.

Bai, Shouyi, ed. *An Outline History of China.* Beijing: Foreign Languages Press, 1976.

Barme, Geremie, and John Minford, eds. *Seeds of Fire: Chinese Voices of Conscience.* New York: Hill and Wang, 1988.

Barrett, David B., ed. *World Christian Encyclopedia.* New York: Oxford University Press, 1982.

Bastid, Marianne. *Educational Reform in Early Twentieth-Century China.* Ann Arbor, Mich.: Center for Chinese Studies, University of Michigan, 1988.

Bays, Daniel H. *Christianity in China: From the Eighteenth Century to the Present.* Stanford, Calif.: Stanford University Press, 1996.

Bellah, Robert N. *The Broken Covenant: American Civil Religion in Time of Trial.* Chicago: University of Chicago Press, 1992.

Bernstein, Richard, and Ross H. Munro. *The Coming Conflict with China.* New York: Alfred A. Knopf, 1997.

Bishirjian, Richard J., ed. *A Public Philosophy Reader.* New Rochelle, New York: Arlington House, 1978.

Bodde, Derk. *Chinese Thought, Society, and Science: The Intellectual and Social Background of Science and Technology in Pre-Modern China.* Honolulu: University of Hawaii Press, 1991.

———. *Essays on Chinese Civilization.* Princeton, N.J.: Princeton University Press, 1981.

Borthwick, Sally. *Education and Social Change in China: The Beginnings of the Modern Era.* Stanford, Calif.: Hoover Institution Press, 1983.

Boyle, Kevin, and Juliet Sheen. *Freedom of Religion and Belief*. New York: Routledge, 1997.

Brinton, Crane. *The Shaping of Modern Thought*. Englewood Cliffs, N.J.: Prentice Hall, 1963.

Brook, Timothy. "Capitalism and the Writing of Modern History in China." In *China and Historical Capitalism: Genealogies of Sinological Knowledge*, ed. Timothy Brook and Gregory Blue. Cambridge, England: Cambridge University Press, 1999.

Brook, Timothy, and Gregory Blue, eds. *China and Historical Capitalism: Genealogies of Sinological Knowledge*. Cambridge, England: Cambridge University Press, 1999.

Brook, Timothy, and Hy V. Luong, eds. *Culture and Economy: The Shaping of Capitalism in Eastern Asia*. Ann Arbor: University of Michigan Press, 1997.

Brown, G. Thompson. *Christianity in the People's Republic of China*. Atlanta, Ga.: John Knox Press, 1973.

Brugger, Bill. *Politics, Economy, and Society in Contemporary China*. Stanford, Calif.: Stanford University Press, 1994.

Carlton, Eric. *Ideology and Social Order*. London: Routledge & Kegan Paul, 1977.

Chang, Chun-shu, ed. *The Making of China: Main Themes in Premodern Chinese History*. Englewood Cliffs, N.J.: Prentice-Hall, 1975.

Chen, Jingpan. *Confucius as a Teacher: Philosophy of Confucius with Special Reference to Its Educational Implications*. Beijing: Foreign Languages Press, 1990.

Chen, Kang. "The Failure of Recentralization in China: Interplays among Enterprises, Local Governments, and the Center." In *Markets and Politicized Economic Choice*, ed. Arye L. Hillman. Boston: Kluwer Academic Publishers, 1991.

Cheng, Chu-yuan. *Behind the Tiananmen Massacre: Social, Political, and Economic Ferment in China*. Boulder, Colo.: Westview Press, 1990.

Cheng, Peter P., ed. *Marxism and Capitalism in the People's Republic of China*. Lanham, Md.: University Press of America, 1989.

Chesneaux, Jean. *China from the 1911 Revolution to Liberation*. New York: Pantheon Books, 1977.

———. *China from the Opium Wars to the 1911 Revolution*. New York: Pantheon Books, 1976.

Chi, Chao-ting. "Key Economic Areas in Chinese History: From the Huangho Basin to the Yangtze Valley." In *The Making of China: Main Themes in Premodern Chinese History*, ed. Chun-shu Chang. Englewood Cliffs, N.J.: Prentice-Hall, 1975.

Chi, Wen-shun. *Ideological Conflicts in Modern China: Democracy and Authoritarianism*. New Brunswick, N.J.: Transaction Books, 1986.

Chien, Mu. *Traditional Government in Imperial China: A Critical Analysis*. New York: St. Martin's Press, 1982.

Ching, Julia. *Chinese Religions*. Maryknoll, N.Y.: Orbis Books, 1993.

———. "Ethical Humanism as Religion?" In *Christianity and Chinese Religions*, ed. Hans Kung and Julia Ching. New York: Doubleday, 1989.

———. *Probing China's Soul: Religion, Politics, and Protest in the People's Republic of China*. San Francisco: Harper & Row, 1990.

Chossudovsky, Michel. *Towards Capitalist Restoration? Chinese Socialism after Mao.* New York: St. Martin's Press, 1986.
Chow, Tse-tsung. *The May Fourth Movement: Intellectual Revolution in Modern China.* Stanford, Calif.: Stanford University Press, 1967.
Christiansen, Flemming, and Shirin M. Rai. *Chinese Politics and Society: An Introduction.* New York: Harvester Wheatsheaf, 1996.
Chu, Godwin C., and Yanan Ju. *The Great Wall in Ruins: Communication and Cultural Change in China.* Albany: State University of New York Press, 1993.
Cleverley, John F. *The Schooling of China: Tradition and Modernity in Chinese Education.* Boston: G. Allen & Unwin, 1985.
Cohen, Paul A. *Between Tradition and Modernity: Wang T'ao and Reform in Late Ch'ing China.* Cambridge, Mass.: Harvard University Press, 1987.
Coleman, James, and Donald Cressey. *Social Problems.* New York: Harper & Row, 1984.
Connolly, William E. *Political Theory and Modernity.* Ithaca, N.Y.: Cornell University Press, 1993.
Cotterell, Arthur. *China: A Cultural History.* New York: Penguin Books, 1990.
———. *Chinese Civilization: From the Ming Revival to Chairman Mao.* New York: St. Martin's Press, 1977.
———. *The Early Civilization of China.* New York: Putnam, 1975.
———. *The First Emperor of China: The Greatest Archeological Find of Our Time.* New York: Holt, Rinehart, 1981.
Cousineau, Madeleine. *Religion in a Changing World.* Westport, Conn.: Praeger, 1998.
Covell, Ralph R. *Confucius, the Buddha, and Christ: A History of the Gospel in Chinese.* New York: Orbis Books, 1986.
Crane, Edward H. "Civil Society versus Political Society: China at a Crossroads." In *China in the New Millennium*, ed. James A. Dorn. Washington, D.C.: CATO Institute, 1998.
Creel, Herrlee Glessner. *Chinese Thought: From Confucius to Mao Tse-tung.* Chicago: University of Chicago Press, 1953.
Cuervo, Robert F. "The Definition of Public Philosophy: Lippmann and Murray," in Richard J. Bishirjian, *A Public Philosophy Reader.* New Rochelle, N.Y.: Arlington House, 1978.
Dardess, John W. *Confucianism and Autocracy: Professional Elites in the Founding of the Ming Dynasty.* Berkeley: University of California Press, 1983.
Davis, Derek H. *Original Intent: Chief Justice Rehnquist and the Course of American Church-State Relations.* New York: Prometheus Books, 1991.
De Bary, William Theodore. *Confucianism and Human Rights.* New York: Columbia University Press, 1988.
———. *The Liberal Tradition in China.* New York: Columbia University Press, 1983.
Deng, Xiaoping. *Selected Works of Deng Xiaoping: 1975–1982.* Beijing: Foreign Languages Press, 1984.
———. "Speech at the National Conference on Education (April 22, 1978)." In *Selected Works of Deng Xiaoping: 1975–1982.* Beijing: Foreign Languages Press, 1984.
Dettmer, Lowell. *China under Reform.* Boulder, Colo.: Westview Press, 1994.

Ding, Jingping. *China's Domestic Economy in Regional Context*. Washington, D.C.: Center for Strategic and International Studies, 1995.

Ding, X. L. *The Decline of Communism in China: Legitimacy Crisis, 1977–1989*. New York: Cambridge University Press, 1994.

Dirlik, Arif. "Post-Socialism? Reflections on Socialism with Chinese Characteristics." In *Marxism and Capitalism in the People's Republic of China*, ed. Peter P. Cheng. Lanham, Md.: University Press of America, 1989.

Dirlik, Arif, and Maurice Meisner, eds. *Marxism and The Chinese Experience: Issues in Contemporary Chinese Socialism*. Armonk, N.Y.: M.E. Sharpe, 1989.

Djung, Lu-Dzai. *A History of Democratic Education in Modern China*. Shanghai, China: Commercial Press, 1933.

Dorn, James A., ed. *China in the New Millennium*. Washington, D.C.: CATO Institute, 1998.

Drachkovitch, Milorad M., ed. *Marxist Ideology in the Contemporary World: Its Appeals and Paradoxes*. New York: Pall Mall Press, 1966.

Editorial Committee. *Achievement of Education in China: Statistics 1949–1983*. Beijing: People's Education Press, 1984.

———. *Education and Science*. Beijing: Foreign Languages Press, 1983.

Edwards, R. Randle, Louis Henkin, and Andrew J. Nathan. *Human Rights in Contemporary China*. New York: Columbia University Press, 1986.

Elman, Benjamin A., and Alexander Woodside, eds. *Education and Society in Late Imperial China, 1600–1900*. Berkeley: University of California Press, 1994.

Elvin, Mark. *The Pattern of the Chinese Past*. Stanford, Calif.: Stanford University Press, 1973.

Ernst, Morris L., and David Loth. *Report on the American Communist*. New York: Capricorn Books, 1962.

Falkenheim, Victor C., ed. *Chinese Politics from Mao to Deng*. New York: Paragon House, 1989.

Fang, Li-chih. *Bringing Down the Great Wall: Writings on Science, Culture, and Democracy in China*. New York: Knopf, 1990.

Fenn, William Purviance. *Christian Higher Education in Changing China: 1880–1950*. Grand Rapids, Mich.: William B. Eerdmans Publishing Company, 1976.

Ferwerker, Albert. *The Chinese Economy: 1912–1949*. Ann Arbor, Michigan: Michigan Papers in Chinese Studies, 1968.

Fitzgerald, John. *Awakening China: Politics, Culture, and Class in the Nationalist Revolution*. Stanford, Calif.: Stanford University Press, 1996.

Fraser, Stewart E. *Education and Communism in China: An Anthology of Commentary and Documents*. Hong Kong: International Studies Group, 1969.

Friedman, Edward. *National Identity and Democratic Prospects in Socialist China*. Armonk, N.Y.: M.E. Sharpe, 1999.

Fukuyama, Francis. *The End of History and the Last Man*. New York: Maxwell Macmillan International, 1992.

———. *The Great Disruption: Human Nature and the Reconstitution of Social Order*. New York: Free Press, 1999.

———. *Trust: The Social Virtues and the Creation of Prosperity*. New York: Free Press, 1995.

Gabriel, Ralph H. *American Values: Continuity and Change*. Westport, Conn.: Greenwood Press, 1974.

Gardner, H. Stephen. *Comparative Economic Systems*. Fort Worth, Tex.: The Dryden Press, 1998.

Gernet, Jacques. *China and the Christian Impact: A Conflict of Cultures*. Cambridge, England: Cambridge University Press, 1985.

———. *A History of Chinese Civilization*. New York: Cambridge University Press, 1982.

Giddens, Anthony. *The Third Way: The Renewal of Social Democracy*. Cambridge: Polity Press, 1998.

Gilbert, Rozman, ed. *China's Modernization*. Jiangsu Province, China: People's Publishing House, 1998.

Goodin, Robert E., and Hans-Dieter Klingemann, eds. *A New Handbook of Political Science*. Oxford, England: Oxford University Press, 1996.

Greel, H. G. "The Eclectics of Han Thought." In *The Making of China: Main Themes in Premodern Chinese History*. Englewood Cliffs, N.J.: Prentice Hall, 1975.

Gregor, A. James. *Marxism, China, and Development: Reflections on Theory and Reality*. New Brunswick, N.J.: Transaction Publishers, 1995.

Habermas, Jurgen. *Between Facts and Norms: Contributions to a Discourse Theory of Law and Democracy*. Cambridge, Mass.: MIT Press, 1996.

Hanter, Alan, and Kim-Kwong Chan. *Protestantism in Contemporary China*. Cambridge, England: Cambridge University Press, 1993.

Harris, Peter. *Political China Observed: A Western Perspective*. New York: St. Martin's Press, 1980.

Hawkins, John N. *Mao Tse-Tung and Education: His Thoughts and Teachings*. Hamden, Conn.: Linnet Books, 1974.

Hayhoe, Ruth. *China's Universities and the Open Door*. Armonk, N.Y.: M.E. Sharpe, 1989.

———. *China's Universities 1895–1995: A Century of Cultural Conflict*. New York: Garland Publishing, 1996.

Hegel, G.W.F. "The Childhood of History." In *The Pattern of Chinese History: Cycles, Development, or Stagnation?* ed. John Meskill. Westport, Conn.: Greenwood Press, 1965.

Henkin, Louis. "The Human Rights Idea in Contemporary China: A Comparative Perspective." In *Human Rights in Contemporary China*, ed. R. Randle Edwards. New York: Columbia University Press, 1986.

Hepburn, Mary A., ed. *Democratic Education in Schools and Classrooms*. Washington, D.C.: National Council for the Social Studies, 1983.

Hillman, Arye L., ed. *Markets and Politicized Economic Choice*. Boston: Kluwer Academic Publishers, 1991.

Ho, John E. *East Asian Philosophy: With Historical Background and Present Influence*. New York: Peter Lang, 1992.

Ho, Ping-Ti. "Social Composition of Ming-Qing Ruling Class," in *The Making of China: Main Themes in Premodern Chinese History*, ed. Chun-shu Chang. Englewood Cliffs, N.J.: Prentice Hall, 1975, p. 298.

Hook, Brian, ed. *The Individual and the State in China*. Oxford: Clarendon Press, 1996.

Hoover, J. Edgar. *Masters of Deceit: The Story of Communism in America and How to Fight It*. New York: Henry Holt and Company, 1958.

Housten, Richard Van, ed. *Wise as Serpents, Harmless as Doves*. Pasadena, Calif.: William Carey Library, 1988.

Hsiao, Kung-chuan. *A Modern China and a New World*. Seattle: University of Washington Press, 1957.

Hsu, Cho-yun. "The Transition of Ancient Chinese Society," in *The Making of China: Main Themes in Premodern Chinese History*. Englewood Cliffs, N.J.: Prentice Hall, 1975.

Hsu, Immanuel C. Y. *China without Mao: The Search for a New Order*. Oxford: Oxford University Press, 1990.

———. *The Rise of Modern China*, 5th ed. New York: Oxford University Press, 1995.

Hu, Chang-tu. *Chinese Education under Communism*. New York: Bureau of Publications, 1962.

Hu, Shaohua. *Explaining Chinese Democratization*. Westport, Conn.: Praeger Publishers, 2000.

Hu, Shi Ming, and Eli Seifman, eds. *Education and Socialist Modernization: A Documentary History of Education in the People's Republic of China, 1977–1986*. New York: AMS, 1987.

Hua, Shiping. *Scientism and Humanism: Two Cultures in Post-Mao China*. Albany, N.Y.: State University of New York Press, 1995.

Hudson, Christopher. *The China Handbook*. Chicago: Fitzroy Dearborn Publishers, 1997.

Hunter, Alan, and Kim-Kwong Chan. *Protestantism in Contemporary China*. Cambridge, England: Cambridge University Press, 1993.

Huntington, Samuel P. *The Clash of Civilizations and the Remaking of World Order*. New York: Simon & Schuster, 1996.

———. *The Third Wave: Democratization in the Late Twentieth Century*. Norman, Okla.: University of Oklahoma Press, 1991.

Ichisada, Miyazaki. "The Four Ages of Chinese History." In *The Pattern of Chinese History: Cycles, Development, or Stagnation?*, ed. John Meskill. Westport, Conn.: Greenwood Press, 1965.

Jian, Bozan, Shao Xunzheng, and Hu Hua. *A Concise History of China*. Beijing: Foreign Languages Press, 1981.

Jie, Chen, and Peng Deng. *China since the Cultural Revolution: From Totalitarianism to Authoritarianism*. Westport, Conn.: Praeger, 1995.

Jochim, Christian. *Chinese Religions: A Cultural Perspective*. Englewood Cliffs, N.J.: Prentice-Hall, 1986.

Johnson, Chalmers, ed. *Ideology and Politics in Contemporary China*. Seattle: University of Washington Press, 1973.

Johnson, David, Andrew J Nathan, and Evelyn S. Rawski, eds. *Popular Culture in Late Imperial China*. Berkeley: University of California Press, 1985.

Jones, Francis P., ed. *Documents of the Three-Self Movement: Source Materials for the Study of the Protestant Church in Communist China*. New York: National Council of the Churches of Christ in the U.S.A., 1963.

Jonsson, John N. "Introduction." In Kwong Chunwah, *Hong Kong's Religions in Transition*. Waco, Texas: Tao Foundation, 2000.

Joshua, Mingchien. *Modern Democracy in China*. Shanghai, China: Commercial Press, 1923.

Ju, Yanan. *Understanding China: Center Stage of the Fourth Power*. Albany, N.Y.: State University of New York Press, 1996.

Kapur, Harish. *As China Sees the World: Perceptions of Chinese Scholars*. New York: St. Martin's Press, 1987.
King, Martin Luther, Jr. *I Have a Dream*, ed. Lotte Hoskins. New York: Grosset & Dunlap, 1968.
Kung, Hans, and Julia Ching. *Christianity and Chinese Religions*. New York: Doubleday, 1989.
Kuo, Tai-Chun, and Ramon H. Myers. *Understanding Communist China: Communist China Studies in the United States and the Republic of China, 1949–1978*. Stanford, Calif.: Hoover Institution Press, 1986.
Lang, Graeme. "Religions and Regimes in China." In *Religion in a Changing World*, ed. Madeleine Cousineau. Westport, Conn.: Praeger, 1998.
Lardy, Nicholas R. *China's Unfinished Economic Revolution*. Washington, D.C.: Brookings Institution Press, 1998.
———. *Foreign Trade and Economic Reform in China, 1978–1990*. New York: Cambridge University Press, 1992.
Lees, Francis A. *China Superpower: Requisites for High Growth*. New York: St. Martin's Press, 1997.
Leng, Shao Chuan, and Norman D. Palmer. *Sun Yat-sen and Communism*. Westport, Conn.: Greenwood Press, 1976.
Lewin, Keith, Su Hui, Angela Little, and Zheng Jiwei. *Educational Innovation in China*. Burnt Mill, Harlow, England: Longman House, 1994.
Li, Cheng. *Rediscovering China: Dynamics and Dilemmas of Reform*. New York: Rowman & Littlefield Publishers, 1997.
Lieberthal, Kenneth. *Governing China: From Revolution through Reform*. New York: W.W. Norton & Company, 1995.
Lieberthal, Kenneth G., and David M. Lampton, eds. *Bureaucracy, Politics, and Decision Making in Post-Mao China*. Berkeley: University of California Press, 1992.
Liew, Leong. *The Chinese Economy in Transition: From Plan to Market*. Brookfield, Vt.: Edward Ekgar, 1997.
Lin, Mousheng. *Men and Ideas: An Informal History of Chinese Political Thought*. New York: Hohn Day, 1942.
Lin, Zhiling, and Thomas W. Robinson, eds. *The Chinese and Their Future: Beijing, Taipei, and Hong Kong*. Washington, D.C.: AEI Press, 1994.
Lindau, Juan D., and Timothy Cheek, eds. *Market Economics and Political Change: Comparing China and Mexico*. New York: Rowman & Littlefield Publishers, 1998.
Linebarger, Paul Myron Anthony. *The Political Doctrines of Sun Yat-sen: An Exposition of the San Min Chui*. Westport, Conn.: Hyperion Press, 1936.
Link, Perry, Richard Madsen, and Paul G. Pickowicz, eds. *Unofficial China: Popular Culture and Thought in the People's Republic*. Boulder, Colo.: Westview Press, 1989.
Lippmann, Walter. *Essays in the Public Philosophy*. Boston: Little, Brown and Company, 1955.
———. *An Inquiry into the Principles of the Good Society*. Boston: Little, Brown and Company, 1943.
Liu, Alan P. L. *Mass Politics in the People's Republic: State and Society in Contemporary China*. Boulder, Colo.: Westview Press, 1996.

Liu, Shia-ling. *U.S. Foreign Policy toward Communist China in the 1970's: The Misadventures of Presidents Nixon, Ford, and Carter.* Taibei: Kuang Lu Publishing Company, 1988.

Liu, Xiangyan. "Wenping Re." In *Five Waves.* Beijing: People's University Press, 1989.

Liu, Xiuwu R. *Western Perspectives on Chinese Higher Education: A Model for Cross-Cultural Inquiry.* New York: Associated University Presses, 1996.

Lopez, Donald S., ed. *Religions of China in Practice.* Princeton, N.J.: Princeton University Press, 1996.

Luo, Zhufeng, ed. *Religion under Socialism in China.* New York: M.E. Sharpe, 1991.

Lutz, Jessie G., and R. Ray Lutz. "Karl Gutzlaff's Approach to Indigenization: The Chinese Union." In *Christianity in China: From the Eighteenth Century to the Present,* ed. Daniel Bays. Stanford, Calif.: Stanford University Press, 1996.

Mackerras, Colin, Pradeep Taneja, and Graham Yong. *China since 1978: Reform, Modernization and Socialism with Chinese Characteristics.* New York: St. Martin's Press, 1993.

Mao Zedong, "Rectify the Party's Style of Work" (February 1942). In *Selected Works of Mao Zedong.* Vol. 2. Beijing: Foreign Languages Press, 1965.

———. *Selected Works of Mao Zedong.* Vol. 2. Beijing: Foreign Languages Press, 1965.

Marsh, Christopher. *Making Russian Democracy Work: Social Capital, Economic Development, and Democratization.* Lewiston, N.Y.: Edwin Mellen Press, 2000.

Massonnet, Philippe. *The New China: Money, Sex, and Power.* Boston: Tuttle Publishing, 2000.

McCormick, Barrett L. *Political Reform in Post-Mao China: Democracy and Bureaucracy in a Leninist State.* Berkeley: University of California Press, 1990.

McGovern, Arthur F. *Marxism: An American Christian Perspective.* Maryknoll, N.Y.: Orbis Books, 1980.

McLellan, David. *Ideology: Concepts in Social Thought.* Minneapolis: University of Minnesota Press, 1986.

———. *Marxism after Marx: An Introduction.* New York: Harper & Row, 1980.

———. *Marxism and Religion: A Description and Assessment of the Marxist Critique of Christianity.* New York: Harper & Row, 1987.

Meisner, Maurice J. *Marxism, Maoism, and Utopianism: Eight Essays.* Madison: University of Wisconsin Press, 1982.

Meissner, Werner. "New Intellectual Currents in the People's Republic of China." In *China in Transition: Issues and Policies,* ed. David C. B. Teather and Herbert S. Yee. New York: St. Martin's Press, 1999.

———. "Western Political Science in China." In *Chinese Thought in a Global Context,* ed. Karl-Heinz Pohl. Boston: Brill, 1999.

Melden, A. I., ed. *Human Rights.* Belmont, Calif.: Wadsworth Publishing Company, 1970.

Meskill, John, ed. *The Pattern of Chinese History: Cycles, Development, or Stagnation?* Westport, Conn.: Greenwood Press, 1965.

Montaperto, Ronald N., and Jaya Henderson, eds. *China's Schools in Flux.* Armonk, N.Y.: M.E. Sharpe, 1979.

Moody, Peter R. *Political Opposition in Post-Confucian Society.* New York: Praeger, 1988.

Mote, F. W. *A History of Chinese Political Thought.* Princeton, N.J.: Princeton University Press, 1979.
Mueller, J. Theodore. *Great Missionaries to China.* Grand Rapids, Mich.: Zondervan Publishing House, 1947.
Myers, Ramon H, ed. *Two Societies in Opposition: The Republic of China and the Peoples' Republic of China after Forty Years.* Stanford, Calif.: Hoover Institution Press, 1991.
Nathan, Andrew J. *Chinese Democracy.* New York: Knopf, 1985.
———. "Sources of Chinese Rights Thinking." In *Human Rights in Contemporary China,* ed. R. Randle Edwards. New York: Columbia University Press, 1986.
Nathan, Andrew J., and Robert S. Ross. *The Great Wall and the Empty Fortress: China's Search for Security.* New York: W.W. Norton & Company, 1998.
Naughton, Barry. *Growing out of Plan: Chinese Economic Reform, 1978–1993.* Cambridge, England: Cambridge University Press, 1995.
Neuhaus, Richard John. "From Civil Religion to Public Philosophy." In *Civil Religion and Political Theology,* ed. Leroy S. Rouner. Notre Dame, Ind.: University of Notre Dame Press, 1986.
Niemeyer, Gerhart. *Between Nothingness and Paradise.* Baton Rouge: Louisiana State University Press, 1971.
Novak, Michael. *Choosing Our King: Powerful Symbols in Presidential Politics.* New York: Macmillan, 1974.
O'Brien, Kevin J. *Reform without Liberalization: China's National People's Congress and the Politics of Institutional Change.* New York: Cambridge University Press, 1990.
Ogden, Suzanne. *China's Unresolved Issues: Politics, Development, and Culture.* Englewood Cliffs, N.J.: Prentice Hall, 1995.
Ong, Aihwa, and Donald M. Nonini, eds. *Ungrounded Empires: The Cultural Politics of Modern Chinese Transnationalism.* New York: Routledge, 1997.
Overholt, William H. *The Rise of China: How Economic Reform Is Creating a New Superpower.* New York: W.W. Norton & Company, 1994.
Overmyer, Daniel L. *Religions of China.* San Francisco: Harper & Row, 1986.
Padover, Saul K. *On Religion: Karl Marx.* Sydney: McGraw-Hill, 1974.
Paine, Lynn. "The Educational Policy Process: A Case Study of Bureaucratic Action in China." In *Bureaucracy, Politics, and Decision Making in Post-Mao China,* eds. Kenneth G. Lieberthal and David M. Lampton. Berkeley: University of California Press, 1992.
Parker, Franklin, and Betty June Parker. *Education in the People's Republic of China, Past and Present: An Annotated Bibliography.* New York: Garland Publishing, 1986.
Pei, Minxin. *From Reform to Revolution: The Demise of Communism in China and the Soviet Union.* Cambridge, Mass.: Harvard University Press, 1994.
Pepper, Suzanne. *China's Education Reform in the 1980s: Policies, Issues, and Historical Perspectives.* Berkeley, Calif.: Center for Chinese Studies, 1990.
Petterson, George. *Christianity in Communist China.* Waco, Texas: Word Books Publisher, 1969.
Pierard, Richard V., and Robert D. Linder. *Civil Religion and the Presidency.* Grand Rapids, Mich.: Academic Books, 1988.
Pohl, Karl-Heinz. *Chinese Thought in a Global Context.* Boston: Brill, 1999.

Priestley, K. E. *Education in China.* Hong Kong: Green Pagoda Press, 1961.
Prime, Penelope B. "China's Economic Progress: Is It Sustainable?" In *China Briefing: The Contradictions of Change,* ed. William A. Joseph. Armonk, N.Y.: M.E. Sharpe, 1997.
Pullapilly, Cyriac K., ed. *Chinese Politics and Christian Missions: The Anti-Christian Movements of 1920–28.* Notre Dame, Indiana: Cross Cultural Publications, 1988.
Pye, Lucian W. *The Mandarin and the Cadre: China's Political Cultures.* Ann Arbor: University of Michigan, 1986.
———. "The State and the Individual: An Overview Interpretation." In *The Individual and the State in China,* ed. Brain Hook. Oxford, England: Clarendon Press, 1996.
Rawski, Thomas G., and Lillian M. Li, eds. *Chinese History in Economic Perspective.* Berkeley: University of California Press, 1992.
Reichley, A. James. *The Life of the Parties: A History of American Political Parties.* New York: Free Press, 1992.
Reynolds, Bruce L., ed. *Chinese Economic Policy: Economic Reform at Midstream.* New York: Paragon House, 1988.
Robinson, Thomas W., ed. *Democracy and Development in East Asia.* Washington, D.C.: AAEI Press, 1991.
Ropp, Paul S., ed. *Heritage of China: Contemporary Perspectives on Chinese Civilization.* Berkeley: University of California Press, 1990.
Rosen, Stanley. "Education and Economic Reform," In *The China Handbook,* ed. Christopher Hudson. Chicago: Fitzroy Dearborn Publishers, 1997.
Rosenbaum, Arthur Lewis. *State and Society in China: The Consequences of Reform.* Boulder, Colo.: Westview Press, 1992.
Rouner, Leroy S., ed. *Civil Religion and Political Theology.* Notre Dame, Ind.: University of Notre Dame Press, 1986.
Rubin, Vitaly A. *Individual and State in Ancient China: Essays on Four Chinese Philosophers.* New York: Columbia University Press, 1976.
Sambaugh, David, ed. *Greater China: The Next Superpower.* Oxford, England: Oxford University Press, 1995.
Sandel, Michael J. *Democracy's Discontent: America in Search of a Public Philosophy.* Cambridge, Mass.: Belknap Press, 1996.
Sandoz, Ellis. *A Government of Laws.* Baton Rouge: Louisiana State University Press, 1990.
Schafer, Edward H. "The Glory of the Tang Empire." In *The Making of China: Main Themes in Premodern Chinese History,* ed. Chun-shu Chang. Englewood Cliffs, N.J.: Prentice-Hall, 1975.
Schell, Orville. *Mandate of Heaven: The Legacy of Tiananmen Square and the Next Generation of China's Leaders.* New York: Simon & Schuster Trade, 1995.
Schmidt, Thomas C. "Organization and Structure." In *China's Schools in Flux,* eds. Ronald N. Montaperto and Jaya Henderson. White Plains, N.Y.: M.E. Sharpe, 1979.
Schwartz, Benjamin Isadore. *China's Cultural Values.* Mesa, Ariz.: Lionheart Press, 1993.
———. *Communism and China: Ideology in Flux.* Cambridge, Mass.: Harvard University Press, 1968.

Selden, Mark. *The Political Economy of Chinese Development.* Armonk, N.Y.: M.E. Sharpe, 1993.
Sheldon, Garret Ward. *The Political Philosophy of Thomas Jefferson.* Baltimore, Md.: Johns Hopkins University Press, 1991.
Shi, Tianjian. *Political Participation in Beijing.* Cambridge, Mass.: Harvard University Press, 1997.
Shiffrin, Harold Z. *Sun Yat-sen, Reluctant Revolutionary.* Boston: Little, Brown and Company, 1980.
Shirk, Susan L. "The Chinese Political System and the Political Strategy of Economic Reform." In *Bureaucracy, Politics and Decision Making in Post-Mao China,* eds. Kenneth G. Lieberthal and David M. Lampton. Berkeley: University of California Press, 1992.
———. *The Political Logic of Economic Reform in China.* Berkeley: University of California Press, 1993.
Shklar, Judith N. *Political Theory and Ideology.* London: Macmillan, 1970.
Solomon, Richard H. "From Commitment to Giant: The Evolving Functions of Ideology in the Revolutionary Process." In *Ideology and Politics in Contemporary China,* ed. Chalmers Johnson. Seattle: University of Washington Press, 1973.
Spence, Jonathan D. *Chinese Roundabout: Essays in History and Culture.* New York: W.W. Norton & Company, 1993.
Starr, John Bryan. *Ideology and Culture: An Introduction to the Dialectic of Contemporary Chinese Politics.* New York: Harper & Row, 1973.
Stavis, Benedict. *China's Political Reform: An Interim Report.* New York: Praeger Publishers, 1987.
Stevenson, Harold W. *The Learning Gap: Why Our Schools Are Failing and What We Can Learn from Japanese and Chinese Education.* New York: Summit Books, 1992.
Strauss, Julia C. *Strong Institutions in Weak Polities: State Building in Republican China.* Oxford, England: Clarendon Press, 1998.
Tanner, Murray Scot. *The Politics of Lawmaking in Post-Mao China: Institutions, Processes, and Democratic Prospects.* Oxford, England: Oxford University Press, 1998.
Teather, David C. B., and Herbert S. Yee, eds. *China in Transition: Issues and Policies.* New York: St. Martin's Press, 1999.
Teiser, Stephen F. "Introduction: The Spirits of Chinese Religion." In *Religions of China in Practice,* ed. Donald S. Lopez. Princeton, N.J.: Princeton University Press, 1996.
Thomas, James R. *Chinese Politics,* trans. Gu Shu and Dong Fan. Jiangsu, China: People's Publishing House of Jiangsu, 1992.
Thompson, Laurence G. *Chinese Religion: An Introduction,* 4th ed. Belmont, Calif.: Wadsworth Publishing Company, 1989.
Thurman, Robert A. F. *Inner Revolutions: Life, Liberty, and the Pursuit of Real Happiness.* New York: Riverhead Books, 1998.
Tong, Yanqi. *Transitions from State Socialism: Economic and Political Change in Hungary and China.* New York: Rowman & Littlefield Publishers, 1997.
Tu, Wei-ming. *Centrality and Commonality: An Essay on Confucian Religiousness.* Honolulu: University Press of Hawaii, 1976.

———, ed. *China in Transformation*. Cambridge, Mass.: Harvard University Press, 1994.

———. *Confucian Traditions in East Asian Modernity: Moral Education and Economic Culture in Japan and the Four Mini-Dragons*. Cambridge, Mass.: Harvard University Press, 1996.

———. *The Living Tree: The Changing Meaning of Being Chinese Today*. Stanford, Calif.: Stanford University Press, 1994.

Van der Veer, Peter, and Hartmut Lehmann, eds. *Nation and Religion: Perspectives on Europe and Asia*. Princeton, N.J.: Princeton University Press, 1999.

Vyver, Johan D. van der, and John Witte Jr., eds. *Religious Human Rights in Global Perspective: Legal Perspectives*. Boston: Martinus Nijhoff Publishers, 1997.

Wallerstein, Immanuel. "The West, Capitalism, and the Modern World-system." In *China and Historical Capitalism: Genealogies of Sinological Knowledge*, ed. Timothy Brook and Gregory Blue. Cambridge, England: Cambridge University Press, 1999.

Wang, Gung-hsing. *The Chinese Mind*. New York: John Day Company, 1946.

Wang, Gungwu. *The Chinese Way: China's Position in International Relations*. Stockholm: Scandinavian University Press, 1995.

Wang, Hui. *Gradual Revolution*. Beijing: China Planning Publishing House, 1998.

Waters, Harry J. *China's Economic Development Strategies for the 21st Century*. Westport, Conn.: Quorum Books, 1997.

Webster, James B. *Christian Education and the National Consciousness in China*. New York: E.P. Duttton & Company, 1923.

White, Gordon. *Riding the Tiger: The Politics of Economic Reform in Post-Mao China*. Stanford, Calif.: Stanford University Press, 1993.

White, Gordon, Jude Howell, and Shang Xiaoyuan. *In Search of Civil Society: Market Reform and Social Change in Contemporary China*. Oxford, England: Clarendon Press, 1996.

Whitehead, Raymond L., ed. *No Longer Strangers: Selected Writings of K. H. Ting*. New York: Orbis Books, 1989.

Wilson, Richard W., Sidney L. Greenblatt, and Amy Auerbacher Wilson, eds. *Moral Behavior in Chinese Society*. New York: Praeger, 1981.

———. *Value Change in Chinese Society*. New York: Praeger, 1979.

Wilson, Thomas A. *Genealogy of the Way: The Construction and Uses of the Confucian Tradition in Late Imperial China*. Stanford, Calif.: Stanford University Press, 1995.

Winckler, Edwin A., ed. *Transition from Communism in China*. Boulder, Colo.: Lynne Rienner Publishers, 1999.

Womack, Brantly. *Contemporary Chinese Politics in Historical Perspective*. Cambridge: Cambridge University Press, 1991.

Wong, K. K. "The Challenge of Sustainable Development." In *China in Transition: Issues and Policies*, ed. David C. B. Teather and Herbert S. Yee. New York: St. Martin's Press, 1999.

Wood, James E., Jr. *Church-State Relations in the Modern World*. Waco, Texas: J.M. Dawson Institute of Church-State Studies, 1998.

Woodiwiss, Anthony. *Postmodernity USA: The Crisis of Social Modernism in Postwar America*. New Park, Calif.: Sage Publications, 1995.

Wronka, Joseph. *Human Rights and Social Policy in the 21st Century.* New York: University Press of America, 1992.

Yabuki, Susumu. *China's New Political Economy: The Giant Awakes.* Boulder, Colo.: Westview Press, 1995.

Yang, C. K. *Religion in Chinese Society: A Study of Contemporary Social Functions of Religion and Some of Their Historical Factors.* Berkeley: University of California Press, 1961.

Yim, Kwan Han, ed. *China and U.S., 1964–1972.* New York: Facts on File, 1975.

Yu, David C. *Religion in Postwar China: A Critical Analysis and Annotated Bibliography.* Westport, Conn.: Greenwood Press, 1997.

Zeigler, Harmon. *The Political World of the High School Teacher.* Corvalis, Oreg.: University of Oregon, 1966.

Zheng, Shiping. *Party vs. State in Post-1949 China: The Institutional Dilemma.* New York: Cambridge University Press, 1998.

ARTICLES

Barmie, Geremie R. "Spring Clamor and Autumnal Silence: Cultural Control in China." *A Current History* (September 1998): 257–62.

Barshefsky, Charlene. "China's Entry into WTO Important to Global Community." 7 November 2001. Available on-line at http://www.china-embassy.org.eng/20478.html.

Brook, Timothy. "Rethinking Syncretism: The Unity of the Three Teachings and Their Joint Worship in Late-Imperial China." *Journal of Chinese Religions* 21 (Fall 1993): 13–14.

Bureau of Democracy, Human Rights, and Labor, U.S. Department of State. *China: Country Report on Human Rights Practices for 1997.* Released January 30, 1998.

———. *1999 Country Reports on Human Rights Practices.* Released February 25, 2000. Available on-line at http//www.state.gov/www/global/human_rights/1999_hrp_report/china.html.

———. *2000 Country Reports on Human Rights Practices.* Released February 23, 2001. Available on-line at http://www.state.gov/g/drl/rls.hrrpt/2000eap/index.cf?docid + 684.

Chakrabarty, Dipesh. "Postcoloniality and the Artifice of History." *Representations* 37 (1992): 1–26.

Chamberlain, Heath B. "Civil Society with Chinese Characteristics?" *China Journal* 39 (January 1998): 69–81.

Chen, Chin-Tsao. "The Necessities, Possibilities, and Difficulties of Establishing a Wholly Foreign-Owned Private School in the People's Republic of China." Ph.D. diss., Wilmington College, 1997. Available on-line at http://wwwlib.umi.com/dissertations/fullcit/9729130.

Chen, Jain. "The China Challenge in the Twenty-first Century." *Peaceworks* 21 (1998): 4.

Chen, Kang, Cary H. Jefferson, and Inderjit Singh. "Lessons from China's Economic Reform." *Journal of Comparative Economics* 16 (June 1992): 221.

Cheng, Linshu. "The Basic Functions of Religion." *Studies on World Religions* 41, no. 3 (1990): 84–93.

China Daily, August 4, 1983.

China Education Daily, October 27, 2000.

Cui, Caimu. "Mao Zedong's Traditionalism." Ph.D. diss., University of Tennessee, 1997. Available on-line at http://wwwlib.umi.com/dissertation/fullcit/9809934.

Cui, Yuwen. *Academic Journal of Beijing Normal University*, no. 1, 2000.

Dallas Chinese News, September 15, 2000.

Davis, Derek H. "Christian Faith and Political Involvement in Today's Culture War." *Journal of Church and State* 38 (Summer 1996): 477–85.

———. "Religious Pluralism and the Quest for Unity in American Life." *Journal of Church and State* 36 (Spring 1994): 245–59.

———. "Thoughts on Religious Persecution around the Globe: Problems and Solutions." *Journal of Church and State* 40 (Spring 1998): 279–287.

Davis, Derek H., and Robert H. Haener III. "An Examination of Church-State Curriculum in American Higher Education." *Journal of Church and State* 38 (Winter 1996): 155–69.

Dickson, Bruce J. "China's Democratization and the Taiwan Experience." *Asian Survey* 38 (April 1998): 349–64.

Dittmer, Lowell, and Lu Xiaobo. "Personal Politics in the Chinese 'Dan Wei' under Reform." *Asian Survey* 36 (March 1996): 246–67.

Dzur, Albert W. "Value Pluralism versus Political Liberalism?" *Social Theory and Practice* 24 (Fall 1998): 375.

Fairbanks, James David. "The Priestly Functions of the Presidency: A Discussion on the Literature on Civil Religion and Its Implications for the Study of Presidency Leadership." *Presidential Studies Quarterly* 11 (1981): 214.

Ferdinand, Peter. "Social Change and the Chinese Communist Party: Domestic Problems of Rule." *Journal of International Affairs* 49 (Winter 1996): 478–92.

Galston, William A. "Expressive Liberty, Moral Pluralism, Political Pluralism: Three Sources of Liberal Theory." *William and Mary Law Review* 40 (March 1999): 869.

Garten, Jeffrey E. "The Rise of the Chinese Economy: The Middle Kingdom Emerges." *Harvard Business Review* 76 (May-June 1998): 167–75.

Goldman, Merle. "Politically Engaged Intellectuals in the Deng-Jiang Era: A Changing Relationship with the Party-State." *China Quarterly* 138 (June 1994): 35–52.

Goldstein, Steven M. "China in Transition: The Political Foundations of Incremental Reform." *China Quarterly* 144 (December 1995): 1105–32.

Goldstone, Jack A. "The Coming Chinese Collapse." *Foreign Policy* 99 (Summer 1995): 43.

Gore, Lance L. P. "The Communist Legacy in Post-Mao Economic Growth." *China Journal* 41 (January 1999): 25–54.

Gu, Edward X. "Cultural Intellectuals and the Politics of the Cultural Public Space in Communist China (1979–1989): A Case Study of Three Intellectual Groups." *Journal of Asian Studies* 58, no. 2 (May 1999): 389–444.

Guang, Shuang. "Education and Economic Development: Evidence from China." *Comparative Economic Studies* 39 (Fall/Winter 1997): 69.

Gvosdev, Nikolas K. "Finding the Roots of Religious Liberty in the 'Asian Tradition'." Waco, Tex: Baylor University, 2000. Mimeographed.

Harland, Bryce. "For a Strong China." *Foreign Policy* 94 (Spring 1994): 48–52.
He, Zuo. "China's Education: The Type of People It Brings Up." *Beijing Review* 1 (January 1980): 22–23.
Hughes, Neil C. "Smashing the Iron Rice Bowl." *Foreign Affairs* (July/August 1998): 71.
Kan, Baoping. "The Christian Church in Its Chinese Context." In *Contemporary Religious Trends within the Socio-Political Climate of East Asia*, ed. John N. Jonsson. Waco, Tex.: Baylor University, 1996. Mimeographed.
Kent, Ann. "Waiting for Rights: China's Human Rights and China's Constitutions, 1949–1989." *Human Rights Quarterly* 13 (1991): 174.
Kessler, Sanford. "Tocqueville on Civil Religion and Liberal Democracy." *Journal of Politics* 39 (1977): 131.
Kolodner, Eric. "Religion Rights in China: A Comparison of International Human Rights Law and Chinese Domestic Legislation." *Human Rights Quarterly* 16 (1994): 470.
Kwan, C. H. "The Role of the Chinese Communist Party Coming to an End." *Voice*, July 2000, p. 2.
Lardy, Nicholas R. "The Role of Foreign Trade and Investment in China's Economic Transition." *China Quarterly* 144 (December 1995): 1065–82.
Li, Shaomin, Mingfang Li, and J. Justin Tan. "Understanding Diversification in a Transition Economy: A Theoretical Exploration." *Journal of Applied Management Studies* 7 (June 1998): 77–95.
Li, Weil. "The Impact of Economic Reform of the Performance of Chinese State Enterprises, 1980–1989." *Journal of Political Economy* 105 (October 1997): 1082.
Lin, Justin Yifu. "The Needham Puzzle: Why the Industrial Revolution Did Not Originate in China." *Economic Development and Cultural Change* 43 (January 1995): 269–92.
Lin, Justin Yifu, Fang Cai, and Zhou Li. "The Lessons of China's Transition to a Market Economy." *Cato Journal* 16, no. 2 (Fall 1996): 212.
Lubman, Stanley. "Introduction: The Future of Chinese Law." *China Quarterly* 138 (March 1995): 1–21.
Mao Zedong, "Instruction on the Question of Consolidating the Anti-Japanese Military and Political College" (October 6, 1966), *Current Background* 897 (December 10, 1969), pp. 10–16.
———. "Summary of Talk with Mao Yan-hsing" (July 5, 1964), *Current Background* 888 (August 1969), p. 14.
———. "A Talk Delivered in 1958," *Current Background* 888 (August 1969), p. 7.
Markoff, John, and Daniel Regan. "The Rise and Fall of Civil Religion: Comparative Perspectives." *Sociological Analysis* 42 (1982): 334–53.
Marsh, Christopher. "One Down, One to Go: The 2000 Election and Russia's First Presidential Turnover." *Analysis of Current Events* 12, no. 3–4 (May 2000): 3–5.
Marsh, Christopher, and Laura Whalen. "The Internet, E-Social Capital, and Democratization in China." *American Journal of Chinese Studies* 8 (April 2000).
Mazarr, Michael J. "Trust: The Social Virtues and the Creation of Prosperity." *Washington Quarterly* 19 (Spring 1996): 177–88.
McGee, Robert W., and Danny Kin-Kong Lam. "Hong Kong's Option to Secede." *Harvard International Law Journal* 33, no. 2 (Spring 1992): 438–52.

Naughton, Barry. "China's Macroeconomy in Transition." *China Quarterly* 144 (December 1995): 1083–104.

New York Times, April 21, 1981.

Nolan, Peter, and Robert F. Ash. "China's Economy on the Eve of Reform." *China Quarterly* 144 (December 1995): 980–98.

Office of U.S. Trade Representative. *USTR on China's WTO Accession Market Access Commitments*. April 8. Available on-line at http://www.usinfo.org/wf/990412/epf103.htm.

Oi, Jean C. "The Role of the Local State in China's Transitional Economy." *China Quarterly* 144 (December 1995): 1132–50.

Pearson, Margaret M. "China's Emerging Business Class: Democracy's Harbinger?" *Current History* (September 1998): 268–72.

People's Daily, August 12, 1979; March 11, 1999; July 13, October 26, 2001.

Potter, Pitman B. "Riding the Tiger: Legitimacy and Legal Culture in Post-Mao China." *China Quarterly* 138 (June 1994): 325–58.

"Proposal of the Central Committee of the Chinese Communist Party for the Seventh Five-Year Plan for National Economic and Social Development (September 23, 1985)." *Beijing Review* 40 (October 1985): 15.

Putterman, Louis. "The Role of Ownership and Property Rights in China's Economic Transition." *China Quarterly* 144 (December 1995): 1047–64.

Pye, Lucian W. "An Introductory Profile: Deng Xiaoping and China's Political Culture." *China Quarterly* 135 (September 1993): 412–43.

Rawski, Thomas G. "Implications of China's Reform Experience." *China Quarterly* 144 (December 1995): 1150–72.

———. "Reforming China's Economy: What Have We Learned." *The China Journal* 41 (January 1999): 139–56.

Rhys, J. Howard W. "Religion and National Identity." *Faculty of Religious Studies* 19 (Spring 1991): 47–58.

Sachs, Jeffrey D., and Wing Thye Woo. "Structural factors in the Economic Reforms of China, Eastern Europe, and the Former Soviet Union." *Economic Policy* 18, no. 1 (1994): 102–45.

Segal, Gerald. "Does China Matter?" *Foreign Affairs* (September/October 1999): 24–36.

Shu, Zhaozhi. "Political Reform Is the Precondition of State-Owned Enterprises." *Zheng Ming* 265 (November 1999): 49.

Sicular, Terry. "Redefining State, Plan and Market: China's Reforms in Agricultural Commerce." *China Quarterly* 144 (December 1995): 1020–46.

State Council of China. "1997 White Paper." *China's Religion* 12 (Spring 1998): 7.

Sun, Laixiang, and Liang Zou. "State-Owned versus Township and Village Enterprises in China." *Comparative Economic Studies* (Summer/Fall 1999): 151–75.

Tanzer, Andrew. "This Time It's for Real." *Forbes* 152 (August 1993): 58–62.

Taylor, Rodney L. "The Religious Character of the Confucian Tradition." *Philosophy East and West* 48 (January 1998): 85.

Ting, K. H. "Greetings to the Sixth National Chinese Christian Conference." *Chinese Theological Review* 12 (1996): 23.

Tucker, Mary Evelyn. "Religious Dimensions of Confucianism: Cosmology and Cultivation." *Philosophy East and West* 48 (January 1998): 10–18.

U.S. Congress, House Committee on Foreign Affairs. *The Future of United States–*

China Policy: Joint Hearings before the Subcommittees on Economic Policy, Trade, and Environment; International Security, International Organizations, and Human Rights; and Asia and the Pacific, of the Committee on Foreign Affairs, House of Representatives. 103d Cong., 1st sess., May 20, 1993.

Walder, Andrew G. "China's Transitional Economy: Interpreting Its Significance." *China Quarterly* 144 (December 1995): 963–79.

Wang, Ming. "Chinese Opinion on Human Rights." *Orbis* 42 (Summer 1998): 361–75.

Wang, Weifan. "A Church Leader of Vision." *Chinese Theological Review* 10 (1994): 89.

Wang, Xiaoyun. "The Debt-Growth Dynamics of Developing Countries: A Case Study of China." Ph.D diss., New School for Social Research, 1998. Available on-line at http://wwwlib.umi.com/dissertations/fullcit/9900456.

Washington Post, March 13, April 26, 2001; January 10, January 18, 2002.

Whaling, Frank. "Christianity and Confucianism and Our Coming World Civilization: A European View." *Ching Feng* 38 (March 1995): 13.

Whyte, Bob. "The Future of Religion in China." *Religion in the Communist Lands* 8 (1980): 7.

Whyte, Martin King. "The Fate of Filial Obligations in Urban China." *China Journal* 38 (July 1995): 1–32.

———. "The Social Roots of China's Economic Development." *China Quarterly* 144 (December 1995): 999–1019.

Williams, Rhys H., and Susan M. Alexander. "Religious Rhetoric in American Populism: Civil Religion as Movement Ideology." *Journal for the Scientific Study of Religion* 33 (March 1994): 4.

Wood, James E., Jr. "Religion and the State in China: Winter Is Past." *Journal of Church and State* 28 (Autumn 1986): 394.

Wu, Bangguo. "Chinese Economy in the Twenty-first Century." *Presidents & Prime Ministers* 9 (January 2000): 16.

Wu, Renhong. "Which Way for the Chinese Economy?" *World and I* 13 (October 1998): 46–52.

Xinhua News Agency, May 24, 1999; October 11, December 16, December 27, 1999; February 28, March 2, March 9, April 3, April 5, April 14, May 12, May 22, May 30, June 26, October 28, 2000.

Xu, Xiaoqun. "The Dilemma of Accommodation: Reconciling Christianity and Chinese Culture in the 1920s." *Historian* 60 (Fall 1997): 22.

Yang, Zhong, Jie Chen, and John Scheb. "Mass Political Culture in Beijing: Findings from Two Public Opinion Surveys." *Asian Survey* 38 (August 1998): 774.

Yu, Chonqing. "Discussion on Religions in the Socialist Period: Again on the Essence and Social Role of Religion." *Studies on World Religions* 30, no. 3 (1987): 126.

Zhang, Gaojiao. "Higher Education Front." *China Report* 24 (March 13, 1985): 37–40.

Zhang, Xiaochuan. "The Political Economy of Foreign Direct Investment in China." Ph.D diss., University of Maryland at College Park, 1992. Available on-line at http:wwwlib.umi.com/dissertations/fullcit/9234697.

Zhuo, Xinging. "The Significance of Christianity for the Modernization of Chinese Society." *Crux* 33 (March 1997): 31–37.

Index

About the Author

JINGHAO ZHOU is Assistant Professor in the Department of Asian Languages and Cultures at Hobart and William Smith Colleges in Geneva, New York. His research interests include Chinese culture, religion, politics, and Sino-U.S. Relations, focusing on China's democratization in a global context.